Edward Lewes Cutts

History of Early Christian Art

Edward Lewes Cutts

History of Early Christian Art

ISBN/EAN: 9783337260750

Printed in Europe, USA, Canada, Australia, Japan

Cover: Foto ©ninafisch / pixelio.de

More available books at **www.hansebooks.com**

HISTORY
OF
EARLY CHRISTIAN ART.

THE GOOD SHEPHERD.
Lateran Museum, about A.D. 300.   *Frontispiece.*

SIDE-LIGHTS OF CHURCH HISTORY.

HISTORY

OF

EARLY CHRISTIAN ART.

BY THE
REV. EDWARD L. CUTTS, D.D.,

AUTHOR OF
"A DICTIONARY OF THE CHURCH OF ENGLAND," "TURNING-POINTS OF
CHURCH HISTORY," ETC.

PUBLISHED UNDER THE DIRECTION OF THE TRACT COMMITTEE.

LONDON:
SOCIETY FOR PROMOTING CHRISTIAN KNOWLEDGE,
NORTHUMBERLAND AVENUE, CHARING CROSS, W.C.;
43, QUEEN VICTORIA STREET, E.C.
BRIGHTON : 135, NORTH STREET.
NEW YORK: E. & J. B. YOUNG AND CO.
1893.

PREFACE.

THE special object of this book is to make more widely known the results which the study of the remains of Early Christian Art has attained in throwing light upon the early history of the Church.

While making free use of the mass of material open to every student, the writer has exercised an independent judgment, and hopes that he has contributed to put some things in a clearer light, e.g. the externals of the worship of the Churches before the time of Constantine.

Some care has been taken to show how the early phase of the Church's life links on to the beginnings of our own English Church history.

Grateful acknowledgments are hereby tendered to the authorities of the Science and Art Department at South Kensington, for permission to make use of reproductions of the woodcuts of sarcophagi, etc. from its "Monuments of Early Christian Art," by Dr. Appell; and to Messrs. Hatchette, of Paris, for permission to use reduced copies of some of the plates of the Count M. de Vogüée's important work on the architectural remains of Central Syria.

CONTENTS.

CHAPTER I.
EARLY CHRISTIAN ART.

Definition of "Christian art"—Early Christian art was Greek art; in its decadence; its historical interest—Scope of this book 1

CHAPTER II.
THE CHURCH IN THE HOUSE.

The Upper Room at Jerusalem reconstructed; a service in it; dignity of the room and service; it was the Church of the Apostles—The first Churches were the Cœnacula or Atria of the houses of wealthy Christians—Examples at Antioch in the Recognitions of Clement; at Rome in the Acta of St. Pontus; at Bourges in Gregory of Tours, in the Dialogues of Lucian—Plan of a Grecian and Roman house—These rooms in houses were often given to or acquired by the Church; and continued to be used as public Churches; and rebuilt on the same site 5

CHAPTER III.
THE PUBLIC CHURCHES BEFORE CONSTANTINE.

That the Churches worshipped in the catacombs during the ages of persecution an error—The persecutions partial and brief; in the intervals the Church living and worshipping freely—First public church in Rome probably in the time of Alexander Severus (222-235)—Toleration of Gallienus—Church organization in Rome—Forty public churches in Rome in the time of Diocletian; in other places—The arrangements of the first public churches derived from the houses in which the Christians had been accustomed to assemble 24

CHAPTER IV.

ARCHITECTURE OF THE PUBLIC CHURCHES BEFORE CONSTANTINE.

Churches in the East; in Central Syria; in North Africa; Egypt and Nubia—Description of a Basilican Church—The Church at Tyre—Church symbolism 34

CHAPTER V.

THE CHURCHES OF CONSTANTINE.

Rome no longer the capital of the empire, and not the centre of Christian influence—Constantine's Churches at Rome—Basilicas not converted into Churches—Temples seldom converted into Churches; their materials used in building Churches on their sites—Description of St. Peter's, St. Paul's, and St. Agnes' at Rome—Constantine's Churches in the East; at Bethlehem, Jerusalem, Constantinople—Effect of Constantine's conversion on Christian art 48

CHAPTER VI.

THE CHURCHES AFTER CONSTANTINE.

The colonnades with the Greek architrave; with the Roman arch; with an upper tier of columns—St. Clement's, Rome—St. Ambrose's, Milan—Churches of Central Syria: Babouda; Qualb Louzeh; Tourmanin—Domestic architecture of Central Syria—Churches at Nisibis; Thessalonica—The Golden Gate of Jerusalem—Churches of Egypt and Nubia, Thamugas—Ravenna: Tomb of Galla Placidia; St. Apollinare Nuova; St. Apollinare in Classe; St. Vitale—Parenzo in Istria—Churches of Gaul: Lyons; St. Martin's, Tours; Clermont—Existing remains of the classical style in Gaul—The dome in Persia; in Central Syria; St. Ezra; Bozra—The Byzantine dome; Sta. Sophia—Domes in the West—Traces of the basilican style of architecture in Britain, at Canterbury, Frampton, Silchester—The Celtic churches ... 65

CHAPTER VII.

THE BAPTISTERIES.

Primitive baptisms — Baptisteries in catacombs — When the *Atrium* was the Church, possibly the *Baptisterium* of the bath was the baptistery—Public baptisteries; of the Lateran;

at Aquileia; at Nocera dei Pagani; at Ravenna; at Deir Seta; in Italian cities—Fonts in churches—Illustrations of the subject in England—Baptistery at York; Canterbury—Holy wells—Fonts—Chapter houses 90

CHAPTER VIII.

THE CATACOMBS.

Literature of the subject—Incremation—Columbaria—Roman subterranean sepulchral chambers—Jewish burial customs—The Church adopted the custom of burial—Christian catacombs—Description of those at Rome—Family catacombs of wealthy Christians put at the disposal of the Church—Burial clubs—Public Christian catacombs became places of pilgrimage—Jerome's description of them—Prudentius's description of them, and of the *Confessio* of Hippolytus—The removal of relics—The catacombs deserted and forgotten 101

CHAPTER IX.

TOMBS AND MONUMENTS.

Tombs and monuments at Rome, Jerusalem, and elsewhere—Christian tombs: of Constantia, Helena—Syrian tombs at Kerbet Hass, Hass, Kokanaya—Subterranean chamber at Mondjéléia—Twin columns at Sermeda, Dana, Bechindelayah—Pillar stones in Britain—Tombs used for funeral rites—Primitive regard for the dead—Funeral feasts—*Confessio* of the martyrs; in the catacombs: above ground—Story of Theodotus of Ancyra—Basilica of SS. John and Paul, Rome—St. Alban, his *martyrion*—Early tombs represented in the paintings and sculptures of the Raising of Lazarus—Abyssinian tomb—Visits to tombs, and names scratched on them—Prayers to the saints 130

CHAPTER X.

PAINTINGS.

Classical paintings at Rome and Pompeii—Christian paintings in the sepulchral chambers and catacombs—In churches—Wider range of Scripture subjects introduced in the fourth century—Canons of Illiberis—Churches at Nola—Pictures of martyrdoms—St. Nilus—Painting in English churches: at Wearmouth and Jarrow—Scripture subjects in the decoration of houses; testimony of Asterius, Palace of Constantine; House of SS. John and Paul, Rome—Subjects of paintings at different periods: Symbolical, historical, apocalyptic, Passion subjects, Madonnas—Style of the early Christian school of painting; of the Byzantine school—Repetition of a narrow cycle of subjects—Originated in the East—The ΙΧΘΥΣ; the ΧΡ; the ΑΩ—The origin of the emblems: lamb, dove, etc.—Conventional treatment of subjects—The "Guide to Painting"—Came from the East—Clement of Alexandria—The Apostolical Constitutions—St. Ephrem; St. Gregory of Nyssa; St. Cyril—Paintings in North Africa; in Alexandria   159

CHAPTER XI.

THE LIKENESSES OF CHRIST AND HIS APOSTLES.

The earliest representations conventional—The statuary group at Paneas; the likenesses by St. Luke; the Veronica legend; Eusebius on the subject; Publius Lentulus's description—The two types of likeness, the classical and the Byzantine—St. Peter and St. Paul—The four evangelists   186

CHAPTER XII.

SYMBOLISM.

Emblems: the cross; the crucifix; the "Graffito Blasfemo;" the monogram—Symbolical subjects: the shepherd; the lamb; the fish; a fisherman; the ship; anchor; amphora; vine; olive; palm; doves; sheep; goats; peacock; phœnix; Orpheus; mount with four streams; stag drinking; nimbus; aureole—Symbolical subjects from the Old and New Testaments: their meaning; Daniel; the Three Children; Jonah; Lazarus; Noah; sacrifice of Isaac; healing the paralytic; the infirm woman; the blind man; the passage of the Red Sea; giving the Law; the burning bush; gathering manna (?); seizure of Moses (?); striking the rock; Job; creation of Eve; fall of man; Adam and Eve clothed; Abel and Cain; translation of Elijah; baptism of Christ; entry into Jerusalem; arrest of Christ—Eucharistic symbols: feeding the multitude; miracle of Cana; manna; table with fish and bread; fish and bread—List of subjects on sarcophagi in the Lateran and Vatican collections—Groups of subjects: on ceilings, gilded glass, arcosolia   195

CHAPTER XIII.

SYMBOLISM—*continued.*

The representation of individual persons—Representations of deceased ; oranti ; oranti with saints—The so-called Madonna of the Cemetery of Priscilla ; the so-called Madonna of St. Agnes—Funeral feasts—Personal emblems: fossors; sculptor; painter, etc.—Punning emblems: a dragon for Dracontius, etc.—Instruments of martyrdom (?) 234

CHAPTER XIV.

SCULPTURE.

Classical sculpture—Christian statuary: the Good Shepherd, at Rome, Constantinople, and Athens; the St. Hippolytus ; the St. Peter—Sarcophagi: Egyptian, Etruscan, Roman, Christian ; kept ready made—The subjects sculptured on them—Sarcophagi of Empress Helena ; Constantia ; Petronius Probus ; Junius Bassus ; Anicius Probus, etc.—Sarcophagi in Gaul, Spain, etc.—Pagan sarcophagi used for burial of Christians—English examples—Survival of style and subjects in stone crosses and fonts 253

CHAPTER XV.

THE MOSAICS.

History of mosaic decoration ; its subjects—Examples: at Rome ; St. Constantia ; St. George Salonica ; Sta. Maria Maggiore ; Sta. Pudentiana ; Vatican ; SS. Cosmas and Damian ; S. Praxedes, etc.—At Ravenna: tomb of Galla Placidia ; the two baptisteries; St. Vitalis; St. Apollinare Nuovo; in Classe —At Constantinople, etc.—At Aix-la-Chapelle ; St. Mark's, Venice—Fragments in the catacombs 283

CHAPTER XVI.

IVORIES.

Consular Diptychs ; Church Diptychs—Diptych of St. Gregory—Chair of St. Maximinus ; of St. Peter—Book-covers—Pyxes and relic-boxes—Caskets and shrines—Doors 297

CHAPTER XVII.

GILDED GLASS VESSELS.

Where found ; mode of execution ; subjects ; inscriptions—Engraved glasses—Original use: memorial application ... 304

CHAPTER XVIII.
ILLUMINATED MANUSCRIPTS.

Earliest books, sacred and profane—Sacred MSS.—The Syrian Gospels of Rabula—Early MS. in England: the Genesis of the Cotton Library; the C.C.C. Cambridge and Bodleian Gospels—The Irish and Saxon MSS. 312

CHAPTER XIX.
GOLD AND SILVER VESSELS—HOLY OIL VESSELS—SACRED EMBROIDERY.

The altar and its canopy; altar vessels, etc.; censers; crosses; lamps—Holy oil vessels; their use; examples at Monza—Superstitions connected with: continued to the present day—Sacred embroidery; hangings in churches; clerical vestments 319

CHAPTER XX.
RELIGIOUS SUBJECTS IN DOMESTIC USE.

Religion in daily life—Use of religious subjects in decorating houses; dress; water-vessels; wine-cups; buckles—Lamps 329

CHAPTER XXI.
COINS, MEDALS, AND GEMS.

Coin of Severus with Noah's ark; of Trajan with XP; of Salonina with EN EIPHNH—Coins with Christian symbols: of Constantine, etc.—Medals: pectoral crosses—Gems: primitive use of them with Christian symbols—Clement of Alexandria—Examples in the British Museum, etc. 336

CHAPTER XXII.
INSCRIPTIONS.

History and character of inscriptions; prayers for the departed, and requests for their intercession; euphemisms; examples 348

CHAPTER XXIII.

SOME CONCLUSIONS 357
INDEX 365

LIST OF ILLUSTRATIONS.

	PAGE
THE GOOD SHEPHERD, LATERAN MUSEUM, ABOUT A.D. 300	*Frontispiece*
CAPITAL OF PILASTER SUPPORTING THE "TRIUMPHAL ARCH" OF THE CHURCH OF SS. COSMAS AND DAMIAN, DIARBEKR	35
CHURCH AT CHAQQA, SYRIA	37
ARCH OF CONSTANTINE, ROME	50
THE MAISON CARRÉE AT NÎMES	55
THE CHURCH OF ST. PAUL WITHOUT THE WALLS, ROME. AFTER THE FIRE	59
THE CHURCH OF BETHLEHEM	62
PLAN OF ST. CLEMENT'S, ROME	67
THE CHURCH OF ST. CLEMENT, ROME	68
CHURCH OF BABOUDA, SYRIA	71
CHURCH OF BAQOUZA	72
CHURCH OF TOURMANIN, SYRIA	73
FROM A HOUSE FRONT, CENTRAL SYRIA	74
PLAN OF ST. GEORGE, EZRA, SYRIA	81
CHURCH OF ST. GEORGE, EZRA, SYRIA	82
ROMAN FUNERAL URN	102
AMBULACRUM WITH LOCULI AND ENTRANCE INTO CUBICULA, CEMETERY OF ST. CÆCILIA, ROME	109
A LOCULUS CLOSED WITH SLABS OF STONE	110

LIST OF ILLUSTRATIONS.

	PAGE
A Loculus partly opened	110
A Loculus closed with an Inscribed Marble Slab	110
The Tomb of the Empress Helena	133
Tomb at Hass, Central Syria	134
Subterranean Sepulchre at Mondjéléia, Central Syria	137
A Christian Monument at Prymnessos, Phrygia	139
Plan of Chapel in the Cemetery in Via Ardentiana, Rome	147
Tomb at Adowa, Abyssinia	148
The Raising of Lazarus	154
Wall-painting of St. Cornelius, Bishop of Rome, from the Cemetery of Callistus, Rome	157
Painted Ceiling of One of the Chambers of the Cemetery of St. Callistus	161
Ceiling, from the Catacombs	163
Fresco Painting, from the Cemetery of St. Callistus	174
Our Lord as the Giver of the Divine Word. Fifth Century	193
Wall-painting, from the Cemetery of Pontianus, Rome	197
Wall-painting, from the Church of the Nativity, Bethlehem	198
Scribbling on the Wall, Palatine Hill, Rome	199
Miniature Painting, from the MS. Syrian Gospels, by Rabula	202
Monumental Inscription at Sivaux, France	203
Monumental Inscription in the Roman Catacombs	203
The Sacred Monogram	203
Glass Vessel embedded in the Mortar of a Loculus, with Palm Branch	208
Orpheus. From the Cemetery of Domitilla, Rome	211
Wall-painting, Cemetery of St. Callistus, Rome	227
Wall-painting, Cemetery of St. Marcellinus. An Orante clad in Chasuble	235
Wall-painting, Cemetery of St. Soter, Rome	236
Inscription on Marble	236
Wall-painting, Cemetery of St. Cæcilia, Rome	237

LIST OF ILLUSTRATIONS.   xv

	PAGE
PAINTING FROM THE UPPER CEMETERY OF ST. GENNARO, NAPLES	239
WALL-PAINTING, CEMETERY OF ST. CALLISTUS, ROME	243
ORANTE AND CHILD, THE SO-CALLED MADONNA OF THE CEMETERY OF ST. AGNES	244
WALL-PAINTING, CEMETERY OF ST. CALLISTUS, ROME	245
THE GOOD SHEPHERD. STATUE IN THE LATERAN MUSEUM	254
FROM A SARCOPHAGUS IN THE CATHEDRAL, TORTONA, FOURTH CENTURY	257
STATUE OF ST. HIPPOLYTUS, LATERAN MUSEUM	258
FROM THE SARCOPHAGUS OF JUNIUS BASSUS, A.D. 359	263
SARCOPHAGUS OF JUNIUS BASSUS, A.D 359	269
SARCOPHAGUS OF ANICIUS PROBUS, A.D. 395	271
SARCOPHAGUS IN THE LATERAN MUSEUM, LATE FOURTH OR FIFTH CENTURY	273
SARCOPHAGUS IN THE LATERAN MUSEUM	275
SARCOPHAGUS IN THE LATERAN MUSEUM	277
END OF SARCOPHAGUS OF ARCHBISHOP THEODORUS, ST. APOLLINARE IN CLASSE, RAVENNA. SEVENTH CENTURY	278
MOSAICS IN THE APSE OF THE ANCIENT CHURCH OF THE VATICAN	289
MOSAIC FROM THE TOMB OF GALLA PLACIDIA, RAVENNA	292
UPPER GALLERY, CHURCH OF ST. VITALIS, RAVENNA	293
THE EMPRESS THEÓDORA: ST. VITALIS, RAVENNA	294
IVORY DIPTYCH AT THE CATHEDRAL, MONZA ... *To face*	298
A PAX OF THE EIGHTH CENTURY, CIVIDALE, FRIULI	300
GILDED GLASS VESSEL, FROM THE ROMAN CATACOMBS. SIDE VIEW	305
GILDED GLASS VESSEL, FROM THE ROMAN CATACOMBS. FULL VIEW	305
GILDED GLASS VESSEL: "POMPEIANE, TEODORA, VIB(V)ATIS"	306
GILDED GLASS VESSEL: "ANGNE"	307
GILDED GLASS VESSEL. BUST SURROUNDED BY TWELVE FIGURES	308
THE ASCENSION: FROM THE SYRIAN GOSPELS, BY RABULA, A.D. 586 (?)	315

LIST OF ILLUSTRATIONS.

	PAGE
AMPULLÆ, AT MONZA	324
WATER-VESSEL FROM NORTH AFRICA	331
BUCKLE OF A BELT. DANIEL IN THE LIONS' DEN, AND AN ORANTE	332
CLAY LAMP, WITH XP ORNAMENT	334
COIN OF SEPTIMUS SEVERUS	337
COIN OF CONSTANTINE THE GREAT	338
COIN OF CONSTANS	340
COIN OF JUSTIN I.	341
COIN OF LICINIA EUDOXIA, WIFE OF VALENTINIAN III.	341
MEDALLION OF THE EIGHTH OR NINTH CENTURY	342
ST. PAUL AND ST. PETER (BRONZE)	343
LEADEN MEDALLION	343
EARLY CHRISTIAN RINGS	345

HISTORY
OF
EARLY CHRISTIAN ART.

CHAPTER I.

EARLY CHRISTIAN ART.

Definition of "Christian art"—Early Christian art was Greek art; in its decadence; its historical interest—Scope of this book.

IT may be well to explain, to begin with, that by the phrase Christian art is meant art applied to Christian uses. The Christianity is in the subjects, not in the style. Artists cannot invent a new style to order, or at will. A man must utter his thoughts, however novel they may be, in the language of his time. The Evangelists and Apostles had a new revelation to convey, but they had perforce to express its mysteries in the Greek which was the *lingua franca*

B

of their age. So if a man undertake to express facts or thoughts in painting or sculpture, it must be in the art of his time; the early Christian artists had to present their subjects in the style of art which was then in current use. Language indeed grows and changes, but slowly, under certain influences; so does art change, slowly, under the influence of new needs, materials, methods of construction, moods of thought, and feeling; and the climax of the history of early Christian art is the actual emergence of a new phase of art under the gradual influence of all these causes.

Art all over the civilized world at the time of the Christian era was Greek art. The Macedonian conquests had spread Greek civilization and art over the East; the Romans had adopted them from conquered Greece, and carried them forward with less genius of conception and less refinement of taste; and, beyond the slow process of natural decadence, art underwent no changes in Roman hands. At the beginning of the Christian era this art had already passed its highest point of excellence; but the architects of the time of Augustus could still decorate the Forum with temples imitated from and hardly inferior to the best of the ancient temples of Greece; the sculptors produced fine replicas of the great works of earlier art; and the original statues of imperial and noble persons which peopled Rome had great dignity in the pose, skill in the broad handling of the robes, and especially great power of portraiture. Few examples of the painting of the period have survived, and those chiefly the less serious works which were used in domestic decoration; enough, however, remains in the house of Livia on the Palatine, at Pompeii, and elsewhere, to prove that the artists possessed great technical skill and abundant graceful fancy.

But by the time that the Christian Church needed to employ the arts in its service, the decadence of classical art had fully set in, and the decline continued through several centuries. Moreover, the Christian art work which has survived is not equal to the contemporary work of heathen art. The circumstances of the early Church made it unlikely that it should obtain, "for love or money," the services of the greater artists who were busy building and adorning the palaces of Roman patricians, and of plundering proconsuls and procurators. So that the early art we have to do with here is poor and debased compared with the earlier classical art, and effete and feeble compared with that of later ages, when Christian civilization had at length wrought out for itself a new style in which to express its mind and soul. This early Christian art, with all its defects, is, however, of the highest interest to us, because it is the autograph record in art language of the history of the Church of those times, its doctrines, worship, manners and customs, hopes and aspirations. And those times were times of especial interest in the history of the Church: first, the three ages before the Church was allied with the State; then the three ages during which all the great

Doctors and Fathers of the Church taught; while the Church was still in external unity, and its life-blood circulated freely throughout its vast extension.

In the latter part of the period of the decline of classical art the phenomena are not merely those of decline; there present themselves indications of a new initiative—new modes of treatment, a growing boldness and vigour of originality, new plans in architecture, new subjects in pictorial art, a disregard of the naturalistic conception and treatment of Greek art and in its place the mystic conception and suggestive treatment of the Byzantine art. There is a wide borderland between the two, in the upper part of which Byzantine feeling is making itself felt, and in the lower classical tradition still survives. A history of early Christian art is bound to note the rise of the Byzantine school while it pursues with interest the late survivals of the earlier school.

CHAPTER II.

THE CHURCH IN THE HOUSE.

The Upper Room at Jerusalem reconstructed; a service in it; dignity of the room and service; it was the Church of the Apostles—The first Churches were the Cœnacula or Atria of the houses of wealthy Christians—Examples at Antioch in the Recognitions of Clement; at Rome in the Acta of St. Pontus; at Bourges in Gregory of Tours, in the Dialogues of Lucian—Plan of a Grecian and Roman house—These rooms in houses were often given to or acquired by the Church; and continued to be used as public Churches; and rebuilt on the same site.

HE history of Christian art, *i.e.* art applied to Christian uses, begins with the birth of the Church, on the great Day of Pentecost, in the upper room of Mary's house at Jerusalem.

Let us try to reconstruct this upper room. A typical Eastern house of the better class is usually built round an open court, which is paved with marble, and has a marble tank or fountain in the middle. Sometimes trees planted near the tank rise to a considerable height, seeking air and sun, and spread out their foliage, giving a pleasant shade;

round the sides of the court are disposed shrubs in great boxes, or a border of flower beds; and climbing plants half clothe the walls. In one corner is a kind of room, open on one side to the court, rising through the two stories of the house up to the flat roof, its floor raised two or three feet above the pavement of the court, with a stone or marble bench round its three sides. This is the divan, where the master of the house usually receives visits of courtesy or of business.* An external stone stair along another side of the court gives access to a balcony † at the height of the second story. And from this balcony opens a large room which is the great reception-room on occasions of ceremony or festivity. This is our Upper Room, in Greek ὑπερῷον, in Latin *cœnaculum*.

Now Mary, the mistress of the house, apparently at this time a widow, was the sister of Barnabas the Levite. Josephus states at the beginning of his Autobiography that the priests were the aristocratic caste of his nation; the Levites were the second order of this aristocratic caste; and Mary was of a Levitical family. Her brother Barnabas had not only the emoluments of his office, but was also a landowner in Cyprus, and appears from the whole narrative to

---

* Our Lord was probably sitting here when they let down the paralytic through the roof above, so that the sick man alighted on this raised platform at the feet of Jesus, between those who sat round the divan and the crowd who stood in the court (Luke v. 18, 19).

† On the Day of Pentecost the Apostles probably came out of the upper room upon this balcony, and thence Peter addressed the crowd in the court below, and perhaps on the flat housetops around. The fountain in the middle of the court would afford water for the baptism of the three thousand (Acts ii. 14).

have been a person of some distinction. Mary, his widowed sister, was probably a person of some social consideration and wealth, for she resided in the capital, and her house was a large one, since its *cœnaculum* would contain at least one hundred and twenty persons. Herod the Great, half a century before, had introduced into Jerusalem a taste for sumptuous architecture in the prevailing classical style of art, and the large and lofty reception-room of Mary would possibly be in the prevailing taste; adorned with pilasters and cornices, its wall-panels and ceiling ornamented with painting. It would make a very convenient church, as the Royal Chapel at Whitehall did, which was built for a banqueting hall.

An Eastern reception-room has little more permanent furniture than the low bench which runs along one or more of its sides, so that there was nothing to interfere with an assembly of people; and since Eastern congregations always stand to worship, there was nothing lacking for their accommodation.

Having reconstructed the room, let us go a little further and assist at one of the Christian assemblies in it—the early morning assembly for the Breaking of the Bread. On this occasion some furniture is required; at least a plate for the bread, a cup for the wine, and a table to place them upon.

Now, the people of those times did not possess the facilities which we have for investing surplus wealth at interest. The accumulated wealth of well-to-do people was not in the shape of scrip and shares, but of actual silver and gold and gems. But instead of keeping all this precious metal and these beautiful stones hidden, it was the custom to use them much more largely than we are in the habit of doing in the form of personal decorations and of ornamental furniture. A wealthy household would have a very much larger display of precious vessels in common use than a household of similar station and means among ourselves. In supplying the vessels necessary for the solemn Memorial of the Sacrifice of the Son of God a natural feeling of reverence would lead Mary to select the best in her possession. We know the kind of vessels in common use at the time, and recognize that the first "paten" and "chalice" would very possibly be a tazza and a cup of silver or gold, perhaps adorned with gems, and made beautiful in form and ornamentation by the best skill of the goldsmith. The tables of the same time often consisted of a marble slab supported by an ornamental frame of bronze; and such a one would be convenient for the use in question.

Convenience would dictate that the table should be placed at the upper end of the room. The Apostles would naturally stand behind it as the ministrants, while the people would stand in reverent order in the body of the room, the men by themselves and the women by themselves; this was the arrangement directed by our Lord in the miracles of the feeding of the multitudes, which were types of this spiritual feeding of the people. Look at the dress of the Apostles, for it is the earliest authority for "clerical vestments." The usual dress of the higher and middle classes at that time in Judæa, as elsewhere, was the tunic and pallium;* on occasions of religion and ceremony their colour was white, and the long tunic was worn, the sleeves of which reached to the wrists and the skirts to the ankles. This is the dress assigned to the Apostles in the earliest pictorial representations, even when the successors of the Apostles had adopted other fashions of episcopal costume,† and it is highly probable that it is that which they actually wore;‡ it is a costume of such statuesque simplicity of line and breadth of fold, that artists to this day employ it to give dignity to their sacred figures.

This, then, is the first presentation of Christian art in the Church; and in the magnitude and architectural character of the place of assembly, in the costly beauty of the sacred vessels, in the habit of the ministers, in the order of the congregation, there was nothing lacking to the dignity of the Divine service.

We have taken pains to realize this assembly of the Apostolic Church in the upper room at Jerusalem in order to combat at the outset the vulgar error that the early Church affected a studious plainness and informality in Divine worship and its appointments. There is not a word of evidence to that effect in the

---

* The pallium was a large oblong piece of cloth, lately come into use instead of the old toga, and was disposed in certain folds about the person.

† As in the mosaic in SS. Cosmas and Damian at Rome, of the time of Felix IV. (526-530), and in the mosaics of the same century at Ravenna.

‡ In the "Recognitions of Clement," viii. 6, about 150 A.D., St. Peter is represented as saying, "My dress is what you see, a tunic with a pallium."

Scriptures, or in the early Christian writers, and the probabilities are to the contrary. The first Christians were Jews, and had been trained in the principles of Divine worship amid the splendours of the Temple, and continued to attend the Temple worship. Even the synagogues for their "prayer-meetings" were handsome buildings and suitably furnished. But the worship of the Church was the continuation of the solemn liturgical worship of the Temple, not of the prayer-meetings of the synagogue. When the Churches could do no better they worshipped in the open air or in a cave, and knew that their worship "in spirit and in truth" would be acceptable to the Most High; but when they could do better, they thought the best which they could do was only a suitable outward expression of their reverence. This principle of Christian worship is sanctioned by our Lord's approval of Mary of Bethany's act of worship in anointing His feet with the precious ointment, and by His implied rebuke of Simon the Pharisee's neglect of the ceremonious courtesies usually offered to an honoured guest.

It is highly probable that this Upper Room was the usual place of assembly of the innermost circle of the disciples; that there the Lord celebrated the last Passover and instituted the memorial of the breaking of the bread;* there the disciples assembled on the evening of the great Easter Day,† and on the following Sunday;‡ there the election of Matthias to the

* Luke xxii. 12.   † John xx. 19.   ‡ John xx. 26.

Apostleship* took place; there the disciples assembled every day after the Ascension in prayer for the coming of the promised Comforter; † and there, on the day of Pentecost, they were baptized with the Holy Ghost and with fire, and the Church began to be.

It is highly probable that the Upper Room thus consecrated continued to be used for the assemblies of the Church and for its worship; that it was there "at the house" that the disciples daily broke the bread, that is to say, celebrated the Eucharist; ‡ that this was the house which was supernaturally shaken in answer to their prayers; § there the Church kept up its ceaseless intercession for Peter while in prison; ‖ there the seven deacons were ordained; ¶ there the first council was held.** For there is an early tradition that the house of Mary was at length entirely given over to the Church; and under the name of the Cœnaculum, or of the Church of the Apostles, it continued to be the most venerated of the churches of Jerusalem down to the fourth century and later.††

We meet with other notices in the writings of the New Testament of the use of these upper rooms for Christian assemblies. Dorcas was "laid out" to

---

* Ac's i. 15.   † Acts ii.   ‡ Acts ii. 46.
§ Acts iv. 23–31.   ‖ Acts xii. 12.   ¶ Acts vi. 6.
** Acts xv. 4–6.

†† St. Cyril, Bishop of Jerusalem (A.D. 347), seems to say that the "Upper Church of the Apostles" of his time was this Upper Room ("Catechetical Lectures," xvi. 4). In the group of buildings on the southern brow of Zion, now known as the Cœnaculum, is a large upper room fifty feet by thirty, which is supposed to represent, if not actually to be, this venerable room.

receive the last honours in an upper room,* very possibly that in which the Christians of Joppa were accustomed to assemble. The Church at Troas was used to assemble in an upper room, on the first day of the week, for the breaking of the bread.† It is probable that in all the cases in which we have notices in the New Testament of the Church in the house of Such-an-one, what is implied is not the prayer-meeting of a circle of Christian friends, but the general assembly of the Church of that city, regularly held in the house of some wealthy convert.‡

For there is sufficient evidence that in the period before the Christian communities were able to erect public churches for their meetings, it was the regular practice everywhere to hold the assemblies for Divine worship in the house of one of the brethren; usually (as was natural) in the house of a Christian of wealth and distinction, because its large rooms afforded ample accommodation to the Church. There were probably more early converts of the higher classes than is popularly apprehended. St. Paul indeed says § that "not many wise, not many mighty, not many noble," were among the disciples of his time; but some there were. At the very first, among those who believed in the Christ were the nobleman of Capernaum,‖ who is probably the same as Chuza, Herod's steward;¶ the centurion of Capernaum; Joseph and Nicodemus, members of the Sanhedrim;

---

* Acts ix. 37.   † Acts xx. 8.
‡ Acts xviii. 7; Rom. xvi. 15; 1 Cor. xi. 18, 22; xiv. 23; xvi. 19; Col. iv. 15.
§ 1 Cor. i. 26.   ‖ John iv. 46.   ¶ Luke viii. 3.

later, the treasurer of Ethiopia and the centurion of Cæsarea—one of the patrician Cornelii; still later, Sergius Paulus, the proconsul of Cyprus, the "most excellent Theophilus" of Antioch, Dionysius the Areopagite, to say nothing of the "chief women" of Thessalonica, and the "honourable women which were Greeks not a few" at Berea; lastly, members of the noble Roman families, Pudentian, Pomponian, Anician, and others, culminating in "them of Cæsar's household," a phrase in which recent discoveries * have enabled us to include Flavius Clemens and his wife Flavia Domitilla, the former the cousin and the latter the niece of the Emperor Domitian.

Other recent discoveries in the Roman catacombs † have proved that the Manius Acilius Glabrio, who was included in the same indictment and sentence with Flavius Clemens, was also a Christian with members of his family. This family attained celebrity about 200 years B.C., when Acilius Glabrio the consul conquered the Macedonians. Towards the end of the Republic they were established on the Pincian Hill, where they had a palace and large gardens, and were so greatly esteemed that Pertinax, in the memorable sitting of the senate in which he was elected emperor, declared them to be the noblest race in the world. Manius Acilius Glabrio was consul with Trajan in the year 91 A.D., and in this very year he was compelled by Domitian to fight with a lion and two bulls in the amphitheatre adjoining the emperor's villa at Albanum. He survived the combat, and was

* See p. 115. † See p. 117.

banished. But four years afterwards, A.D. 95, he was tried, condemned, and executed, together with Flavius Clemens and others, on the charge of having embraced the customs and persuasion of the Jews.

Recent discoveries have also put it beyond a doubt that Pomponius Græcina, the wife of Aulus Plautius, the conqueror of Britain, was a Christian. An inscription bearing the name ΠΟΜΠΟΝΙΟC ΓΡΗΚΕΙΝΟC has been found in the cemetery of Callistus, together with other records of the Pomponii Attici and Bassi. Some scholars think that Græcina, the wife of Aulus Plautius, is no other than Lucina, the Christian matron, who interred her brethren in Christ in her own property, at the second milestone of the Appian Way.

Other evidence of the conquests made by the gospel among the patricians is given by an inscription discovered in 1866, in the catacombs of Prætextatus, near the monument of Quirinus the martyr. It is a memorial raised to the memory of his departed wife by Postumius Quietus, consul A.D. 272. Here also was found the name of Urania, daughter of Herodes Atticus, by his second wife Vibullia Alcia, while on the other side of the road, near St. Sebastian, a mausoleum has been found, on the architrave of which the name URANIOR[VM] is engraved.

Eusebius, in speaking of the martyrs of the Flavian family, quotes the authority of the historian Bruttius. He evidently means Bruttius Præsens, the friend of the younger Pliny, and the grandfather of Crispina the Empress of Commodus. In 1854, near the entrance to the Flavian crypt, was found a fragment of a stone sarcophagus with the name of Bruttius Crispinus, so that the Flavian family and that of their historian were united in the proximity of their villas and tombs and by community of religion.

There also occur the names of several Cornelii, Cæcilii, and Æmilii, the flower of Roman nobility, grouped near the graves of St. Cæcilia and Pope Cornelius; of Liberalis, a *consul suffectus* * and a martyr, whose remains were buried in the Via Salaris; of Jallia Clementina, a relative of Jallius Bassus, consul before A.D. 161; of Catia Clementina, daughter or relative of Catius, consul A.D. 230, not to speak of persons of equestrian rank whose names have been collected in hundreds.†

The subject of these domestic churches is of such general interest that it is worth while to illustrate it in some detail.

The "Recognitions of Clement," written soon after the middle of the second century, says that "At Antioch, by the preaching of St. Peter, within seven days more than 10,000 men were baptized, so that Theophilus,‡ who was more exalted than all the men of power that were in that city, consecrated the great hall of his house for a church,§ and a chair (*cathedra*)

---

* Elected to supply the place of a consul dying or retiring in his year of office.

† Lanciani, "Pagan and Christian Rome," ii. 9.

‡ The "most excellent Theophilus" of St. Luke's dedication of the Gospel and Acts; "most excellent" was an official title. Tradition says that St. Luke was a resident in Antioch.

§ "*Domus suæ ingentem basilicam ecclesiæ nomine consecraret*" (x. 71).

was placed in it for the Apostle, and the whole multitude assembled daily to hear his word."

The writer of a novel, for such is the nature of the "Recognitions," does not necessarily narrate truths, but he is careful to make his narrative truth-like; we infer, therefore, that it was in accordance with the known facts of the history of the Church, that a man of rank and wealth should give up "the basilica of his house" for a church.*

The "Acta" of St. Pontus supplies, in the course of a charming contemporary sketch of Roman life, another example of the church in an upper room. It relates that one day, in his boyhood, as Pontus was passing at dawn through the streets of Rome, on the way to his preceptor, accompanied by his pedagogue and a young companion, he heard singing from an upper room of one of the houses which they were passing, and distinguished the words, "Our God is in heaven. . . . Their idols are silver and gold, the work of men's hands," etc. (Ps. cxv.). Seized with a sudden impulse, he knocked at the door of the house. Some looked down from above through a window,† and saw that it was a child who knocked. Bishop Pontianus (A.D. 230–235), who was present,

---

* The house would probably be the same building, called by Eusebius ὁ τῆς Ἐκκλησίας οἶκος, "the house of the Church," in which Paul of Samosata made so much display of episcopal state, and which he refused to give up on his deposition from the bishopric for heresy, until compelled by the intervention of the Emperor Aurelian, A.D. 272.

† The principal windows of an Eastern house look into the interior courtyard, but there is often a small projecting window overlooking the street, so that the inhabitants can, as in this instance, ascertain who comes and goes and knocks.

bade that he should be admitted, "for of such," he said, "is the kingdom of God." Pontius, with his companion Valerius (who is the author of the narrative), having been admitted, ascended to the *cœnaculum* (the upper room), and seeing that they were celebrating the Divine mysteries, turned aside till the service was concluded; then Pontianus talked with him, and laid the foundation of his conversion.

Gregory of Tours relates that the missionaries who planted the church at Bourges in the middle of the third century, when they had made some converts, began to cast about for a place for their assemblies for worship, and sought to obtain possession of the private house of some citizen for the purpose of converting it into a church; but all the senators and wealthier people of the place were still heathen. So they had recourse to one Leocadius, a man in the highest position and related to the family of Vettius Epagathus, who had suffered in the famous persecution at Lyons a century earlier, and offered to purchase his house. He became a Christian, and gave his house for use as a church. The existing cathedral of Bourges is the magnificent representative, on the same site, of the atrium of Leocadius.

The satire of an opponent of Christianity affords us still another example. In the "Dialogue of Philopatris," which goes by the name of Lucian, but is probably by a later writer, and of date A.D. 363, the time of the Emperor Julian, one of the characters relates that he was persuaded to visit some men, who, he was told, would teach him all mysteries. He passed through iron doors and by brazen ways, and having ascended a long roundabout route, he came to a chamber with gilded ceiling, such as Homer tells of the house of Menelaus.* He saw no Helen, however, but only a number of men with pale countenances bent towards the earth. In short, he had been induced to visit a Christian assembly. This description of the satirist is no doubt imaginary, but it is better evidence for our purpose than an isolated fact, because his story would certainly be founded upon what was known to be the general custom of the Christians.

The Christians at Cirta, North Africa, were using a house for their assemblies at the time of the outbreak of the Diocletian persecution.

The houses of Greece and Rome were built on a different model from the Eastern house which has been described, and in houses of this plan it would be the atrium which would be used for the place of assembly, and it is this atrium which afforded the type of the churches of the first six centuries.

In the sketch plan of a Greek or Roman house given in Smith's "Dictionary of Greek and Roman Antiquities," † the visitor passes first through an outer court, which is sometimes surrounded by a colonnade, and has a fountain in the middle. He

---

* "There was a radiance like that of the sun or moon throughout the huge vaulted hall of renowned Menelaus, ... the gleam of bronze and of gold, of amber and of ivory" ("Odyssey," bk. iv.).

† The prehistoric palace at Tiryns (Smith's "Dictionary of Greek and Roman Antiquities") and the first-century houses at Pompeii (Lanciani, "Pagan and Christian Rome," 114), bear witness to the persistency of this normal plan.

enters into the *atrium*, the common reception-room. It is always large in proportion to the size of the house, for, as in the halls of our Saxon ancestors, the indoor life of the family was for the most part transacted in it. Frequently it was divided into a nave and aisles by two rows of columns, which sustained the roofs. Beyond it was the *tablinum*, or supper-room, which was only divided from the *atrium* by a curtain. The *outer court*, *atrium*, and *tablinum*, formed the principal body of the house; besides these, were usually a room on each side of the tablinum, some small rooms on each side of the atrium opening from it, and receiving their only light through their doors; and sometimes a second story of small rooms over these. The houses of Pompeii afford many examples of houses of this plan still standing.

At Corinth, when St. Paul desisted from his preaching in the synagogue, he separated the believers, and formed them into a Church, which " came together into one place" for worship (1 Cor. xiv. 23), probably in the house of Justus (Acts xviii. 7). Now, Justus was a Gentile, and the house of a well-to-do Gentile in the lately rebuilt city of Corinth would be of the usual plan and architectural style of the period. The Christian congregation would pass through the outer court into the atrium. The reader may accompany them, and study the place and people. On the further side of the open-air court, by a short passage through the house, he enters the atrium. It is a large and lofty hall; two rows of pillars support the roof, which is open in the middle for light and air; the walls are divided by pilasters to correspond with the columns, and the wall panels are decorated with paintings, like those in the house of Livia, or in the houses at Pompeii. At the further end, when the curtain is withdrawn, the eye travels into the tablinum,* which is like a chancel; its table is already conveniently placed for the approaching Breaking of the Bread, the necessary vessels are already placed upon it, and the Apostle Paul and his assistant ministers, Silas and Timotheus, are seated behind it, waiting for the time to begin. The hall would be destitute of furniture, and the people would stand, the men on the left hand and the women on the right, the men with their heads uncovered, the women with the usual head-veil, which partly concealed the face. Mere convenience would dictate that the Divine service should be performed in the tablinum, and the sermon preached thence; the people would come up to the tablinum, and there, standing, would receive the consecrated food, as they now do in all the churches of the East. Thus naturally grew the plan of the church and the order of its service.

There is abundant evidence that the Churches continued to assemble for Divine worship in private houses, not only during the ages of persecution, but long after the decrees of Constantine had given

* This custom of screening the tablinum from the atrium by a curtain was perhaps the origin of the custom of the early Church to place a curtain before the apse, which was drawn and withdrawn in different portions of the services.

universal peace to the Church. It was natural that it should be so. The buildings, as we have seen, whether upper room or atrium, were sufficiently spacious to contain a considerable congregation, sufficiently dignified architecturally for a church, and endeared to the Christian community by long years of the most sacred associations. There, in the tablinum, saints and martyrs had celebrated the Divine mysteries and had preached the Word; there, in the atrium, this and that illustrious person had stood to worship; there their parents and relatives had worshipped; there they themselves had first been brought to the assembly of the faithful. No wonder that the place had become to them a sacred place, "none other than the House of God, and the very gate of heaven." It is probable that in some cases the whole house had been given to the Church. We see something like this adumbrated very early in the case of Mary's house at Jerusalem. The owners of the house, *ex hypothesi* zealous Christians and wealthy people, would be moved by natural piety to feel that a building so long dedicated to sacred purposes should not return to secular uses, and would give it to the Church; or the Church, desirous to retain a building so endeared to them by its venerable associations, would seek to possess it, if necessary by purchase. The place so long used for the assembly of the congregation would still be used as the church, and the rest of the house would afford a dwelling-place to the bishop, or to some of the clergy, or would serve some similar Church use. Thus there is an extant letter of Pius I. (A.D. 142–157), Bishop of Rome, in which he states that Euprepia, a pious widow, had assigned her house over to the Church, "where dwelling with the poor we celebrate the Divine offices."

The natural sequel would be that, in course of time, these houses would be taken down and larger churches would be built upon their venerable sites. The ancient and credible tradition at Rome is that several of its most ancient churches were thus built upon the sites of houses in which first the Church assembled by permission of the owner, then the owner gave the house to the Church, and lastly, larger churches were built upon the site.

St. Prisca is traditionally said to occupy the site of the house in which St. Prisca was baptized by St. Peter, and the first church to have been built by Bishop Eutychianus, A.D. 280. The interesting church of St. Clement is said to have been built upon the site of the house of Flavius Clemens, of the imperial family. The Pudens saluted by St. Paul, in his Epistle to Timothy (2 Tim. iv. 21), is said to have been the distinguished senator of that name, in whose house St. Paul is said to have lived; and the grandson of this Pudens, Pius I., Bishop of Rome from A.D. 142 to 157, is said to have converted part of the family mansion* into a church, of which the existing church of St. Pudentiana is the successor. Its proper name is the Church of Pudens, and it is so called in an inscription on the book held by the figure of our

---

* Part of the house still remains (Lanciani).

Lord in the apse, for the early Christians called their churches after the name of their founder. Part of the Anician Villa on the Via Latina was converted into a church in the fourth century by Demetrias, the daughter of Anicius Hermogenianus, prefect of the city (368-370), and of Tyrrania Juliana, the friend of Augustine and Jerome. The remains of villa and church were discovered in 1857.*

    * Lanciani, "Pagan and Christian Rome."

CHAPTER III.

THE PUBLIC CHURCHES BEFORE CONSTANTINE.

That the Churches worshipped in the catacombs during the ages of persecution an error—The persecutions partial and brief; in the intervals the Church living and worshipping freely—First public church in Rome probably in the time of Alexander Severus (222-235)—Toleration of Gallienus—Church organization in Rome—Forty public churches in Rome in the time of Diocletian; in other places—The arrangements of the first public churches derived from the houses in which the Christians had been accustomed to assemble.

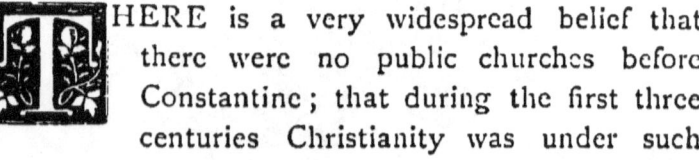HERE is a very widespread belief that there were no public churches before Constantine; that during the first three centuries Christianity was under such continuous persecution, that its adherents were driven to worship in secrecy and concealment in caves and catacombs, or in holes and corners of one another's houses.

The error has an important bearing upon our subject, for a community in such a condition could have no thought to spare for art. It has a more important bearing upon the whole history of the

Church, for men in the condition supposed, however fervent their personal piety, could have no freedom to embody their principles in institutions, to develop their beliefs and sentiments and aspirations into manners and customs, to express their inner life of thought and feeling, as free human nature will do, in their surroundings. In such a case, we should have had to reckon with two results: first, that the condition of the Church before Constantine could not be accepted as a model of what the Church, freely and fully grown and developed, should be; and next, that the Church after Constantine would lie under the suspicion of having suddenly developed, not freely and independently, but under the influence of imperial patronage.

Whereas the truth is that, while Christians were always liable to individual molestation, and local Churches did suffer from occasional persecutions, and while this might serve to keep off the half-hearted and to brace the spiritual nerve of those who really believed, there was not enough of continuous general persecution to warp or hamper the natural growth of the life of the Church.

There are two points to be noticed—the chronic danger in which all Christians lived, and the special danger of the occasional systematic persecutions.

Christianity was at first a "new superstition," exclusive, unsocial, mysterious, which excited suspicion and dislike. Being a *religio illicita*, a religion unrecognized by the law, its professors were liable at any moment to be brought before the magistrates on that charge. The condition of the Christians, till after the edict of Gallienus (A.D. 260), was always precarious, and there were many examples of suffering for conscience sake in all parts of the empire. Informers sometimes, moved by cupidity or malice, brought the accusation against individuals; the fanaticism of the people sometimes, on the occasion of public calamity, clamoured against the Christians as atheists, who provoked the anger of the gods against those who tolerated them. But the emperors Trajan and Hadrian issued edicts against these individual delations and these riotous outbreaks; and the Christians in time lived down the popular suspicion and dislike, and, except in times of systematic persecution, exercised their religion freely and lived unharmed among their neighbours.

The authorized persecutions were few in number, brief in duration, and occupied in the aggregate a very small space out of the three centuries over which they extended. Nero's persecution in the year 64 A.D. was a solitary act of wanton tyranny which did not extend beyond Rome. It is not till halfway through the three centuries that Marcus Aurelius ordered the first general procedure against the professors of the new faith, which extended over about twenty years (161–180) of his reign, and ceased at his death. Septimius Severus, about two years before the close of his reign (209–211), provoked at finding men and women of the highest rank becoming Christians, issued an edict forbidding his subjects to become Jews or Christians, and renewed the law against "close associations;" but this edict was rescinded by his successor. Alexander Severus (222–235) had a statue of Christ, among those of other great religious teachers, in his private oratory, and favoured Christianity; and Philip the Arabian (244–249) was so friendly to Christians that he was suspected of being a secret convert. There were partial outrages against Christians under Maximin (235–238). Decius made a serious attempt to destroy Christianity entirely, but his action was directed chiefly against the clergy, and did not continue above a year (251). The persecution was renewed during the last three years and a half of the reign of Valerian (253–260), but on his capture by Sapor (260), his son Gallienus suspended the persecution, and shortly after restored the confiscated buildings and property of the Churches, and gave the Christians freedom of worship; there is reason to believe that his wife Salonina was a Christian. Diocletian himself during the first twenty years of his reign (284–305) showed great favour to the Christians. Eusebius tells us that of the freedmen whom he employed in the management of the affairs of the empire many were Christians; he entrusted to Christians the government of provinces, and exempted them from the customary sacrifices which it was their official duty to attend; his wife and daughter were secretly attached to the faith; the bishops were recognized and treated with respect by the magistrates of their cities. In short, the Church was looking with hope and expectation for the conversion of the emperor, when, under the influence of the brutal Gallerius, the last and most dreadful persecution began. The first persecuting edict was issued in 303. The tolerance of Constantius and Constantine mitigated the severity of the persecution in the provinces of Gaul, Spain, and Britain, over which they ruled. The persecution lasted in the East till 308, and the last two years were the most prolific of bloodshed. All fear of persecution ceased in the West with the conversion of Constantine in 312; vexatious proceedings were continued in the East until the final victory of Adrianople (323) made Constantine sole master of the Roman world.

If the reader will take the trouble to consider this brief summary he will find that there was no general official action against the Christians till 161, and that it ceased with the death of Marcus Aurelius in 180. From the death of Marcus Aurelius to the reign of Decius the Church had peace for eighty years, with the short interruption of Severus's unfavourable action, which only lasted about two years; the Decian and Valerian persecutions occupy about eight years (251–260); and again, from the death of Valerian to the beginning of the Diocletian persecution, there was another interval of forty years of unbroken peace, and during those years the Church was not only tolerated by official indifference but was sometimes encouraged by imperial favour.*

* In times of persecution most likely the Churches met in secret places. Thus Gregory of Tours (lib. x. 31) says that Gatianus, the first Bishop of Tours, in the time of Decius, concealed himself on account of the attack of great men who overwhelmed him with ill-treatment, and celebrated secretly in crypts and hiding-places the

During these long intervals of peace the Church was freely and independently growing in numbers, wealth, and consideration. The congregations assembled without any secrecy in the houses where their worship was conducted; and later on they built churches in the cities, and possessed themselves of suburban cemeteries in which they erected chapels and monuments; till at length this great organization, rapidly growing in numbers, wealth, and influence in every part of the world, including all ranks and classes, bound together by a bond of sacred fraternity, possessed of a spirit of self-devotion to the cause, and a burning zeal of proselytism, seemed to Roman statesmen to constitute a serious danger to the State.

In these long intervals of peace the Churches made free use of the arts and applied them to their requirements; while the individual martyrdoms and general persecutions have left their marks upon the art history of the times.

To return to the special question of Christian architecture before Constantine, it was probably in the interval of peace after the death of Septimius Severus, under the favour of Alexander Severus, that the Christian communities first openly began to build churches.

In the reign of Alexander Severus (222–235) there was a dispute between the Christians of Rome and the Guild of the Popinarii—the Taverners—about the

Mystery of the Solemnity of the Lord's Day to the few converts whom he had made.

possession of a plot of land, on which one proposed to build a church and the other a tavern; it was referred to the emperor, who gave his decision in favour of the Christians, saying that it was better that God should be worshipped in any form in the place, than that the place should become the scene of the license of a tavern. Tradition says that the church built on this site was dedicated by Bishop Callistus, and is now represented by the Church of St. Maria in Trastavere.

It is very possible that the persecution of Decius was in part provoked by this growing boldness of the Church, and would check it for the time;[*] but the edict of Gallienus, restoring to the Church its property and making its worship lawful, was almost an invitation to build places for its worship. It is certain that before the end of the third century churches had been built in many of the cities of the Roman empire, and probably in the eastern countries beyond the boundaries of the empire, in which also the Church was flourishing. Lactantius[†] relates that in the empire, "by the time of the outbreak of the Diocletian persecution, the numbers of the frequenters of the churches had so increased that they pulled down the ancient churches and rebuilt them from the foundation in all the cities, and these buildings were

---

[*] A passage in the "Apostolic Constitutions" (viii. 34) seems to belong to this period. "If it be not possible to go to the church on account of the unbelievers, thou, O bishop, shalt assemble them in a house, . . . if it is not possible to assemble in a house, let every one by himself sing and read and pray, or two or three together."

[†] "De Mortibus Persecutorum," ch. xii.

insufficient to contain the increasing multitudes of worshippers, and in their place more spacious and stately edifices were erected." The publicity of their churches and their architectural character is illustrated by that of Nicomedia, the eastern capital of the empire, which is described as a "magnificent" building, erected on an elevated site in the midst of the other great buildings of the city, in full view from the windows of the imperial palace.

There are some interesting notices which help us to conjecture the growth of Church organization in Rome. An extant letter of Pius I., Bishop of Rome (142–157), states that Felix, a presbyter, had given a "*titulus.*"* As early as the beginning of the third century Bishop Evaristus is said to have divided the "titles" among the priests and appointed seven deacons. Fabian (236–251) divided the fourteen (civic) *regiones* of Rome among the deacons; and there is reason to believe that each region had its *titulus*, or "parish church," and its cemetery; that each cemetery had its chapel or basilica; and that there were two priests to each title, one of whom ministered in the chapel of the cemetery. Dionysius (259–269) is said to have revised this organization; Marcellus (308–310) constituted twenty-five *tituli* in the city of Rome; Optatus of Melevia states that there were forty churches in Rome and its suburbs in the time of Diocletian—twenty-five in the city and fifteen in the suburbs.

* *I.e.* a permanent church to which priests were appointed, and which might not be abandoned (Ducange).

The provinces of Gaul, Spain, and Britain were much behind the ancient, populous, wealthy, and civilized provinces of the East, and behind Italy; but that even in those remote and backward populations there were, before Constantine, Christian communities, who had built for themselves churches, we gather from the statement of Lactantius, that the Cæsar Constantius did not approve of the persecution ordered by Diocletian, and "while he destroyed the churches in his provinces, which could be rebuilt, the true temple which is in men he preserved." That there were public churches and cemeteries in Spain and no hindrance to their free use seems to be proved by certain Canons of the Council of Illiberis (300 or 301 A.D.); for Canon 21 censures those who should be absent from church for three Sundays; Canon 36 prohibits the painting on their walls of sacred persons or saints; and Canon 35 forbids women to attend the night vigils in the cemeteries, because it was found to lead to abuses. We have also proof of the existence of churches in Africa in the fact that when Constantine became Emperor of the West he gave the clergy of those regions money for the rebuilding of their churches which had been destroyed.

When the Church began to erect independent buildings for its worship, it adhered to the plan to which it had so long been accustomed, with such modifications as convenience suggested. Its architects found this modified plan ready to their hands in the basilicas of the Roman magistrates. For the official basilica was an enlargement of the usual reception-rooms of a Roman house, adapted to the needs of a large public assembly. There the great patrician received the crowd of clients who waited upon him daily to pay their respects or to prefer their requests; there the Roman magistrate received the crowd of courtiers and suitors, administered justice, and transacted his general public business.* It retained the open court on what we may conveniently call the west. The great hall was divided by its two rows of columns, only instead of the centre of the nave being left open to the weather, it was usually completely roofed over. The ancient tablinum was modified into an apsidal tribune, which, for the sake of convenience and dignity, was raised above the level of the hall, and the opening between them was spanned by a lofty arch. The curule chair of the magistrate was placed upon the elevated platform, on the chord of the apse, conveniently overlooking the great hall; and a stone bench round the curve of the apse afforded seats for assessors, officials, or visitors of distinction. A curtain was drawn before the tribune while the judges consulted. A transverse aisle or transept sometimes separated the tribune from the rest of the hall. Such a basilica was "Herod's judgment hall", at Cæsarea, where Festus, sitting in his chair of office, with Agrippa and Bernice on chairs beside him, and the chief captains and principal men of the city on the bench behind, permitted St. Paul to speak for himself.

* Compare the basilica of the house of the "most excellent Theophilus" at Antioch, p. 15.

CHAPTER IV.

ARCHITECTURE OF THE PUBLIC CHURCHES BEFORE CONSTANTINE.

Churches in the East; in Central Syria; in North Africa; Egypt and Nubia—Description of a Basilican Church—The Church at Tyre—Church symbolism.

HEN the architects were required to build churches for public worship, we have seen that they adopted the basilican plan, which retained the architectual arrangement to which the congregations were accustomed, with just such modifications as made it still better suited to Christian worship. We find the plan almost universally in use from Britain to Nubia, from Spain to Mesopotamia, and it continued in use for centuries, and indeed continues, in a modified form, down to the present day. In the thirteenth century it became usual, in England, to enlarge the semicircular tribune into the long square-ended chancel, in order to transfer the choir into it out of the atrium; but the nave and aisles of mediæval and modern churches

are the old atrium, with Gothic, instead of Grecian, details.

In looking for the earliest existing examples of these public churches, we do not necessarily turn to Rome, where the people, and especially the noble families, were among the latest to abandon the worship of

Capital of pilaster supporting the "Triumphal Arch" of the Church of SS. Cosmas and Damian, Diarbekr.

the ancient gods; nor necessarily to the empire at all. There are several other countries where we might search with better reason. Tradition indicates a very early acceptance of Christianity by the kings of Osrhoene, and it is confirmed by the fact that the

Abgarus who reigned at Edessa from 160 to 170 replaced the old symbols of the national worship on his coinage by the symbol of the cross. The Edessans are said in their chronicle to have had a church (*templum ecclesiæ Christianorum*) which was destroyed by a flood in 202 A.D. A church still exists at Urfa (Edessa) of basilican plan and with details of good classical character.* The Church had been planted in Parthia in Apostolic times, and, sometimes protected, sometimes persecuted by the Great King, it had attained considerable magnitude before the age of Constantine. Two churches exist at Diarbekr † with capitals of fine and pure classical design; at Nisibis is a basilica of early date and in perfect preservation; these may be among the earliest existing churches, but we need fuller and more accurate information about them. Gregory, called Thaumaturgus, is said to have built a church at Neo-Cæsarea in Pontus in 258. Gregory the Illuminator caused three churches to be built at Etchmiadzin, about 300 A.D., and under his preaching Armenia had embraced Christianity as the national religion before the age of Constantine; among the ancient churches of these countries it is possible that some very early examples may still exist.

The earliest existing examples which we are able with any confidence to claim are in Central Syria and in North Africa.

In Northern and Central Syria are more than a

---

* "Christians under the Crescent," p. 81.
† Ibid., p. 101.

hundred ruined—or rather deserted—cities; for in many of them houses, public buildings, churches, and tombs are so far perfect that a very little labour in replacing fallen stones, putting on roofs and adding doors, would restore them to their original condition. They were built in the third, fourth, fifth, and sixth centuries, were deserted probably at the time of the Mohammedan conquest early in the seventh century, have never since been occupied, and remain unaltered by the hand of man. We shall have to return to this

Church at Chaqqa, Syria.

interesting series of examples of Christian architecture, but for the present we have only to introduce two of them which belong to the period with which we are here immediately concerned. M. de Vogüé* thinks that at Chaqqa to be the earliest, and assigns it to the end of the second or beginning of the third century. It differs from the conventional basilican type. It is 1830 metres from east to west, and 1980 from north to south, the height of the façade

* "Syrie Centrale," by Count M. de Vogüé.

being 8·36. The internal colonnades are not, as usual, of equally spaced columns, but each colonnade consists of a wide central arch with one narrower arch on each side. De Vogüé says that there was a gallery on each side over the side aisles. The construction is rude, of stone without cement, except in the façade and pillars. The basilica at Taffka, which has the remarkable feature of a tower at the north corner, is assigned by M. de Vogüé to the third century. The section across the church shows that the arches of the nave reached to the roof; while the side aisles are divided into two stories, of which the upper forms a gallery. The entire construction is of stone; the roof, the floors of the galleries, even the shutters of the windows (of which two remain *in situ*), are of stone.

In North Africa there are also ancient cities so far perfect that they are more correctly described as deserted than ruined, as Lambœsis, Thamugas, Theveste, in Algeria, south of the slopes of the Aures, and Sufetulu, in Tunisia; an account of the remains of the early churches in these countries would occupy a chapter; their foundations may be traced in nearly every town, and occasionally portions of the superstructure remain. These also are all (or with very rare exceptions) of the basilican type.

In Egypt, and so far south as Nubia, very ancient churches are found. The church at Ermet in Egypt, and that at Ibrim in Nubia, are, perhaps, of the end of the third or beginning of the fourth century. The fine basilica of Theveste, built not later than the first century, has certainly been a church since the reign of Justinian, but it was perhaps originally built for a civil basilica, and subsequently converted to Christian uses. One of the earliest which we can claim as having been built for a church, is at Djemla, in Algeria. It is a rectangular hall, 92 feet long by 52 feet wide, divided by pillars into a nave and aisles, with a lofty square enclosure at the upper end, on the usual site of the chancel. Its floor is covered with a fine mosaic pavement, so purely classical in design as to leave no doubt of its early date. Another very early church at Announa, also in Algeria, is of the common basilican plan, a body and aisles, about 95 feet square, with a semicircular apse at the upper end. A basilica at Orleansville, the ancient Castellum Tingitanum, erected, according to an inscription, in 252 (probably a local era corresponding to A.D. 325), is 80 feet long by 52 wide, divided by four rows of pillars into a nave with double aisles, and has an apse at the lower as well as the upper end. A church of the usual basilican plan at Oued Gilma, of the fourth or fifth century, has the novel features of external buttresses and small windows in the aisle walls.

It is clear, then, that the Christian communities from the first were accustomed to worship in the spacious and handsome upper rooms, or in the stately pillared atria, of the houses of wealthy converts; and that at a comparatively early period, they built public churches, in which they imitated the domestic buildings to which they had become accustomed, not only in general architectural plan and design, but in the use of marble and bronze, mosaic pavements, and mural paintings. There is reason to believe that the sumptuous appointments of the private houses were also imitated in the furniture of the public churches; and that the greater churches sometimes possessed considerable wealth in gold and silver vessels for the Eucharistic service, silver lamps, and silken hangings.*

The following is a detailed description of a basilican church :—

The court was usually approached from the west by a pronaos or entrance more or less ornamented. It was a large open area surrounded by a pillared cloister, and in the middle was a cantharus or fountain, at which the people washed their hands as they came to worship. This was the original of the holy-water stoop outside the doors of our mediæval churches, into which the people dipped their fingers.

The church presented on the side of the court an unpretending façade. A low portico, a continuation of the cloister of the atrium, stretched across the front, and sometimes a long narrow porch beyond that called the *narthex*, a term whose derivation is uncertain. Above the portico were usually three long round-headed undivided windows, symmetrically arranged, and above them a round window in the pediment; windows of the same kind were introduced

* See chapter xix.

in both side walls immediately under the eaves, which admitted abundance of light. The portals were usually square-headed, and often decorated with sculptured architraves taken or copied from older buildings. The church itself, we have seen, was a large hall divided by colonnades. The pillars often supported an architrave which carried the wall above; but the arch was more frequent. In either case the structure was not adapted to vaulting, and was roofed with timber; the rude timber beams which we see in some cases are not necessarily original, it is probable that the original roofs were more ornamentally finished with timbers carved, coloured, and gilded, or sheathed in metal; we know that the basilica of Ulpia, for example, was roofed with beams of gilded bronze. At the upper end of the nave was placed the choir elevated some feet above the pavement, and enclosed by *cancelli* from which we get the name of chancel. In the early Oriental churches these *cancelli* were made of wood; in the West all the examples which remain are of marble, very generally adorned with that kind of mosaic which is called *opus Alexandrinum*. On either side of the choir stood the *ambones*, or pulpits, the loftier and more richly adorned was usually on the (ritual) north side from which the deacon read the Gospel, the other on the south side from which the subdeacon read the Epistle. From the Gospel pulpit also the Bidding Prayers were read, and the bishop or priest preached; a small pillar in front of it supported the Paschal candle.

The sanctuary in the larger churches was divided from the nave by the *triumphal arch*. The altar—there was only one—stood on the raised platform of the apse, on the chord of the apse, or a little before or behind that line, but always well forward from the east wall, surmounted by its tabernacle or baldachino. A stone chair, elevated on some steps against the centre of the east wall, was the throne of the bishop, and the stone bench round the curve of the wall formed the seat of his presbyters.

We are able to conclude this series of the ante-Constantine churches by a contemporary description of one of them, the earliest detailed description of a church and its furniture which has come down to us. A new church was built at Tyre between the years 313 and 332; it was built on the site of a former church—though that was not the most advantageous position which could have been found for it—on account of the attachment of the people to the old site. It was built, not by the imperial bounty, for it must be borne in mind that the imperial favour was not extended to the Church in the East till the defeat of Licinius in A.D. 323, but by the voluntary donations of the people themselves, under the pious care of Paulinus, the aged bishop. It is not to be supposed that all churches were of like magnitude and splendour, for we are expressly told that this was by far the most noble church at that time in Phœnicia. Eusebius, Bishop of Cæsarea, the well-known historian of the early Church, as metropolitan of the province, dedicated the church, and preached the dedication sermon, and, with a pardonable vanity for which we are very grateful, preserved his sermon in his History; and in his sermon the description of the church occurs. We give a paraphrase * of Eusebius's account as more generally intelligible than the rhetorical and somewhat obscure original :—

"Eusebius states that the bishop surrounded the site of the church with a wall of enclosure. This wall, according to Dr. Thomson ('The Land and the Book,' p. 189, chap. xiii.), can still be traced, and measures 222 feet in length by 129 in breadth. In the east side of this wall was a large and stately entrance, which gave access to a quadrangular atrium; this was surrounded by ranges of columns, the spaces between which were filled by net-like railings of wood; in the centre of the court was a fountain, at which those who were about to enter the church purified themselves (*i.e.* washed their hands and feet).

"The church itself was entered through interior porticoes, perhaps a narthex, but whether distinct from the portico which bounded the atrium on that side, does not appear. Three doorways led into the nave; the central of these was by far the largest, and had doors covered with bronze reliefs; the other doorways gave entrance to the side aisles. Above these aisles were galleries, well lighted (doubtless by external windows), and looking upon the nave; these galleries were adorned with beautiful work in wood. The passage is a little obscure, but it seems most probable that the passage from the galleries into the nave

* From the "Dictionary of Christian Antiquities."

was protected by a balustrade of wood. The nave was constructed of still richer materials than the rest, and the roof was of cedar of Lebanon. Dr. Thomson states that the remains of five granite columns may still be seen, and that 'the height of the dome was eighty feet, as appears by the remains of an arch.' Nothing which Eusebius says leads to the supposition that there was a dome, and the arch was probably the triumphal arch, through which, as in many basilican churches, a space in front of the apse, something like a transept, was entered.

"The building having been in such manner completed, Paulinus, we are told, provided it with thrones in the highest places for the honour of the presidents, and with benches according to fitness, and, placing the most holy altar in the midst, surrounded the whole with wooden net-like railings of most skilful work, so that the enclosed space might be inaccessible to the crowd. The pavement, he adds, was adorned with marble decoration of every kind. Then, on the outside, he constructed very large external buildings and halls, which were attached to the sides of the church, and connected with it by entrances in the hall lying between. These halls, we are told, were destined for those who still required the purification and sprinkling of water and of the Holy Ghost.

"It may not be out of place to extract the passage of the sermon in which the preacher makes an elaborate parallel between the material and the spiritual Church of Tyre. 'The exterior wall he compares to the great mass and multitude of the people. The doors, to the ostiaries who admit the people into the building. These he has supported by the four pillars which are placed without around the quadrangular atrium, by initiating them in the first elements of the literal sense of the Four Gospels. Then he stations around on both sides of the royal temple, those who are yet catechumens and that are yet making progress and improvement, though not very far separated from the inmost view of Divine things enjoyed by the faithful. Receiving from among these the souls that are cleansed like gold by the Divine washing [baptism], he likewise supports and strengthens those with columns far better than these external ones, viz. by the inner mysteries and hidden doctrines of the Scriptures. He also illuminates them by the openings to admit the light, adorning the whole temple with one grand vestibule (?) of adoration to the one only God, the universal Sovereign; exhibiting however, as the second splendour, the light of Christ and of the Holy Spirit on each side of the Father's authority, and displaying in the rest, throughout the whole building, the abundance and the exceeding great excellence of the clearness and brilliancy of truth in every part. Having also selected from everywhere and every quarter the living and moving and well-prepared stones of the mind, he has built a grand and truly royal edifice of all, splendid and filled with light within and without.

"'And in this temple there are also thrones and many seats and many benches [for the bishop, priests, and deacons], and in all the souls in them the gifts of the Holy Spirit reside, such as anciently were seen in the holy Apostles, to whom cloven tongues as of fire appeared and sat upon each of them. But in the chief of all [the bishop] Christ Himself resides as it were in His fulness. In those that rank next to Him [the priests] each one shares proportionately in the distribution of the power of Christ and of the Holy Ghost. The souls of those to whom is committed the care of instruction [the deacons, etc.] may be seats for angels. Nobler and grand and unique is the altar, such as should be, sincere and most holy, the mind and spirit of the priest of the whole congregation [the celebrant]. That great High Priest of the universe, Jesus, the only-begotten Son of God, Himself standing at His right hand, receives the sweet incense from all, and the bloodless and immaterial sacrifices of prayer, with a bright and benign eye; and with extended hand bears them to the Father of heaven and God over all. He Himself first adoring Him, and the only one that gives to the Father the worship that is His due, and then interceding with Him for us, that He may always continue propitious and favourable to us.'"

Notwithstanding a little obscurity of language here and there, we easily catch the meaning of this interesting early example of ecclesiastical symbolism. The preacher reaches his climax when he proceeds to remind his hearers that the material Temple which they are dedicating, is a figure of the universe, and this worship of the Church on earth but a faint echo of the worship which all His intelligent creatures offer through Christ to God:—

"'Such is the character of this great Temple which the mighty creative Word hath established throughout the whole world, constituting this again a kind of intellectual image on earth of those things beyond the vault of heaven. So that in all His creation, and by all His intelligent creatures on earth, the Father should be honoured and adored. But those regions beyond the heavens are also displays of what are here; and that Jerusalem above, and that heavenly Sion, and that City of the Living God beyond our earth, in which are the innumerable choir of angels, and the assembly of the Firstborn written in heaven, extol their Maker and the Universal Sovereign of all with praises and hymns inexpressible. These surpass our comprehension, neither could any mortal tongue be adequate to express that glory. For eye hath not seen, and ear hath not heard, neither hath it entered into the heart of man to conceive those things which God hath prepared for them that love Him.'"

CHAPTER V.

THE CHURCHES OF CONSTANTINE.

Rome no longer the capital of the empire, and not the centre of Christian influence—Constantine's Churches at Rome—Basilicas not converted into Churches—Temples seldom converted into Churches; their materials used in building Churches on their sites—Description of St. Peter's, St. Paul's, and St. Agnes' at Rome—Constantine's Churches in the East; at Bethlehem, Jerusalem, Constantinople—Effect of Constantine's conversion on Christian art.

WHEN Constantine entered Rome, after the victory at the Milvian Bridge (A.D. 312), it was as an avowed convert to Christianity and champion of the Christian cause. He made open profession of his new faith by causing to be placed in the hand of his statue in the Forum a copy of the Labarum, the standard embroidered with the symbolic XP under which he had gained his decisive victory; and the senate, probably with no very great enthusiasm, decreed a triumphal arch to the victor.

The arch of Constantine is in a sense a Christian monument, the earliest of his reign, and the only one which has come down to us unaltered and uninjured, and it is quite worth while to include it among our illustrations, if only as a standard of architectural comparison, and to say a few words about it.

After the victory of the Milvian Bridge, which gave to Constantine the Empire of the West, and secured the victory of Christianity, the Roman senate decreed to their new sovereign the honour of a triumphal arch. It was the work of the senate, which was still, and for long afterwards continued to be, conservative of the religion of the gods of Rome; but it is a monument of the victory of Christianity, and its ambiguous inscription bears witness to the politic compromise which the senate made between their own beliefs and the new religion of the emperor to whose honour it was dedicated. It is sufficiently well known, and the woodcut sufficiently represents its general features to make a detailed description unnecessary. But there are some remarkable features in its construction which illustrate the state of art at the time which we have elsewhere had occasion to mention. Portions of the monument, notably the bas-reliefs and statues which adorn its faces, are of the age of Trajan, and probably belonged originally to an arch dedicated to that emperor; while others of the bas-reliefs introduced are in a style of art greatly inferior, and are no doubt the work of the sculptors employed at this date by the senate. The usual explanation is that the senate destroyed an arch of Trajan, and used the materials in the construction of their monument to Constantine, which would be in accordance with the custom of the time to rifle ancient monuments of their precious materials for the construction of new buildings, of which we find so many examples in the Christian Churches for centuries afterwards, and, in harmony with another custom, to appropriate old imperial

Arch of Constantine, Rome.

statues to new emperors by the simple expedient of cutting off the heads of the old statues, and replacing them by new portraits. But we take leave to offer another conjecture which we venture to think more probable. The fine design and pure architectural details of this noble monument seem to be beyond the capabilities of the debased art of the beginning of the fourth century. Moreover it does not on examination give evidence of being, as a whole, a new design worked up out of old materials. The work looks like a fine and homogeneous whole, with a few debased details manifestly added. We suggest that an arch dedicated to Trajan was bodily "annexed" by the senate; a few new bas-reliefs substituted for others which were unsuitable for its present appropriation; and a new inscription placed over the central arch, which dedicated it to the glory of the new master of Rome.

The inscription on the south front is as follows:—

IMP . CAES . FL . CONSTANTINO . MAXIMO .
P. F. AVGVSTO . S. P. Q. R.
QVOD . INSTINCTV . DIVINITATIS . MENTIS
MAGNITVDINE . CVM . EXERCITV . SVO
TAM . DE . TYRANNO . QVAM . DE . OMNI . EIVS
FACTIONE . VNO . TEMPORE . JVSTIS
REMPVBLICAM . VLTVS . EST . ARMIS .
ARCVM . TRIVMPHIS . INSIGNEM . DICAVIT

"To the Emperor Cæsar Flavius Constantinus, Maximus, Pius, Felix, Augustus, who, by the inspiration of the Divinity and the greatness of his genius, together with his army, has avenged, by his just arms, the Republic at the same time from the Tyrant and all his faction, the Roman Senate and People have dedicated this eminent Arch of Triumph."

Inside the centre arch are also the inscriptions: LIBERATORI . VRBIS, on one side, and on the other, FVNDATORI . QVIETIS. To the Liberator of the City; To the Founder of Peace. There used to be a question whether the words INSTINCTV . DIVINITATIS were not a later insertion, a correction of some allusion to a Pagan deity; but at the instance of the Emperor Napoleon III., architects and savans were allowed to ascend the arch and make a careful examination of the inscription, and they found that the words were beyond doubt an integral part of the original inscription.

The popular notion that Constantine proceeded to give basilicas and temples to be converted into churches, and to make Rome the centre of the Christian world, is erroneous.

Rome was at that time, and continued to be for two centuries longer, the chief stronghold of the ancient religion; its temples occupied the most commanding situations, and were among the great architectural glories of the city; their worship was maintained with all its wonted splendour. The great nobles adhered to the old religion as part of the ancient order to which they belonged, and the citizens as a body showed the same attachment. The vast population of the city, drawn from all parts of the world, afforded converts enough to make up the most numerous Church of any city in the empire, but they were chiefly of the lower orders of the people. The Church was overshadowed in Rome by the dominant State religion.

Nor was the Church of Rome distinguished among the Churches of Christendom; it had not yet produced a single name great in theological learning or ecclesiastical statesmanship. The Churches of the East constituted by their wealth, learning, and civilization, the most important part of Christendom, and for many generations to come they looked down upon the comparatively recent, rude, unlearned Churches of the West. Moreover, Rome had long ceased to be the political centre of the empire. The Eastern conquests had made the shores of the Bosphorus the most convenient centre of affairs; there, on the Asiatic shore, Diocletian had built a new capital at Nicomedia, and Constantine shortly removed it to the western shore at Byzantium; and the secondary capital of the Augustus of the West had been established at Milan.

This will explain the fact that Constantine remained less than three months at Rome on this occasion, and did not revisit it again till he celebrated there his decennalia. No doubt the conqueror during those three months showed his good will to his new faith by benefactions to the Church of Rome. Notably he founded two noble churches over the resting-places of the Apostle-martyrs, the founders and patron-saints of the Roman Church, St. Peter's at the Vatican and St. Paul's without the Walls; and several other churches are, with less certainty, attributed to him. When it is said that the emperor built churches, at Rome and elsewhere, what is meant is that he contributed the necessary funds, but there is direct evidence that he left the design and execution of the work to the bishops of the places, to whom it naturally belonged.

There is no evidence that he gave any of the civil basilicas in Rome or elsewhere to be converted into churches. It would be difficult to explain why the head of the civil administration of the empire should eject the magistrates from their courts and build new basilicas for them, when it was just as easy to build new churches where they were wanted. There is, in fact, only one known example in which a basilica was turned into a church, and that was at Trèves.*

Constantine did present the Palace of the Lateran, which had come to him through his wife, the Empress Fausta, to the Bishop of Rome, who made it the episcopal residence; and the basilica of the palace, which was probably larger and handsomer than all the earlier churches, was used as a church—the cathedral church of the city—and it still takes precedence of all the churches of Rome. Bishop Sylvester is said to have added a baptistery.

Nor did Constantine give up the ancient temples to be used as churches. It was his wise policy at this time to relieve the public mind of any fear of retaliation for the past persecution of Christianity, or of a crusade against the ancient religions. The only temples whose worship Constantine suppressed were some temples of Venus, on account of the immoralities practised in them, and for like reasons he suppressed the worship of Isis in Egypt. The temples were gradually deserted, until the edict of Valentinian II. (391) put an end to the public ceremonies of the old religions, closed the temples, and appropriated

* E. A. Freeman.

them to various public uses, or left them to gradual decay.*

The building which is given here as a specimen of the ancient temples is that at Nîmes, in France, which is popularly known as the *Maison Carrée*. It is a gem of architecture. The excellence of its proportions, the beauty of its Corinthian columns,

The Maison Carrée at Nîmes.

frieze, and cornice, and its wonderful preservation, make it the finest example of a classical temple remaining in Northern Europe. The date is disputed, but it is probably of the time of Antoninus Pius. The columns scattered around it are the remains of

* Jerome (Ep. cvii. 1, 2) speaks of the temples at Rome as left to neglect, disorder, and decay.

long colonnades, which probably formed part of the forum of the ancient city, into the further end of which the temple projected.

Some of the disused temples of the ancient gods were ultimately converted into churches, but the ordinary plan of a temple was not well adapted to the uses of the Christian assembly. The ancient worship was an outdoor worship. The altar was placed at the base of the porticoed front of the temple. As the people stood assisting at the sacrifice, the pillared façade of the temple formed a background to the altar and an ornamental screen for the cella behind, in which the deity was supposed to be present. Since the cella was not intended to contain a body of worshippers, it was comparatively small and dark. An early church was architecturally a temple turned inside out. It was intended to enclose the whole body of worshippers within its ample area ; its stately colonnades, sculptured friezes, and marble veneering were all inside, while the exterior presented to the outside world only a mass of brick wall, with hardly any attempt to mitigate its blank ugliness.*

There were exceptions such as will readily occur to the mind of the reader. The Parthenon at Athens, and the Temple of Jupiter of the Capitol of Rome, in which the senate held its meetings, and others, had a cella large enough to contain a great congregation; in some other instances, by throwing down the cella and building a wall between the columns

---

* The exteriors of the Syrian churches are an exception to this statement.

which had surrounded it, a capacious church was obtained.*

More frequently the temples left desolate by the expiring heathenism, and handed over to the triumphant Church, were pulled down, and churches were built on the site, and largely out of the old materials. A great number of churches all over Christendom are traditionally said to occupy the sites of heathen temples, and among them St. Peter's, Cornhill, and St. Paul's, London. One of the commonest features of the most ancient churches is that they are largely made up of the spoils of more ancient buildings. The Christian architects had not wealth enough at their disposal to obtain at first hand the shapely monolithic columns of the earlier magnificence of the Roman world, or skill enough to execute the beautifully carved capitals of a purer style of art; but they had taste enough to appreciate them, and they habitually used them in their new buildings. Sometimes the columns did not match, and the architect helped a column which was too short by giving it a taller base. In the same way, the Christian artists used ancient carved ivories to ornament a bishop's chair or form the covers of the sacred books, and ancient gems engraved with classical devices (sometimes strangely incongruous) to enrich chalices and

* The Pantheon and the Church of S. Maria Egiziaca are the only examples at Rome of temples turned into churches (Lübke's "History of Art") (the Pantheon at Rome was consecrated as a church in A.D. 610), and the Church of S. Urbano alla Caffarella in the suburbs of Rome (Lord Lindsay), but very few in Italy; in the East a larger number were thus converted.

shrines. And in doing this they were perhaps moved not only by the artist's instinct to adorn his work with that which was intrinsically precious in material and beautiful in art, but with something of the spirit of a conqueror displaying in his triumphal procession the riches of the conquered people. These were the Church's trophies of its conquest over the heathen worships and godless luxury of the ancient time.

The new churches which were built at this period at Rome, the two basilicas—the one on the site of Nero's Circus, in honour of St. Peter, and the other without the walls, on the Ostian Way, in honour of St. Paul—both have ceased to exist. St. Peter's was destroyed to make way for the present magnificent monument of the Renaissance. Of the old St. Peter's, however, drawings exist which give us a very accurate idea of the great church. The plan shows the atrium, 212 feet by 225, entered by a portico with buildings on each side which may have been added in the Middle Ages. It has the usual columned cloister round the sides and the fountain in the middle. The eastern portico, which formed the narthex, is entered by a little porch. The church itself was 380 feet long by 212 wide; its magnificent dimensions are perhaps best understood from the statement that it covered as large an area as any mediæval cathedral except Milan and Seville. At the upper end is a kind of transept, and the apse was separated from the transept by a row of pillars. Over the colonnades of the nave the side walls were divided into a double tier of panels, each of which contained a picture; above these panels was the clerestory from which the building received its light, and a broad cornice of ornamental work supported the wall-plate of the roof. What was the design of the original roof is matter of pure conjecture; probably it was finished with an ornamental ceiling. The

The Church of St. Paul without the Walls, Rome.   After the fire.

columns with their bases and capitals were taken from earlier buildings.

The first Church of St. Paul without the Walls was a small church of the normal basilican plan—a fore court, a nave with aisles, and an apse flanked by two square chambers.* Having been badly built,

* Lanciani, " Pagan and Christian Rome."

it fell into disrepair. The second church on the same site was begun by Theodosius and finished by his sons Arcadius and Honorius on a much larger scale. It was 419 feet long by 217 wide, and the nave 80 feet high; it had a great court, on the west side of which were five chambers. The noble colonnade was composed of pillars taken from earlier buildings, pillars of the finest and rarest marbles—Greek, Phrygian, and African—some with Corinthian capitals of their own, some with capitals of the time. The two columns of Pentelic marble which supported the triumphal arch were, base and capital included, 45 feet high.

It was almost an exact counterpart of St. Peter's in dimensions and plan, but there was one important structural difference: the pillars which separated the nave from the aisles were surmounted by arches instead of a horizontal architrave, which was an improvement in picturesque effect as well as an advance in the principles of construction. The woodcut gives a sufficient idea of the grandeur of the general effect. It was partially destroyed by an accidental fire in 1822. From existing drawings and from the portions which survived the fire the church has been rebuilt as a reproduction of the original church.

Several smaller churches claim to have been originally built by Constantine or in his reign. One of these, the Church of St. Agnes without the Wall, has preserved its whole construction with very little change, and is in this respect one of the most interesting churches in Rome. It consists of a nave separated from the two aisles by sixteen ancient columns—some of them curiously fluted—with good Corinthian and composite capitals. Above rises a second range of columns of smaller dimensions, upon which rests the wall, pierced with windows and supporting the roof. Over the aisles and at the west end is a gallery which was reserved for the women. Under the high altar, which has a baldachino, is the "confession" of St. Agnes, where the remains of the virgin martyr are deposited. The square chamber at the east end of the south aisle was probably the ancient sacrarium, and the larger chamber (now used as a vestry) at the north-west side of the building was perhaps the baptistery.

Among the other churches in Rome traditionally said to have been founded by Constantine are San Lorenzo and Sta. Croce in Gerusalemme. Both contain portions of the original building and fragments of the greatest interest, but they add nothing to our knowledge of the art of that early period.

When Constantine had won the Empire of the East he caused other churches to be erected at his cost. One at Antioch for its splendour was called the Golden Church; others were at Mamre, at Heliopolis in Phœnicia, and at Nicomedia. When the pilgrimage of his mother, the Empress Helena, had drawn attention to the "Holy Places" of Palestine, the emperor built a church at Bethlehem over the site of our Lord's Nativity, a group of churches on the site of the Holy

Sepulchre, and one on the Mount of Olives, over the supposed site of the Ascension.

The nave of the church at Bethlehem still remains as represented in the accompanying woodcut. It is the only church of Constantine which still exists; all the others have been rebuilt or have disappeared. This seems to be a purely unaltered example of the age, with the advantage that all its pillars and

The Church of Bethlehem.

capitals appear to have been made for the place which they occupy. The dimensions of the whole church are 215 feet long by 103 across. The choir, with its three apses, was probably added or rebuilt by Justinian.

The group on the site of the Holy Sepulchre consisted first of a memorial church, of the usual circular plan, round about the rock-tomb which was believed to be the actual tomb in which our Lord was laid, and to the east of it a basilican church in honour of the Resurrection; and the two were connected by subsidiary buildings. Constantine's directions to the Bishop of Ælia for the Church of the Holy Sepulchre were that it should excel all other churches in beauty, and that not only the building itself, but all its accessories should be such that they should not be surpassed by the fairest structures of any city of the empire. Eusebius gives an elaborate description of the church, and an account of the grand ceremonial of its dedication, A.D. 335. A full description, accompanied by plans of the buildings erected by Constantine, may be seen in Professor Willis's essay in the second volume of Williams's "Holy City." Mr. Fergusson has started the strange notion that the Dome of the Rock on Moriah is Constantine's church; and another site outside the Damascus Gate has lately been put forward as that of the Holy Sepulchre; but it is highly probable that the traditional site is not only that which was pointed out to the Empress Helena, but also that it is the true site of the Sepulchre.

When Constantine built a new capital for the reunited empire on the west shore of the Bosphorus he made it from the first a Christian city; not a single heathen temple was permitted within its walls, but fourteen churches supplied the people with abundant provision for Christian worship. The chief of them, dedicated in honour of the twelve Apostles, which came to be more commonly known after his own name as the *Ecclesia Constantina*, was,

Eusebius says, "vastly high, and yet had all its walls [internally] covered with marble, its roof [ceiling] overlaid with gold, and the outside, instead of tiles, covered with gilded brass." A second great church dedicated to the Holy Wisdom, *Sancta Sophia*, was finished by his son Constantius. The Church of St. John Studens, commonly said to have been rebuilt after the taking of Constantinople by the Latins, is now believed to have retained its original plan and probably much of the original building, the date of which is tolerably well ascertained as A.D. 363. It is a plain basilica, 120 feet long by 85 wide, divided into a nave and aisles by rows of marble columns, supporting an architrave, frieze, and cornice, upon which stand other columns supporting arches; the capitals are semi-classical, ornamented with acanthus leaves. The style is rich, and retains much of the ancient classical form and feeling. It has a semi-octagonal apse and an oblong narthex.

The conversion of Constantine gave a great impulse to the spread of Christianity, especially among the upper class of society, and thereby caused a great increase in church-building and in the employment of all the arts in the service of religion. It would also naturally have the effect of placing at the disposal of the Church the services of the most eminent artists. But this would only ensure that the best of contemporary art would be bestowed upon Christian subjects; it could not possibly produce any sudden change in the style of art.

CHAPTER VI.

THE CHURCHES AFTER CONSTANTINE.

The colonnades with the Greek architrave; with the Roman arch; with an upper tier of columns—St. Clement's, Rome—St. Ambrose's, Milan—Churches of Central Syria: Babouda; Qualb Louzeh; Tourmanin—Domestic architecture of Central Syria—Churches at Nisibis; Thessalonica—The Golden Gate of Jerusalem—Churches of Egypt and Nubia, Thaumugas—Ravenna: Tomb of Galla Placidia; St. Apollinare Nuova; St. Apollinare in Classe; St. Vitale—Parenzo in Istria—Churches of Gaul: Lyons; St. Martin's, Tours; Clermont—Existing remains of the classical style in Gaul—The dome in Persia; in Central Syria; St. Ezra; Bozra—The Byzantine dome; Sta. Sophia—Domes in the West—Traces of the basilican style of architecture in Britain, at Canterbury, Frampton, Silchester—The Celtic churches.

THE great defect, as it seems to us, in the interior design of some of the early basilicas was that the columns were too low in proportion to the great height of the wall which they supported, so that the long-drawn colonnades, which ought to have been the noblest feature of the view, looked dwarfed and overloaded. This was especially the case where the pillars were surrounded by a straight architrave, as in St. Peter's. But it must be borne in mind that

F

painting was very largely used in the decoration of interiors, and that this wall space would be divided into panels corresponding with the intercolumniations; the strong vertical borders of these panels would break up the long wall, and continue the line of the columns upwards; and the panels would be filled with painted designs, so that the whole wall would be alive with interest and rich with colour.

The defect of the disproportion of the height of the columns to the height of the wall was greatly diminished by the substitution for the architrave of a series of round arches, as is seen in the interior view of St. Paul's without the Walls (p. 59). The change abolished the strong horizontal line of the architrave which emphasized the defect, and the extra height of the arches increased the proportionate height of the arcades in fact and still more in effect to the eye; the lines of painted decoration also would naturally follow the curve of the arches and give additional apparent height to the arcades, while it diminished the apparent height of the wall. But in later examples, as we have seen in St. Agnes, the architect frequently got rid of the defective proportion altogether by means of a second tier of columns, which formed what in Gothic churches we call the triforium; and the Roman designer made better use of this space over the aisle than the Gothic builder, by making it a commodious gallery for the accommodation of the women. The architrave over the lower arcade found its constructive use as the front of the floor of the gallery, and carried a low parapet

THE CHURCHES AFTER CONSTANTINE. 67

wall or screen which formed the gallery front. The sloping timber roof, of low pitch, was covered with tiles; internally it was often ceiled, but in any case the main timbers were often carved and gilded and the panels ornamented with painting.

The apses of the aisles were not intended for chapels and had no altars. Paulinus of Nola * describes one of them as the sacristy, and the other as a place where the pious could read the Scriptures and say prayers. There was not more than one altar in a church till centuries later in the Western Church, and in the Eastern Church never.

The Church of St. Clement at Rome was long thought to be the original church built upon the site of the house of the Flavian family, and one of the most unaltered of existing Christian churches. Recent discoveries have shown that the original church was filled in, probably in the twelfth century, in consequence of the great rise in the level of the neighbouring ground; the present church was built on the same site and partly out of the old materials, and the furniture of the old church was replaced in the present. The result is that the present church does retain a less altered appearance than any other, and that its arrangements give a better idea of the interior of a primitive basilica.

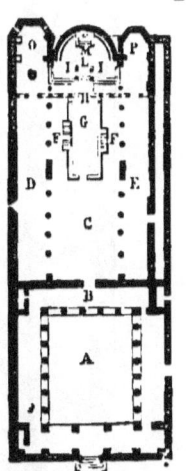

Plan of St. Clement's, Rome.

* Ep. 32.

It has the only perfect court (A) left in Rome. The chancel (G), the earliest remaining example, was probably removed to its present position from the lower church, and is of the time of John VIII., in the

The Church of St. Clement, Rome.

ninth century. The enclosing walls of marble are sculptured with Christian emblems. On the sides of the choir are the anbones or pulpits (F, F). That on the left (looking towards the altar), from which the Gospel was read, is ascended by a double stair, and has a handsome candelabrum of mosaic-work for the Paschal candle; that on the right has two reading-desks, one towards the tribune, the other towards the nave. The presbytery (I) is separated from the choir by a screen of handsomely sculptured marble panels, evidently of the same period as the choir; (B) is the narthex; (L) the altar; (M) the bishop's throne.

The Church of St. Ambrose at Milan still retains very much of the plan and design of a primitive basilica. The fine ninth-century court surrounded by a colonnade is perfect. The church, originally built in the fourth century, was renovated in the twelfth, but it retains its ancient plan, and the tribune retains an ancient episcopal throne; there is a sculptured sarcophagus of the sixth century over which the pulpit is built, the baldachino is of the eighth century, and the gold and silver altar frontal of the Carolingian period.

As we have had to quote a late example of the chancel, so we have to take a late illustration of the arrangement of the apse. The little church at Torcello, in the Venetian Lagune, was originally erected in the seventh century, and was altered and perhaps to some extent rebuilt in the first year of the eleventh; but it still retains much of the original arrangement and character, and is the best example we know of the ancient arrangement of the apse—the bishop's throne elevated so that it overlooks the whole congregation, and the benches of the presbyters arranged like those of an ancient theatre.*

* Fergusson's "History of Architecture," i. 427.

The exteriors of the older basilicas were usually very plain in design, and depended upon magnitude and proportion for any dignity which they possessed. Other buildings attached to the church are occasionally described, or traces of them found, but the provision of an official house for the clergy does not appear to have formed a regular part of the plan, except in the case of monastic churches.

The numerous churches of the deserted cities and monasteries of Central and Northern Syria afford a very interesting and valuable series of examples, fairly perfect and unaltered, of the ecclesiastical art of the period from the third to the seventh centuries. Many of them are given in plan, elevations, and details, in Count M. de Vogüé's work on the "Architecture of Central Syria." The churches have not usually inscriptions or dates, but some of the houses and monuments have, and by comparison M. de Vogüé claims to assign the dates of the churches with trustworthy accuracy. These Syrian architects, while adopting the universal basilican plan, and using the principles and ornamental forms of the old Greek art, display much artistic vigour and freedom. They had not, as the builders in countries of older civilization had, the ruins of temples and palaces to furnish them with columns and capitals ready to their hand, and consequently they had not the example of those older works as a constant check upon their own genius. Moreover, the material with which they had to deal influenced their work to some extent both in construction and ornament; for the absence of timber drove them to employ arches to span their intercolumniations and to cover their areas, and the hard character of the stone was unfavourable for such fine work as Corinthian and Composite capitals, and led them to the use of ornament in low relief. The result is that we do not find their churches—like so many in other countries—made up of interesting but incongruous ancient materials, and we do find original invention in scientific construction and in artistic design. In these churches first occurs the idea of two western towers, which became a characteristic feature of mediæval cathedrals; some of their apses are decorated in a way which found its full development in the Romanesque of the Rhine; and, lastly, we find here the introduction of the square plan surmounted by a dome, which afterwards developed into the characteristic feature of Byzantine architecture.

We can only cite two or three examples of special interest as representatives of the characteristics which we have described.

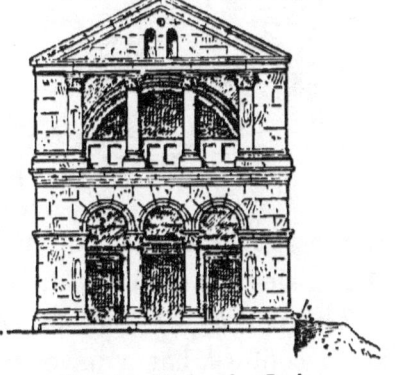

Church of Babouda, Syria.

The little church at Babouda, of the fifth century, has a nave without aisles, an apse, and a narthex. The western elevation is a charming example of the ornate composition of the external designs of these Syrian churches. It will be seen by a study of the elevation that the narthex has an upper story, open to the air westward and to the church eastward, by which the church receives a flood of light; this upper story forms a western gallery. The roof of the church continues over the narthex. The massive piers and their capitals, the ornamented moulding round the arches, and the shafts which carry the

Church of Baqouza.

timbers of the roof are worthy of special notice. The aisles are roofed with horizontal slabs of stone.

The church of Baqouza, of the beginning of the sixth century, has a nave with aisles, an apse, and a chamber on each side of the apse, a narthex, and two porches on each side. The woodcut gives a view of the striking eastern elevation; being built on the slope of a hill, this east end stands on a base which gives it additional dignity. The nave is of six bays divided by circular columns with Corinthian capitals, supporting round arches.

Qualb Louzeh, in remarkable preservation, has a nave and aisles three bays in length, and a narthex flanked by two western towers. The apse is a fine composition, with three windows, ornamented with shafts still more richly than that of Baqouza.

Church of Tourmanin, Syria.

One of the finest of these designs is the church of Tourmanin, which consists of nave and aisles of seven bays, an apse with a chamber on each side, and a narthex with two western towers. Like the church at Baqouza, this stands on a site which gives occasion for a flight of stairs up to the western entrance. It will be seen that here also, as at Babouda, the narthex has an upper gallery, open both to the outer air and to the church. The west end is an especially fine composition.

These Syrian cities give us also illustrations of the influence of Christian feeling in domestic architecture. De Vogüé remarks that the sudden growth of civilization in the district came immediately after the victory of the Church, and that the religious zeal of the people is shown not only in the existence of numerous churches and several monasteries, but in

From a house front, Central Syria. De Vogüé's "Syrie Centrale," Plate XLII.

the fact that on the greater part of the houses Christian symbols are sculptured, and numerous inscriptions of pious sentences and scripture texts, whose choice indicates the general exultation in the recent triumph of the faith. He mentions one in the bourg of Refadi where a certain Christian named Thalasis built himself a house, and on the door engraved his profession of faith: ΧΡΙΣΤΕ ΒΟΗΘΕΙ ΕΙΣ ΘΕΟΣ ΜΟΝΟΣ, "Christ, help; Thou art the one God." At Deir Sanbit some one has painted on the wall of a house, with red distemper, the sacred monogram of Constantine's Labarum XP with the ΑΩ, and repeated it, and written over ΤΟΥΤΟ ΝΙΚΑ.

At Nisibis, beyond the Euphrates, is a triple church which retains the mouldings of its doorways and windows as perfect as when they were erected. "They are identical in style with the buildings of Diocletian at Spalato, and of Constantine [?] at Jerusalem" (Fergusson).

At Thessalonica the Eski Juma, or Old Mosque, is a Christian church probably of the fifth century. It is a simple basilica in plan, with nave and narthex. St. Demetrius is larger, divided into five aisles with internal transept, and accessory buildings.

The Golden Gate in the east wall of the Temple enclosure at Jerusalem is a fine and fairly perfect work. Fergusson assigns it to Constantine, but it is more probably of the fifth to sixth century (De Vogüé), and a good example of the style as it approached the Byzantine.

Basilicas of the fifth and following centuries are still numerous in Egypt and Nubia, the oases of the Libyan Desert, and in the waste lands of Algeria and Tunis. They are usually small, with the peculiarity that the apse is included within a square external wall. At Thamugas in the Aures is one with an inscription which states that it was built in 646—a square building with an apse, divided into nave and aisles by columns of rose-coloured marble.*

* Colonel Playfair's "Travels in the Footsteps of Bruce."

As time went on the basilican plan and arrangement for an ordinary church were still adhered to in the Western Empire, but the architects—especially where they were not influenced by the use of old materials and the presence of old models—began to work with greater freedom, and to feel their way slowly towards a new style.

The most important examples are at Ravenna, which Honorius in 404 had made the capital of the empire. His sister, Galla Placidia, afterwards adorned the city with superb monuments, of which her tomb remains. At a later time, when it fell into the hands of Theodoric the Goth, the enlightened conqueror continued the works which he found in progress and built others. The Church of St. Apollinare Nuova was built in his reign (443-525), and his tomb, with its dome composed of a single stone, is one of the most remarkable of architectural monuments. His daughter Amalasuntha encouraged similar undertakings. When Narses gained the victory over the Goths, Ravenna became the residence of the Exarchs of Justinian. In this reign was built the Church of St. Apollinare in Classe, at the port of Ravenna, about three miles from the city; it was commenced in 538 and dedicated in 549.

These two basilicas still remain in their original condition. They show a considerable development in plan and design; the nave has a tall clerestory above the level of the aisles, an impost over the capitals, arches over the windows, and a tall bell-tower. In St. Apollinare in Classe the exterior has some little relief to the plain side walls of the nave and aisles, in an arcading of shallow pilasters and arches; but the west wall and the great narthex are as unadorned as they possibly could be, in striking contrast to the elaborate and beautiful architectural design of the interior. A woodcut in Fergusson's "History of Architecture," vol. i. p. 423, of the angle where the nave joins the apse, gives some idea of the grandeur of the design and the richness of its ornamentation. Internally, with its twenty-five Greek marble columns, its richly adorned archivolts, and its grand mosaics (hereinafter described), it is a very noble monument of early Christian architecture.

The Church of San Vitale, built A.D. 528–547 under Eastern influences, is the first church in the West which shows a strong Byzantine feeling. It is in plan an octagon, forty-seven feet in diameter, with a choir and apse added to it; massive pillars support the clerestory and dome; between the piers of this central area are niches, with galleries above;* the square piers are cased with marble, and the wall-spaces above are adorned with twisted columns and mosaics.

Another fine example, contemporary with these at Ravenna, is the cathedral at Parenzo in Istria, built by Bishop Euphrasius, A.D. 542. It is a long basilica, with apses to the aisles in addition to the central apse, and retains its atrium; to the west of which is the baptistery—an octagon within a square; and to the west of that a tower, square externally and round

* An arcade of this gallery is given at p. 295.

internally. Some of the capitals are Corinthian, taken from an earlier building; others are of a form and ornamentation influenced by the new Byzantine style, which was very shortly to supersede the long-continued debasement of the classical forms of art. For down to this time the sculptors were still imitating the old capitals, architraves, and cornices, rudely and with variations which, with the occasional exception of deliberate copies of old work, departed more and more from the ancient forms.

Very few examples of the buildings of this early period remain north of the Alps. We know that Southern Gaul was highly civilized, and possessed noble buildings of all kinds, including churches. The basilican plan for the larger churches, at least, was almost universal, and they had marble columns, tessellated pavements, gilded ceilings, glass windows, mosaics and paintings on the walls. Sidonius (Caius Sollius Apollinaris Sidonius), in one of his pleasant letters,* describes a basilica which Patiens, Bishop of Lyons (A.D. 470), built in honour of the popular Gallic saint Justus, for which Sidonius wrote a dedicatory inscription, engraved on a tablet and fixed on the west wall. The church faced "the equinoctial east." "It is light within; the sun is attracted to the gilded ceiling, and wanders, with its yellow glow, over the gilded metal. Marbles of various splendour enrich the ceiling (*camerarius*), the pavement, and the windows; and through the green glass of the windows, beneath vari-coloured figures, an encrustation, grassy and

* Liber ii. 10.

springlike, bends around the sapphire gems.* It has a triple portico (probably along three sides of the atrium), magnificent with Aquitanian marbles, and a similar portico closes the further (eastern) side of the court. A grove of stone scatters its columns far and wide over the interior." It is easy to recognize that the church was of the usual basilican type, with court and narthex, handsomely adorned with marbles, mosaics, and gilding.

Gregory of Tours describes some of the Gallic churches of his time (A.D. 573-594). The new basilica of St. Martin, built by Perpetuus, the sixth successor of Martin in the see of Tours, was 160 feet long by 60 wide, and its height to the ceiling, 45 feet; it had 52 windows, 120 columns, and 8 gates. The church which Namatius, the eighth Bishop of Clermont, built, "which is the principal church there," was 150 feet by 60, and 50 feet high to the ceiling of the nave; in front (*i.e.* to the east) it had a round apse, and on each side stretched aisles of elegant structure, and the whole edifice was disposed in the form of a cross. It had 42 windows, 70 columns, and 8 gates. The wife of the above-named Bishop Namatius built the basilica of St. Stephen, without the walls of the town, and had it painted with paintings which she indicated to the artists out of a book which she pos-

---

* The passage is very obscure. Does it describe a pattern of coloured glass in the windows, or the mosaics on the walls? Here is the original:—

"Ac sub versicoloribus figuris
Vernans herbida crusta sapphiratos
Flectit per prasinum vi'rum lapillos."

sessed. Was it a book with miniature pictures, or a book like that which the Greek artists of later times possessed—a directory of subjects for artists?* The inhabitants of the south and south-east of France long maintained the classical civilization which the Greek colonists had originally planted there; and the classical style of art survived in their buildings to a late period. The actual remains of this classical style in Gaul are the porch of the cathedral of Avignon, St. Paul aux Trois Châteaux, near Avignon, and other fragments in the Rhone Valley, as the apse at Alet, with good Corinthian capitals and cornice; the baptistery at Poictiers, the church of the Convent of Roman Motier, on the Jura, St. Trophimus in Arles, St. Gilles in Languedoc, and others. In the north of Gaul the cathedral at Trèves claims to be of the date of Constantine; four colossal granite columns with Corinthian capitals, and portions of the original walls, still remain. It had a circular building adjoining it, probably a baptistery, on the site of the present Liebfrauenkirche. The church is remarkable for having an apse at the west, as well as at the east end. This feature has its prototype in the basilica of Trajan at Rome; it is found in the early basilica at Orleansville, Algeria, already mentioned; in several other northern churches, *e.g.* at Bemberg, Rothenberg, Maintz, and Laach; and perhaps at Canterbury and Lyminge, Kent.†

* See Miss Stokes' edition of Didron's "Iconographie."
† The small parish church of Heybridge, Essex, also has a western as well as an eastern apse.

THE CHURCHES AFTER CONSTANTINE.

One of the most striking developments of the new style of architecture which was gradually growing up to express the mind of the new Christian world, was the adoption of the square plan, surmounted by a dome, which became the characteristic feature of Byzantine architecture.

Where that grand architectural feature the dome originated is not known; perhaps the earliest example which exists is at the palace of Sarvistan in Persia, constructed in the fourth century, B.C.* It was from Persia probably that the energetic and able builders of Central Syria borrowed it. The earliest church in which it appears is the Church of St. George at Ezra, which is certainly one of the most interesting of all the Christian buildings of this region. Finished in 515 A.D., according to an inscription carved on the lintel of the west door, it has come down to us without alteration, and uninjured in its essential features; always consecrated to the offices of religion, for which it was built, and which are still celebrated beneath its venerable vault.

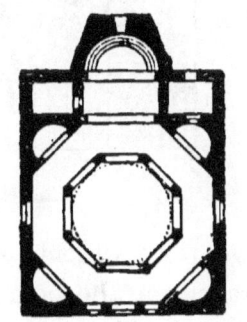

Plan of St. George's, Ezra, Syria.

The plan is extremely simple.† It consists of two regular concentric octagons, inscribed in a square; the central octagon supports a drum and cupola. Projecting from the eastern face of the

---

* "L'Art Antique de la Perse." M. Dieulafoy.
† Plate XX., De Vogüé's "Syrie Centrale."

G

external octagon is built the choir (flanked by two square sacristies), which terminates in an apse, and in each of the angles of the square is a niche; there are three doors at the west, and one on the north and south sides of the square. The diameter of the external octagon is 60 feet; of the interior octagon, 35 feet; the total length of the choir is 27 feet.

The cupola is supported by eight pillars 14 feet high, which carry a drum of 18 feet. The last

Church of St. George, Ezra, Syria.

two rows of this drum are made of slabs, which transform the octagonal drum first into a figure of sixteen sides, and then of thirty-two sides, and so the octagon passes gradually into the circle, which serves as the base of the cupola. The cupola De Vogüé believes to be part of the original structure. Its ovoid form is very unusual, and recalls the monuments of Central Asia. At the base of the cupola is a row of small windows, the first example of a method of lighting which finds its full development in Sta. Sophia at Constantinople. Round the apse are seats for the clergy.

The inscription seen over the west door is to the effect that the abode of demons is become the house of the Lord; the light of salvation enlightens the place which the shadows obscured; the sacrifices to a deity are replaced by the choirs of angels; where the orgies of a false god were celebrated the praises of God are sung. A man who loves Christ, the notable John, son of Diomed, has offered to God, at his cost, this magnificent monument, in which he has placed the precious relic of St. George, the triumphant martyr; the saint having appeared to him, the said John, not in a dream, but in reality. In the ninth indiction in the year 410 (= A.D. 515). The church, we gather from this inscription, was erected on the site of a temple to a pagan deity, probably to Theandrites, a divinity especially worshipped at Ezra.

The cathedral of Bosra is almost of the same date as that of Ezra, and constructed in the same style, but on a much larger scale. The exterior walls alone remain, and in the empty interior a small basilica was subsequently built. The original plan (Plate XXII., "Syrie Centrale") of the cathedral was a great circle of 120 feet diameter, inscribed in a square of 125 feet a side, to which was added on the east a choir of 36 feet, flanked by sacristies and lateral chambers. The dimensions are exactly double those of the cathedral at Ezra, and an imaginary restoration is easily deduced from the latter church, aided by some indications in the existing walls. An inscription states that it was finished under the Archbishop Julian, in 511 of our era, and dedicated to the holy martyrs Sergius Bacchus and Leontius.

Of the completed Byzantine style the dome is the essential and characteristic feature. Where the building is a square, or octagon, or square carried up into an octagon, one dome covers the whole building; where the plan is a cross of equal arms, a central dome covers the crossing and minor domes the arms. The other principal features are the mighty arches and broad wall surfaces. Colonnades which were the principal ornamental feature of the basilicas, hold here only a subordinate position, to screen off aisles or support galleries. The friezes, door and window frames, capitals and bases, everything which lends itself to it, is covered with surface ornamentation, classical in suggestion, skilfully wrought, and elegant in design. The internal walls and piers are veneered with marble; the domes, arches, and niches are adorned with mosaics; the capitals have a convex outline adorned with acanthus leaves which sit close to the bell, are, indeed, incised upon it, and have a reminiscence of the old archivolt in a moulded impost. The general effect of the broad spaces overarched at a great height by the golden hemisphere of the dome is very grand, the sculptured architectural details are original and beautiful, and the mosaics add greatly to the richness and dignity of the effect.

When Justinian, in the middle of the sixth century,

undertook to replace the ruined Church of the Holy Wisdom at Constantinople, originally built by Constantine and rebuilt by Theodosius II., he adopted this idea of a square plan surmounted by a dome. The emperor's ambition was to make it the most splendid temple which the world had ever seen. He entrusted the design to the two most eminent architects of the time, Anthemius of Tralles and Isodorus of Miletus. The body of the building was constructed of brick, and the exterior walls, after the fashion of those ages, were entirely destitute of any attempt at architectural adornment. But the interior was as costly and splendid as power, wealth, and art could make it. The world was ransacked for the most costly materials. Eight great porphyry columns, which Aurelian had carried off from the Temple of the Sun at Baalbec, and which were worth a great fortune, eight green columns said (erroneously) to have been taken from the Temple of Diana at Ephesus, still adorn the building. The most beautiful marbles from all countries were brought to line the walls.

On the day of its consecration, Christmas Eve, A.D. 568, the emperor ascended the pulpit, looked around, and with outstretched arms cried, "God be praised who has deemed me worthy to complete such a work," and added, *sotto voce*, "Solomon, I have outstripped thee."

The plan is a central square surmounted by the dome, contained within a larger square which forms the aisles. The influence of the original basilica plan is seen in a semicircular apse on the east, the narthex on the west, and the western atrium. The sculptured details of the architecture are free from any imitation of the old classical style; they are the most finished examples of the new style which had been gradually growing up in the East, and of which there are numerous earlier tentative examples in the churches of Syria which have been already described. Santa Sophia was the triumph of the new style of Christian art, and exercised an influence over the architecture of the Greek Church which has survived in full vigour to the present day. The structure of this grand church still remains uninjured, waiting till the decadence of the Turkish empire shall once more restore it to the uses of Christian worship for which it was erected.

Meanwhile the conquests of the Barbarians had divided the Western Empire from the Eastern. In the West the new nations took the art whose monuments they saw around them as the starting-point of the new styles which their fresh energy gradually evoked. There are noble examples of the square plan and dome in the West, but only where some exceptional Greek influence was powerful enough to introduce them. After Justinian's conquest of Italy the Church of St. Vitalis at Ravenna was built on the new Greek plan, and became the model of all those erected in Europe for several centuries. Charlemagne's church at Aix-la-Chapelle is one of the most important of them. Others are the Duomo of

Ancona, and St. Fosca Torcelli. St. Mark's, at Venice, is on the same plan, and is an evidence of the extent to which the Eastern associations of that great emporium influenced its art. At the Renaissance the influence of Byzantine art led to the adoption of the dome as the great feature of the new St. Peter's at Rome, and, later, to Wren's adoption of the dome in St. Paul's. But in the West the Greek idea of square plan and dome was always an exotic, and never made its way against the traditional following of the original basilican type.

Of the churches of this period, we have only slight traces in this country, but these traces are very interesting to us. We know, from Bede's history of the re-establishment of the Church in Kent in the sixth century, that there existed at Canterbury, after its conquest by the Jutes, at least two deserted churches of earlier times. One, St. Martin's, was repaired by King Ethelbert for the worship which Bishop Eleutherius and his staff of clergy maintained on behalf of the Christian queen Bertha. The present church is partly built of the old materials, since some of the bricks of the Roman time, easily recognized by their shape and texture, are still visible in its walls; but there is nothing to indicate its original plan and design. Of the other, which Ethelbert gave to Augustine, nothing remains but a description of it at the time of the fire which nearly destroyed it in 1067; but from this description Professor Willis was able to make out that it was a basilica, having a western as well as an eastern apse, like that at Trèves, with an adjoining baptistery. The plan of two other early churches has been preserved by foundations still existing. One at Frampton, Dorset, 31 feet by 21, has an apse; in the tessellated pavement, across the chord of the apse, was a band of circles all filled with scrolls of foliage, except the centre one, which had the sacred monogram XP. Since this symbol seems not to have been used in Rome till about the time of Constantine, the date of this building was probably about the fourth century. The other, at Silchester, Hants (probably the Roman Calleva), was only discovered in 1892. The foundations indicate a nave with apse, two aisles enlarged into quasi-transepts, and a narthex extending along the (ritual) west end. The whole of the nave and apse has been paved with tesseræ; in front of the apse, where the altar would be placed, is a square of finer mosaic, five feet square, in black and white check, with a border of coloured lozenges. There are remains of a tessellated pavement in the narthex. About eleven feet in front of the narthex is a foundation of brick about four feet square, perhaps formerly the base of the fountain in the middle of the atrium. The very interesting church of Brixworth, Northants, is built of Roman brick, and the main walls may possibly be of Roman construction, but there is nothing to prove conclusively that it was a Roman church. The church in Dover Castle, also, is partly of Roman work, but so altered in the eleventh century, and almost rebuilt in the thirteenth, that its original plan and design are lost in the subsequent alterations; and, again, there is nothing to prove that it was originally a church.

The Celtic churches had a plan of their own, the characteristic feature of which is a long square-ended chancel with only a small opening into the nave, and this plan has modified our national type of church. Some eminent Churchmen of the Italian school, like Wilfrid and Benedict Biscop, travelled through Gaul to Italy, and brought back from Rome models for church-building, decoration, furniture, and music; so that the churches of Wilfrid at Hexham and Ripon, and of Benedict at Wearmouth and Jarrow, were imitations of classical basilicas. The Norman builders also used the circular apse of the old basilican type; at Norwich Cathedral the traces still exist of the bishop's stone chair and the presbyters' bench at the east end of the original apse.

CHAPTER VII.

THE BAPTISTERIES.

Primitive baptisms—Baptisteries in catacombs—When the *Atrium* was the Church, possibly the *Baptisterium* of the bath was the baptistery—Public baptisteries; of the Lateran; at Aquileia; at Nocera dei Pagani; at Ravenna; at Deir Seta; in Italian cities—Fonts in churches—Illustrations of the subject in England—Baptistery at York; Canterbury—Holy wells—Fonts—Chapter houses.

N the first age, before public churches and baptisteries were erected, we have to infer the details of the administration of baptism from the incidental notices of it with which we meet. The mode of our Lord's Baptism by John would be likely to influence the mind of the Church; and we suppose that the traditional representation of it is correct, that our Lord went down into the water to a certain depth, and that the Baptist poured water, from his hand or from a shell, over His head. It is thus represented in a painting in the Cemetery of Callistus, of the second century; in a painting of uncertain date, over the font in the Cemetery of Pontianus (Marchi,

Plate XLII.); in the baptistery at Ravenna, called San Giovanni in Fonte, A.D. 450; in the later baptistery, in the same city, called Sta. Maria in Cosmedin, A.D. 553; and in other early works of art. So, probably, Philip baptized the treasurer of Queen Candace in the stream which they came to on their journey. The three thousand who were converted on the Day of Pentecost seem, from the narrative, to have been baptized there and then in Mary's house, perhaps with water poured over their heads from the fountain in the middle of the court of the house (see p. 5); and the jailer of Philippi and his family perhaps in the same way.

Tertullian observes that Peter baptized his converts in the Tiber at Rome, as John had baptized his in Jordan, and that it makes no difference whether one is baptized in the sea or a lagoon, a river or a fountain, a lake or a marsh. In the "Recognitions of Clement" St. Peter is represented as preaching to the people that they might wash away their sins in the water of a river, or a fountain, or the sea; and the writer describes the actual baptism of some converts in certain fountains by the seashore. Justin Martyr seems to say that baptism was usually performed outside the church: "All who believe the things which are taught, and promise to live accordingly, are taught to pray, with fasting, for forgiveness. Then we bring them where there is water, and they receive the washing of water; . . . we bring the person to be washed to the bath ($\tau\grave{o}$ $\lambda o \upsilon \tau \rho \acute{o} \nu$). After thus washing him, we bring him to those who are called brethren, where they are assembled together to offer prayers in common;" and he goes on to describe the celebration of the Eucharist.* The recently discovered "Teaching of the Twelve Apostles," a document whose date is said to be "far nearer the middle of the first century than the middle of the second," directs, "Baptize in living water [*i.e.* water not separated from its source], but if thou hast not living water, baptize in other water —in warm, if thou canst not do it in cold. But if thou hast neither [in sufficient quantity], pour water upon the head three times in the name of Christ." This would seem to contemplate baptism in a spring or river, in the *baptisterium* of a bath, or by affusion only.

Perhaps the earliest font which still exists is that in the Cemetery of Pontianus, already alluded to. The fossores, in extending its underground galleries, came upon a spring of water, and it was natural that they should excavate a little chamber and cistern in the floor of the chamber to make a reservoir for their own convenience, and for the convenience of any who visited the cemetery. It was quite as natural that, in some subsequent time, those who had control over the cemetery, with their minds full of religious symbolisms, should appropriate the subterranean fountain for baptismal purposes, and convert the chamber into a baptistery. The decorations of the little chamber prove that it was thus used. The font consists of a small cistern, or *piscina*, between two

* "First Apology," §§ 61 and 65.

and three feet deep, and six feet broad, constantly supplied by a current of water. It is approached by a flight of steps, between the base of which and the water is a level space, about five feet wide, on which the priest may have stood. Above the water is a painting of our Lord's Baptism, and on another side is a painting of a cross, adorned with gems and throwing out leaves and flowers from its stem; two lighted candelabra stand on the arms of the cross, and the letters $A\Omega$ are suspended from the arms by chains (see woodcut, p. 197). The date of the paintings is probably the seventh century, and may be later than that of the excavation of the cemetery. There is something of the same kind in the catacombs at Naples.*

A careful consideration of all the circumstances, and of these incidental notices, suggests that when churches were in the private houses of well-to-do converts, baptisms were performed in the bath which formed a usual adjunct of such a house; so that as the *atrium* and *tablinum* afforded the type of the future churches, the *baptisterium* afforded the type of the future baptistery. In the old baths at Pompeii the baptistery is square externally, internally a kind of octagon; the circular *piscina*, or basin, in the middle of its floor is 13 ft. 8 in. in diameter and 3 ft. 8 in. deep, coated with white marble, having two marble steps down into it, and a

* In the catacombs of San Gennaro, at Naples, is a church with three arches, supported by columns cut out of the tufa rock, with an altar, episcopal seat, and baptistery of stone, and in another part is a fountain, which was probably used for baptismal purposes.

marble bench all round on which the bather could sit. The diameter of the building leaves a broad margin of floor round the piscina; the roof is vaulted.*
The *piscina* of the baptistery in private baths seems usually to have been circular.†

When the Church built public basilicas it possibly built baptisteries beside them, but the only one we can mention before the time of Constantine is in connection with the new church at Tyre, already described (p. 43); for Eusebius seems to allude to a baptistery when he says that there were spacious *exhedræ* and *oëci* on each side, attached to the basilica and communicating with it, " for those who require yet the purification and the sprinklings of water and of the Holy Spirit." From the beginning of the fourth century a baptistery is usually found attached to a cathedral church, and in Rome alone to many of the churches.

From the beginning the baptisteries are built on a certain fixed general design, from which there are only minor deviations. The plan is usually octagonal,‡ or rarely circular, with an inner octagon of eight columns supporting a second story; the columns surround a piscina, or bath, which is protected by a

---

* See plan, p. 254, and interior, p. 279, in Smith's "Dictionary of Greek and Roman Antiquities," article " Balneæ."

† *E.g.* that of Pliny's villa at Laurentium (Letter xx. to Gallus).

‡ The octagonal form was considered peculiarly applicable to the baptistery—

" Octochorum sanctos templum surrexit in usus:
Octagonus fons est munere dignus eo.
Hoc numero decuit sacri Baptismatis aulam
Surgere, quo populus vera salus rediit."

parapet wall, and support a dome which forms a canopy of honour over the piscina. In some cases the central columns do not form a constructional part of the building, but are smaller shafts fixed in the angles of the parapet wall of the piscina, carrying a light cupola over it. In either case, the shape of the building, the internal circle of columns surrounding the basin, the reflection of the architecture in the still mirror of the sacred bath, must have produced very striking pictorial effects. There was often an anteroom at the entrance of the baptistery, where the catechumens made the renunciation of Satan and confession of faith which formed the introduction to the service;[*] and an apsidal recess opposite the entrance contained an altar at which the newly baptized received their first communion. Baptisteries were also used for assemblies of people, and bishops were not infrequently buried in them.

The earliest remaining example is the building at Rome known as San Giovanni in Fonte,[†] or the baptistery of Constantine, which is said to have been built for the baptism of the two Constantias—the sister and daughter of the emperor. It is an octagonal building of brickwork, in the adornment of which the columns and capitals of earlier buildings have been freely used. The central octagon of eight columns, with Ionic and Composite capitals, carries a cornice which runs round the building, and supports

---

[*] In mediæval times this was done in the porch of the church.
[†] St. John of the Fonts, *i.e.* St. John Baptist. All the Italian baptisteries are similarly dedicated.

eight smaller columns of marble, which again support the octagonal drum of the cupola and lantern of the roof. It has a portico which was so large as to form an entrance hall to the baptistery. The fabric may be of the time of Constantine, altered by later adaptations and adornments, but Lübke is of opinion that the original structure is of the fifth century.

There is an example of this primitive period in ruins at Aquileia* octagonal in form, with a small apse at the east angle, an inner octagon of columns, and a hexagonal piscina.

At Nocera dei Pagani, between Naples and Salerno, is an extremely beautiful circular church of early date almost unaltered, "built undoubtedly for the purpose of a baptistery." An inner circle of doubled columns supports the dome, and forms a circular aisle. The central piscina is twenty feet in diameter and nearly five feet deep, circular within and octagonal without; two stone steps or benches surround the interior; it has a raised parapet of marble, ornamented with incised patterns, and upon the angles of the parapet stood eight columns which probably carried a canopy.†

The most interesting of all the early baptisteries which remain to us is that known as San Giovanni in Fonte, in Ravenna, of the fifth century. It is an octagonal brick building of two stories, very plain externally, but internally richly adorned with marble

---

* Engraved in the "Dictionary of Christian Antiquities," i. 175.
† Plan and section are given in Fergusson's "History of Architecture," i. 433, 434.

columns which support a dome; the walls are lined with marble and the dome with mosaics. It has an octagonal basin, and a stone reading-desk beside it for the convenience of the officiating minister.*

At Deir Seta, in Central Syria, is a hexagonal baptistery, with a hexagonal basin, with columns at its angles which probably supported a canopy.†

There are other interesting baptisteries, all of the same general design, at Bologna, Florence, Torcello, Volterra, Cremona, Verona, Padua, Parma, Pisa, Baveno, etc. The basin was sometimes of fanciful form: in Lusitania it was commonly cross-shaped; in the "Pontifical of Landulph" it is a quatrefoil in plan.

After the eleventh century it became the custom for parish priests to baptize children soon after birth, and fonts were introduced into the parish churches for the purpose; about the middle of the eleventh century, Pope Leo IV. recommended the clergy henceforth to provide fonts in their churches; and very few cathedral baptisteries were subsequently built. In some of the Italian cities, however, as Pisa, Florence, and others, baptism continued, and still continues, to be administered only in the baptistery. We can easily understand the strong sentiment in favour of continuing to baptize the whole population of the city in the one font, the same in which the ancestors of the whole people had been baptized for many

* There are good representations of it in Gally Knight's "Ecclesiastical Architecture of Italy."
† De Vogüé, "Syrie Centrale," Plate CXVII.

generations. The miniature paintings in the "Pontifical of Landulph of Capua," which is of the ninth century, represent two scenes within one of these early baptisteries. In one an adult is standing up to the breast in the piscina, and a priest seems to have poured—or to be about to pour—water over his head; in the other, infants are being baptized by immersion.*

The plan for the church of St. Gall, which is of early ninth century, shows a circular font within the nave, at its west end, surrounded by a screen.

In our own country we have some illustrations of these Church customs. Augustine at Canterbury and Paulinus at Catterick are said to have baptized their converts in the neighbouring river. We have already had occasion to notice that the Romano-British basilica at Canterbury had a baptistery adjoining it. For the baptizing of King Edwin of Northumbria a wooden baptistery was erected over a spring or well, and the cathedral was subsequently built around it, and the well still exists in the crypt. About A.D. 750, Cuthbert, Archbishop of Canterbury, erected a church east of the cathedral, and almost touching it, to serve as a baptistery and for other purposes (*examinationes judicorum*, burial of archbishops, etc.). There are wells in some of our churches and churchyards, which were very possibly used as baptismal fonts. Some of the holy wells are enclosed in a building, and have a screen of columns

---

* They are engraved in D'Agincourt's "L'Art par ses Monumens," and in the "Dictionary of Christian Antiquities," pp. 158 and 171.

supporting a canopy over the water, after the fashion of the old baptisteries; there is a beautiful example at Holy Well, Flintshire, near Chester.*

We have no existing baptisteries attached to our cathedrals, and there are no fonts in our English churches earlier than the eleventh century. It is interesting to note that the small parish church fonts retain some reminiscences of the diocesan baptisteries which they superseded, for their most usual form is an octagonal external plan with a circular bowl; and many of them have, and probably many more once had, a cover in the shape of a canopy of honour. Some of them have the Baptism of Christ sculptured upon them, as at Bridekirk, Cumberland, and Lenton, Notts. On the Norman font at Darenth, Kent, and those at Kirkburn and Thorpe Salvin, Yorkshire, is a representation of baptism in a font.

The chapter houses attached to so many of our cathedrals seem to have been derived from the old cathedral baptisteries. Every monastery had its chapter house, but it was an oblong hall, always adjoining a transept of the church; but the chapter house of cathedrals served by canons was usually a large octagonal building (sometimes of nine sides) with a pyramidal roof, standing alone conspicuously, in the immediate neighbourhood of the church, and sometimes connected with it by a covered way. It would seem that when no longer needed for baptisms, such a building was still wanted for ecclesiastical

* It may very possibly have been used as a baptistery.

assemblies. The modification of its construction by the substitution of a central pillar to support the groining of the roof, in place of the old octagon of columns supporting the dome, is an interesting example of mediæval felicity of design.

CHAPTER VIII.

THE CATACOMBS.*

Literature of the subject—Incremation—Columbaria—Roman subterranean sepulchral chambers—Jewish burial customs—The Church adopted the custom of burial—Christian catacombs—Description of those at Rome—Family catacombs of wealthy Christians put at the disposal of the Church—Burial clubs—Public Christian catacombs became places of pilgrimage—Jerome's description of them—Prudentius's description of them, and of the *Confessio* of Hippolytus—The removal of relics—The catacombs deserted and forgotten.

THEIR tombs are often the most important surviving monuments of the existence of the ancient races of mankind, and the contents of the tombs supply the principal materials left to us for determining what manner

* On the rediscovery of the Roman catacombs at the close of the sixteenth century the first results were published by A. Bosio ("Roma Sotteranea," 1632). Aringhi, Boldetti, and Bottari do little more than work up Bosio's materials. D'Agincourt in his "Histoire de l'Art par ses Monumens," 1823, gives the result of additional discoveries up to his time. A new era opens with Padre Marchi's "Monumenti dell' Arte primitive Cristiane," 1844, followed up by the magnificent works of De Rossi, the "Christian Inscriptions of Rome," and the "Roma Sotteranea." Garucci's "Storia della Arte Christiana" brings of people they were. So of the earliest ages of the Church, the catacombs contain almost the only examples left of the painting and sculpture of several centuries, and afford invaluable illustrations of the beliefs and customs of primitive Christianity.

At the period when the Church began its existence the cremation of the dead had been for some centuries the general custom throughout the Roman world. The law required that the dead should be disposed of without the walls of the towns and cities, and it was the custom to place their monuments beside the suburban roads. The body was burned upon a costly funeral pile, or more economically cinerated in a *ustrinum*—a furnace made for the purpose; a handful of the calcined human remains was carefully rescued from the heap, and en-

Roman funeral urn.

together, in its five great folios, photographic representations of all the principal objects of art of the first centuries. T. Roller has illustrated the Roman catacombs and their contents by photogravure, and discussed them from an anti-Roman point of view. J. H. Parker's photographs of the paintings and sculptures of Rome are a very valuable addition to the student's materials. F. Perret's copies of the paintings are fanciful restorations of what the originals may have been, or ought to have been—of very little archæological value. The photographs are the only trustworthy authorities.

closed in an urn of earthenware, glass, marble, silver or gold, according to the wealth of the deceased. Some Roman cemeteries which have been carefully examined (*e.g.* at Colchester) indicate that large areas of land by the sides of the principal roads leading out of the towns were appropriated as general cemeteries, each with its own ustrinum ; and that the funeral urns (together with other vessels of glass and earthenware, containing perhaps salt, wine, oil, etc., as offerings to the manes, and personal relics of the deceased, as a necklace of beads or the like) were buried in orderly rows in small shallow square graves ; in many cases four of the large flat Roman bricks lined the grave and formed the sides of a rude cist, while another brick formed the lid, which sufficed to ward off the pressure of the surrounding soil and to preserve the frail deposit uninjured to the present day. Over some of these graves were erected monuments of various kinds, as plain upright stones with an inscription, columns, slabs of stone with an effigy of the deceased sculptured in sunk relief, and accompanied by an inscription.

Wealthy families purchased a suburban plot of land, and built a family tomb upon it. A common form of the tomb was a square basement with a round upper story ; the massive walls were internally honeycombed with niches, each of which accommodated a funeral urn ; while the chamber afforded accommodation for the funereal rites, and memorial feasts. Place was often found in the tomb for the funeral urns of dependents of the family. The external shape of the round tower and its internal rows of niches like pigeon-holes obtained for these tombs the name of *columbaria*.

Some however of the Roman families, especially perhaps those who prided themselves on their descent from the ancient Etruscan nobles, adhered to the earlier custom of entire burial. These deposited their dead in chambers hewn out of the sides of the rocky hills, with an architectural façade against the scarped face of the hill; or they excavated chambers in the rocky substrata of the plain, reached by a perpendicular well or a sloping driftway, the entrance to which was protected by an architectural building like a little temple. Of the former kind is the Tomb of the Scipios in the Latin Way, which consists of a chamber hewn in the hillside, with a Doric front; and the Tomb of the Nasos (the family of the poet Ovid) in the Flaminian Way, which is a similar crypt in the hillside, also with a Doric front. Of the latter kind is the group of sepulchral chambers found in recent times on the Latin Way, paved and lined with marble, and adorned with paintings, with the sculptured sarcophagi still remaining undisturbed in their recesses.

The Jewish funeral customs had, no doubt, great influence upon the mode in which the Christian Church disposed of its dead. The Jews clung to the custom of entire burial and laid their dead in chambers hewn out of the rock. The earliest example is the Cave of Machpelah. The neighbourhood of Jerusalem still possesses examples of these tombs.

The hillsides round about the holy city are honeycombed with sepulchral grottoes. The Tomb of Joseph of Arimathea was one of them, hewn in the rock within his suburban garden. The Tomb of Helena, Queen of Adiabene, a proselyte in the reign of Claudius, has a façade to the scarped front of the rock, consisting of a column and two semi-columns, supporting an architrave, cornice, and frieze; its door gives access to an entrance hall, and from the hall open a series of small chambers all excavated out of the interior of the hill. The so-called Tomb of St. James is a chamber excavated out of the side of the cliff, with a façade consisting of two Doric columns and two semi-columns supporting architrave and frieze. The so-called Tomb of the Prophets is a catacomb with a central chamber and radiating and concentric galleries. Individuals of the powerful and wealthy Jewish colonies of Alexandria, Cyrene, Antioch, and Cyprus, may have constructed monuments equally important. But the custom of the less wealthy is illustrated in the Jewish cemeteries of the same period in the neighbourhood of Rome and elsewhere. They adopted the method of which we have seen an example in the Tomb of the Prophets. They obtained possession of a piece of ground, dug down to the rocky stratum beneath the surface soil, and excavated galleries and chambers, extending them from time to time as need required. Three small catacombs on different sides of Rome have been identified, by the inscriptions and symbols which they contain, as belonging to the Jews, and one of them is ascertained to be the earliest of all the numerous catacombs around the city.* Another has been found at Venosa in the south of Italy.

The Church seems at once to have adopted the custom of burying its dead without mutilation. The fact that the nuclei of the Churches were generally groups of converted Jews would naturally incline the Church custom in that direction. The burial of the Lord would afford an influential precedent to His followers. A number of religious considerations, as to the sacredness of the body which had been grafted into the mystical Body of Christ, and had been the temple of the Holy Ghost, and as to the doctrine of the Resurrection, would strengthen the other motives for shrinking from cremation and adopting burial as the custom of the Church. The funeral customs of the early Christians were therefore derived from two sources. The Jewish custom of burial was universally adopted; but the other circumstances of the interment were largely influenced by the general funeral customs. It must be borne in mind that many of the Christians of these early ages were men and women converted in adult age, who had their ingrained notions and habits; that no customs have so tenacious a hold upon the popular mind as those which relate to burial; and that the Church did not set itself against the innocent customs of the people, but rather adopted them, impressed upon

* Julius Cæsar gave the Jews at Rome legal protection for their burial associations and graves.

them a Christian character, and utilized them in the service of religion.

The Christians of Rome appear to have at once followed the example of the Jews of Rome and buried their dead in underground catacombs. There are Christian catacombs in other places besides Rome, indicating that this method of interment was widely adopted by the Church. There are extensive catacombs at Naples; a catacomb at Alexandria only partially explored, at Venosa, Chiusi, Oria, Syracuse, Malta, and other places;* and subterranean chambers of less extent abound about the deserted cities of Central Syria.

The Christian catacombs themselves, independently of the paintings, sculptures, and inscriptions which they contain, are an interesting monument of the primitive age of the Church, and demand a careful description.

The Christian catacombs in the neighbourhood of Rome are not only the most extensive known to us, but they have been the most thoroughly explored, and, what is still more important, the discoveries made in them have, especially during the last few years, been systematically observed and recorded.

The substrata of the soil around Rome consisted chiefly of three formations. The *Pozzolana pura* was a stratum of sharp sand which formed excellent material for the making of mortar, and the Roman

* Some Christian sepulchres were found at Cagliari, in Sardinia, in 1892, which have tombs, inscriptions, paintings of Lazarus, Jonah, etc., of the third and fourth centuries.

builders had for generations been in the habit of quarrying it by means of driftways (*arenaria*) carried beneath the soil, wide enough for the passage of the carts which conveyed the sand. Another stratum was of *Tufa litoide*, which was hard and difficult to quarry. A third stratum was of *Tufa granolare*, not so hard to excavate as the second, not so soft and crumbling as the first; it could be easily worked, and yet was firm enough not to crumble and fall in; it was this last stratum which was selected for the cemeteries.

Some of the cemeteries are now entered by accidental openings where the superincumbent soil has fallen in from the surface, from the *arenaria*, and otherwise; but it seems probable that they all had originally one or more formal entrances, and these entrances had probably some architectural approach—a little building containing chambers above ground for the celebration of funeral rites, and protecting the flight of steps which led down to the subterranean galleries and chambers; or a descending driftway down to the level of the chambers and galleries, with an architectural face to the scarped rock through which the excavated chambers were entered.

Beyond this entrance the catacomb consists of a narrow gallery (*ambulacrum*) cut through the rock, in the sides of which are excavated a series of shelves (*loculi*) like the berths of a ship's cabin, tier above tier, each large enough to contain a single body;* as each loculus was occupied, it was closed by three

---

* In pagan and in Jewish cemeteries, and in that of Alexandria, the loculus is sometimes at right angles to the corridor, so that the bodies were placed in them feet first.

tiles or a slab of marble embedded in mortar; sometimes a name was rudely painted along the front,

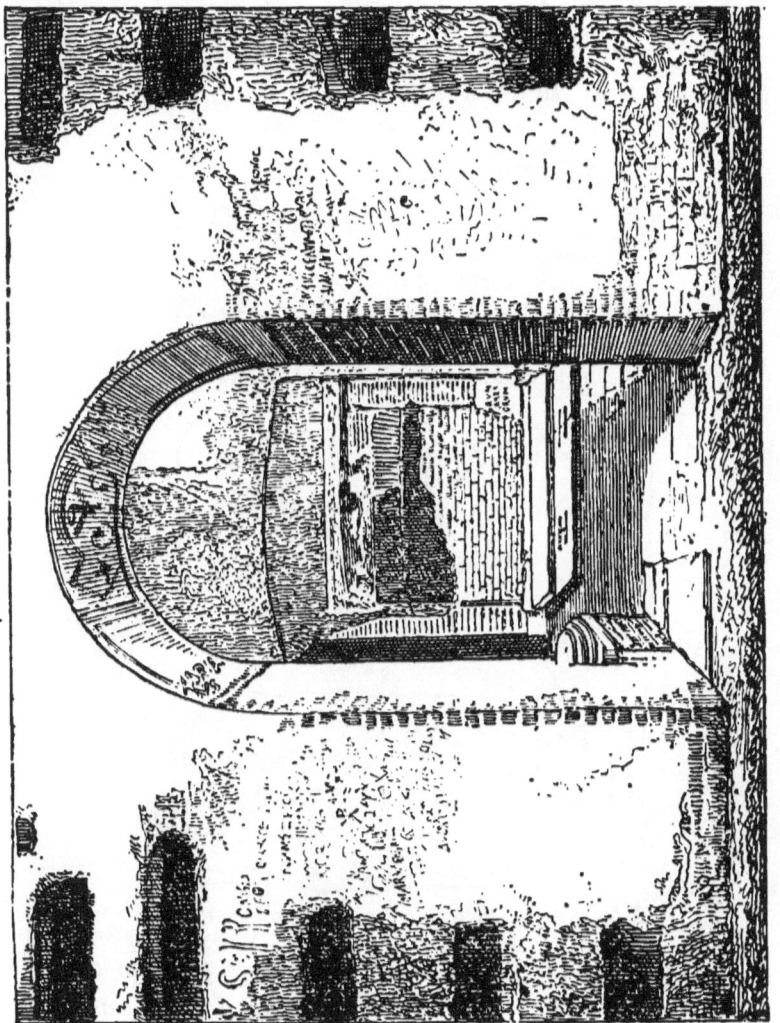

Ambulacrum with loculi and entrance into cubicula, Cemetery of St. Cæcilia, Rome.

with some brief words by way of epitaph, which we shall have to read and comment upon hereafter; or a pictorial emblem of some kind alluding to the deceased's religion or secular occupation. Every here and there a larger niche is formed with an arched head (called an *arcosolium*), beneath which was an excavation in the rock, like a stone coffin, sometimes

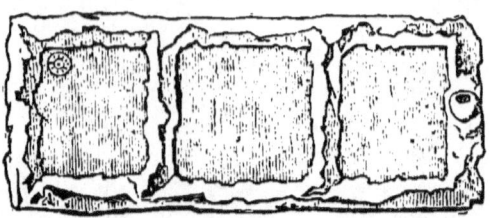

A loculus closed with slabs of stone.

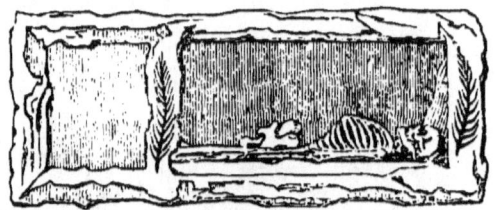

A loculus partly opened.

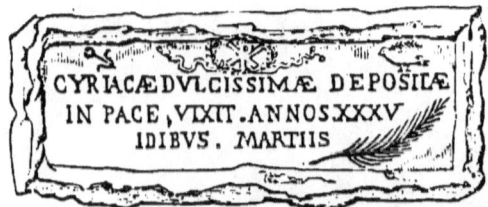

A loculus closed, with an inscribed marble slab.

large enough to contain two bodies—*e.g.* man and wife—side by side. Opening out from the *ambulacra*, like the chambers from the long passages of a modern house, are small sepulchral chambers (*cubiculæ*) excavated out of the rock; they afforded space for sarcophagi on the floor, and *arcosolia* and *loculi*, excavated in their walls, afforded other burial-places.

The earliest of these chambers are of small dimensions, unprovided with shafts for air and light, not adapted to any other purpose than that of family burial-places. The later *cubiculæ*, made about the middle of the third century, are of larger size; and those still later, of the latter half of the third and early part of the fourth century, are spacious quadrangular chambers, double, triple, even quadruple (*i.e.* one opening out of another), with other appendages. In the Cemetery of S. Soteris, of still later date, some of these chambers are polygonal, with apses and vaulted roofs, like subterranean mausoleums.

It will be observed that the narrow passages and small chambers of the " ages of persecution " were not capable of being used as abodes or places of worship, and that it is not till persecution had long ceased that we find these larger chambers, which, like the tombs above ground, were no doubt used for commemorative services; tombs of famous martyrs, at their annual commemorations, would be attended by considerable numbers of people, who would wish to visit the sacred tomb, even if the service were held in a more commodious building above ground. In one case in the *Cœmeterium Ostrianum* (commonly known as that of St. Agnes) at Rome, a series of chambers running at right angles to the general gallery is supposed by some to have been intended for a small church. But this is very unlikely; if a church was wanted there, there was nothing to hinder the excavation of a church of the usual plan. In the catacomb at Naples is a church with three arches supported by columns cut out of the tufa rock, with an altar, episcopal seat, and baptistery of stone. The catacomb at Chiusi also has a small church.

As years went on these subterranean passages and chambers were extended to meet the growing want of room for the dead, and were ramified in all directions to keep them within the area of the estate beneath which they were formed. Additional accommodation was gained by driving a stair down to a lower level and constructing another story of galleries and chambers; there are examples of even three, four, and five stories one beneath the other, communicating with one another by flights of steps. One cemetery sometimes communicated with neighbouring cemeteries, and thus an intricate network of passages and chambers spread under a very large area of ground.

The walls and roofs of some of the burial-chambers and the *arcosolia* were often adorned with paintings, the stone sarcophagi which were placed in their recesses had their fronts carved with bas-reliefs; and these paintings and sculptures not only afford examples of Christian art, but throw light upon the whole condition of the Christian Church of the period. But before we enter upon these works of painting and sculpture, there is still much which is of great interest to be said upon the history of the Christian catacombs of Rome.

Of the sixty catacombs known by name in the environs of Rome the greater number took their ancient name from the name of the proprietor of the land under which they were excavated or of their founder. Others were designated by the name of some well-known neighbouring landmark, as the *Cœmeterium ad Nymphas, ad duas lauras, ad Ursum pileatum, ad septem columnas, ad sixtum Philippi*, etc. That in which the bodies of the martyred Apostles St. Peter and St. Paul are said to have found a temporary resting-place was known as the Cœmeterium ad Catacumbas, *i.e.* at the hollow; and it is suggested that, from the general familiarity of the Christian world with this name, all the subterranean cemeteries obtained the general name of catacombs. Some of the cemeteries seem to have been known to Christians from the first by the name of martyrs of the family to which the cemetery belonged, as those of St. Agnes, St. Priscilla, etc. In course of time the primitive name of many cemeteries was superseded by that of some famous saint subsequently buried there; thus the Cemetery of Domitilla became better known as that of SS. Nereus, Achilleus, and Petronilla, that of Balbinus by the name of St. Marcus, that of Callistus by that of St. Sextus and St. Cecilia.

It seems highly probable that in the earliest times of Christianity the wealthy converts who put their houses at the disposal of the Church as places of assembly for worship, also allowed the use of their cemeteries as places of burial for the faithful. We have seen that it was common for a great family to allow the funeral urns of their servants and dependents a place in the family *columbarium*, and no doubt when the fashion changed they would still be allowed a *loculus* in the family catacomb; it was not unusual also to allow a friend to make a sepulchral chamber for himself and his within the area of the cemetery of a great family; so that there would be nothing very contrary to custom in permitting the congregation to make for itself a special gallery in the suburban catacomb belonging to the city house where they were used to assemble, and whose clients in a sense they were.

The principal cemeteries of the first century are those of St. Peter on the Via Cornelia; of St. Paul on the Via Ostiensis; of Priscilla (one of the family of Pudens) on the Via Salaria Nova; *Ostrianum*, where St. Peter is said to have baptized, on the Via Nomentana; and of Domitilla on the Via Ardeatina, where were buried the martyrs Nereus and Achilleus, near to Petronilla, all three disciples of St. Peter.

The first has been destroyed by the excavations for the foundations of the basilica of St. Peter; some sarcophagi found in it have been preserved. The same fate has overtaken the greater part of the Catacomb of Lucina (or Commodilla, both names occur in ancient records), in which St. Paul was buried, and the rest is choked with earth and ruins. Two inscriptions found here are dated respectively by the consular years corresponding to 107 and 110 A.D.

The Cemetery of Priscilla is said to have been dug in the property of the family of Pudens, converted by the Apostle. In the middle of it is a chapel, clearly constructed before the system of excavation had been devised. It is not simply a chamber hewn out of the tufa, but is regularly built of bricks and mortar. There are no graves in the walls; it was intended to receive sarcophagi only, of which numerous fragments have been found. It was beautifully decorated with ornamental stucco-work worthy of being compared with the best work of the kind of pagan times, and also with frescoes different from the subjects of Christian symbolism which afterwards became so common.

The *Cœmeterium Ostrianum* is on a lower level than that which is known as the Catacomb of St. Agnes. It contains a chamber whose sides are honeycombed with graves, and within it a stone chair said to be that which in the ninth century was believed to be "the chair on which St. Peter first sat."

The Cemetery of Domitilla, the niece of Vespasian, who was banished to Ponza on account of her Christianity, is on the farm called Tor Marancia, on the Via Ardeatina, and is identified by several inscriptions found on the spot, which bear her name; in the same neighbourhood is also a monument of some member of the Flavian family who lived and died in the days of Domitian. The original entrance, which still remains, was in the side of the hill. The scarped rock was faced with a front of fine brickwork, with a cornice of terra-cotta and a pediment. Some chambers were subsequently added on each side of the entrance. The fragments of sarcophagi found here have no subjects carved on them, only ornamental figures of dolphins, sea-horses, etc. Other sarcophagi of terra-cotta found buried beneath the ground seem not to be later than the middle of the second century. In the catacombs behind, the first galleries and chambers are also of ancient date. On a second level of excavation is a wide corridor leading by an antechamber to a large chamber, whose walls are covered with the finest stuccoes and then decorated with ornamental devices, bearing so close a resemblance to the decorations of pagan chambers of the same date, that the whole might be mistaken for a pagan monument, were it not for the figure of the Good Shepherd which occupies the centre of the ceiling. The one original arcosolium is decorated with a landscape painting. The roof of the gallery is covered with graceful designs of trailing vine branches, with birds and winged genii among them; there are also a landscape, two persons sitting at a feast with bread and fish only on the table, a man fishing, a sheep feeding near a tree, Daniel in the lions' den. It might have been the burial-place of the martyred consul Flavius Clemens himself.

In the Cemetery of St. Priscilla, De Rossi found, in 1888, the family burial-place of a Christian branch of the Acilian family.* In exploring that portion of the Catacombs of Priscilla which lies under the Monte delle Grove, near the entrance from the Via Salaria, De Rossi observed that the labyrinth of the galleries converged towards an original crypt shaped

* "Pagan and Christian Rome," ii. 4.

like the Greek letter gamma (Γ) and decorated with frescoes. On a careful search among the earth which filled the place, a fragment of a marble coffin was discovered with a portion of an inscription to Acilio Glabrioni Filio. Four other inscriptions were found among the *débris*, namely to Manius Acilius . . . and his wife Priscilla, Acilius Rufinus, Acilius Quintianus, and Claudius Acilius Valerius, so that there is no doubt as to the ownership of the crypt, and of the chapel which opens at end of the longer arm of the Γ. This part of the cemetery resembled the most ancient part of that of Domitilla; there were no loculi in the walls, but only spaces for sarcophagi; the walls were covered with white plaster and adorned with paintings.

In the Cemetery of Prætextatus De Rossi discovered the tomb of St. Ianuarius, not merely hewn out of the rock, but built with excellent yellow brickwork, ornamented with pilasters of red brick and cornices of terra-cotta, just like the pagan sepulchres on the Latin or Appian Roads, and similar in construction to many of the latter half of the second century. It had originally been lined with marble; the vault, which is elliptical, terminates in a square light hole at the top; it is elaborately painted in fresco on a fine white plaster, in a style not inferior to the best classical productions of the age, with flowers and birds, reapers reaping corn, men gathering olives, men gathering grapes, children gathering flowers; at the back of the arched recess for a sarcophagus is a rural scene, of which the central figure is the

Good Shepherd. Inscriptions proved this to be the burial-place of St. Ianuarius, who was martyred A.D. 162.

On the opposite side of the gallery was found a crypt, which De Rossi assigned as the burial-place of St. Quirinus, *c.* 130. The brickwork was mostly of the time of Hadrian, the sarcophagus had no Christian sculpture, the portrait bust which occupied the centre wore the laticlave.

In another monument in the same gallery the arch of the arcosolium in the side of the gallery had been closed with a slab of marble pierced in a geometrical pattern, and on each side stood a porphyry pillar; the opposite wall of the gallery had been recessed into a semicircular apse, designed for the accommodation of visitors to the tomb.

Messrs. Brownlow and Maitland sum up the characteristics of these earliest catacombs in these words: "Paintings in the most classical style, and scarcely, if at all, inferior in execution to the best specimens of contemporary pagan art; a system of ornamentation in fine stucco, such as has not yet been found in any other Christian subterranean work; crypts of peculiar shape and considerable dimensions, not hewn out of the bare rock, but carefully and even elegantly built with pilasters and cornices of brick or terra-cotta; no narrow galleries with shelf-like graves thickly pierced in their walls, but spacious ambulacra, with painted walls, and large recesses provided only for the reception of sarcophagi; whole families of inscriptions with classical names and very few distinctly Christian forms of speech; and, lastly, actual dates of the first or second century."

When the Church began to build public basilicas it probably at or about the same time began to possess public cemeteries. This could be effected without much difficulty by help of burial clubs. The pagan population generally was very solicitous to obtain proper funeral rites, the absence of which was supposed to entail disadvantages in the next life; the less wealthy classes provided friends to perform the last offices, and money to defray the cost, by associating themselves in *Collegia Funeraticia, i.e.* burial clubs, the members paying a monthly subscription, all the members assisting at the funeral of one of their number, and meeting for the *ferialia*, or days of general sacrifice and feasting at the graves. A building for the celebration of these funeral ceremonies, called a *Schola*, was provided at the cemetery by each *Collegium* for the use of its members. One of these chambers still exists at Pompeii in the street of Tombs. "Close to the villa called the Villa of Diomedes, is a small enclosure presenting to the street a plain front about twenty feet in length, stuccoed and unornamented, except by a low pediment and cornice. The door is remarkably low, not more than five feet high. Entering we find ourselves within a chamber open to the sky, the walls cheerfully decorated with paintings of animals in the centre of compartments bordered by flowers. Before us is a stone triclinium with a massive pedestal in the centre to receive the table, and a short round pillar in advance of it. It is a funeral triclinium for the celebration of feasts in honour of the dead; the pillar probably supported the urn of him in whose honour the feast was given, which it was the custom to place in some conspicuous position, in view of the guests at the funeral feast. The Funeral Association provided all the necessaries for the feast, from the table service to the festal garments, and they were often kept on the spot."

These clubs, permitted at first only in Rome, were allowed by Septimus Severus throughout the empire, and became common from the end of the second century. It is obvious that the Christian community of any locality might form itself into a burial club, and thus secure legal possession of a cemetery, and the protection of the law for its funeral ceremonies. The first public cemetery which belonged to the Roman Church as a corporate body was a considerable area on the Appian Way, obtained by Pope Zephyrinus at the beginning of the third century. The law required that each *Collegium* should have an official agent, who represented it in all legal business which concerned the association. Zephyrinus, as was natural, appointed his deacon, Callistus, to regulate the use of the cemetery, and to transact the necessary business with the legal authorities, and thus the cemetery came to be called the Cemetery of Callistus. One of the earliest sepulchral chambers of this cemetery was thenceforward till 303 used as the ordinary burial-place of the Roman bishops.

The Christian public cemeteries were rapidly multiplied; there is reason to believe that in the time of Fabian (236-251) each *titulus* (*i.e.* public church) had a district of the city assigned to it, as what we should call its parish, that each had its suburban cemetery, and that the cemetery had its *fabrica*, which was probably a chapel for the funeral services and commemorations with other buildings adjoining for the convenience of the officials and mourners.

In 257 Valerian issued the first edict forbidding the Christians to use their cemeteries. In the following year, Pope Sixtus and his four deacons were seized in the Cemetery of Prætextatus, and martyred.* Under Numerian, a number of people who had entered one of the cemeteries on the Salarian Way, near the tombs of the martyrs Chrysanthus and Daria (perhaps for worship in one of the chambers, since they had with them the *vasa sacra*), were blocked in, by the closing of the entrance with a heap of stones and sand, and left to perish.

The decree of Diocletian, in 303, confiscated all the buildings and property of the Church, including the public cemeteries. It would seem that Pope Marcellinus hereupon obtained permission to use the cemetery of the family of Pudens, on the Salarian Way, for the burial of the Christians of Rome, and that he caused an extensive series of new galleries and chambers to be made at a lower level than the existing catacomb, and there they remain to this

* See p. 146.

day, planned and executed with an unusual degree of regularity, as if the work of one mind and hand.

When Constantine restored her property to the Church, burial in the old public cemeteries was resumed. Pope Melchiades recovered the body of his predecessor, Eusebius, who had died in exile in Cyprus (?), and buried him in the Cemetery of Callistus—not in the old crypt of the bishops, which was by this time filled, but in another chamber in the same cemetery, which he had decorated anew: "The roof was painted with a pattern of hexagons and other geometrical figures, containing alternately birds and flowers; the vaulted roofs of the arcosolia were covered with mosaics, and the white walls were faced with various coloured marbles." Pope Melchiades himself was buried in another crypt similarly ornamented. His successors, Sylvester, Mark, and Julius, were all buried in small cellæ, or tombs, built near the entrances to the catacombs, but not within them. Of Mark it is said that he was buried in the Cemetery of Basilius in the Via Ardeatina, in a basilica which he built, and which he constituted a cemetery; there can be little doubt that this means that he attached a priest to it, and made it a public cemetery of the church.

Excepting three new cemeteries made by Pope Julius (336–347), it would seem that, from the end of the third century to the end of the fifth, all that was done in the old catacombs was to make accommodation for persons who had expressly desired to be buried in the catacombs, near the resting-places of the martyrs. For this purpose, people made their arrangements with the *fossores*, the professional grave-diggers, and new loculi and arcosolia and cubiculæ were made, and sometimes crowded round certain famous graves in a way which has caused much defacement to the original features of the catacombs. About the same period, by cutting away whole blocks of rock with their loculi, space was made for small basilicas, so arranged that the apse should include, or immediately adjoin, the grave of some martyr,* and much damage was thus done in the older parts of the catacombs. This fashion, however, did not last long, and after the date (410) of the invasion of Rome by Alaric, there is scarcely an example of it.

By the middle of the fourth century began the important change of burial in brick graves, made in the upper stratum of soil over the catacombs, around the basilicas of the martyrs, and this fashion increased when burial in the catacombs ceased before the year A.D. 410.

When the cemeteries ceased to be used as burying-places, they became the objects of a still more reverential interest. In this and the following centuries, much was done in repairing, decorating, and

---

* The subterranean basilica of Petronilla, erected by Siricius at the end of the fourth century in the Cemetery of Domitilla, is an example; and less perfect examples are the basilicas of S. Agnese, S. Sebastian, S. Lorenzo, and, outside Rome, the basilicas at S. Generosa and Bolsena.

redecorating the chambers which had become objects of special reverence.

Pope Damasus (366-385) took great interest in the catacombs; he faced the cubiculæ of some of the more illustrious martyrs with marble, widened the galleries which led to them, and made new shafts for light and air, put up inscriptions in Latin verse inscribed in large and elegantly formed capital letters,* and thus encouraged the devotional practice of paying visits to the martyrs' tombs.

The present condition of the catacombs gives an impression of desolation which did not belong to them originally. The long narrow galleries must always have been dark, but the light of the lamp which the visitor carried showed perfect walls, and lighted up a constant succession on both sides, in three or four tiers, of brief inscriptions and Christian symbols, with frequent points of special interest—a glass vessel half standing out from the concrete, with its glittering device on gold-foil, a coin imbedded in the concrete to mark a date; here and there an arched recess (*arcosolium*), with a longer inscription at the back of the niche, which the visitor might pause to read; at intervals a *cubiculum*, into which he would turn to examine with interest its painted walls and ceiling, and the sculptured sarcophagi, which then suitably furnished the chamber of the dead.

Jerome,† in a well-known passage, describes the

---

* All these poetical inscriptions are on record, and fragments of the original marbles have been discovered in recent excavations.

† In Ezech. lx.

custom of visiting the tombs of the martyrs in his time: "When I was a boy being educated in Rome [he went there about A.D. 364], I used every Sunday, in company with other boys of my own age and tastes, to visit the tombs of the Apostles and martyrs, and to go into the crypts excavated there in the bowels of the earth. The walls on either side as you enter are full of the bodies of the dead, and the whole place is so dark that one seems almost to see the fulfilment of those words of the prophet, 'Let them go down alone into Hades.' Here and there, a little light admitted from above suffices to give a momentary relief to the horror of the darkness; but as you go forward and find yourself again immersed in the utter blackness of night, the words of the poet come spontaneously to your mind, 'The very silence fills the soul with dread!'"

Prudentius, towards the close of the fourth century, gives a description of the catacombs, and also of one of the crypts which had been sumptuously decorated in honour of the martyr Hippolytus, who was buried in it. "Not far from the city walls, among the well-trimmed orchards, there lies a crypt buried in darksome pits. Into its secret recesses a steep path with winding stairs directs one, even though the turnings shut out the light. The light of day indeed comes in through the doorway, as far as the surface of the opening, and illuminates the threshold of the portico; and when, as you advance further, the darkness as of night seems to get more and more obscure throughout the mazes of the cavern, there occur at intervals apertures cut in the roof, which convey the bright rays of the sun into the cave. Although the recesses, twisting at random this way and that, form narrow chambers and darksome galleries, yet a considerable quantity of light finds its way through the pierced vaulting down into the hollow bowels of the mountain. And thus throughout the subterranean crypt it is possible to perceive the brightness and enjoy the light of the absent sun. To such secret places is the body of Hippolytus conveyed, near to the spot where now stands the altar dedicated to God. The same table (*mensa*) gives the Sacrament and is the faithful guardian of its martyr's bones, which it keeps laid up there in expectation of the Eternal Judge, while it feeds the dwellers on the Tiber with holy food. Wondrous is the sanctity of the place! The altar is at hand for those who pray, and it assists the hopes of men by mercifully granting what they need. Here have I, when sick with ills both of soul and body, oftentimes prostrated myself in prayer and found relief. Yes, O glorious priest! I will tell with what joy I return to enjoy the privilege of embracing thee, and that I know that I owe all this to Hippolytus, to whom Christ our God has granted power to obtain whatever any one asks of him. That little chapel (*ædicula*), which contains the case of garments of his soul [his relics], is bright with solid silver. Wealthy hands have put up tablets glistening with a smooth surface [of silver] bright as a concave mirror; and, not content with overlaying the entrance with Parian marble, they have lavished large sums of money on the ornamentation of the work." He goes on to describe the crowds who visit the tomb on the martyr's festal day: "No doubt the cavern, wide though its mouth be stretched, is too narrow for such crowds; but hard by is another church (*templum*) enriched with royal magnificence which the great gathering may visit." And then follows the description of a basilica, which is supposed by many to be the original basilica of San Lorenzo in Agra Verano.

After the capture of Rome by Alaric (A.D. 410) burial in the catacombs ceased, except in some few special cases; and none of these after A.D. 450. After the sack of Rome by Totila (560) burial in the cemeteries above ground ceased. In A.D. 648 began the removal of relics of saints from the catacombs into the basilicas in the city; in 756 Paul I. removed more than a hundred; and in 817 Paschal I. removed thousands to Sta. Prassede. After this period the cemeteries, deprived of that which had formed their principal attraction, were soon deserted, neglected, and almost forgotten. At the beginning of the fifteenth century only that of the Catacumbas remained open. It was not till the end of the sixteenth century that the accidental rediscovery of one of them attracted the attention of the students of Church history and antiquities.

The catacombs at Naples are excavated in the volcanic tufa, on the face of the hill of Capodimonte. The only entrance now open is at the Church of

S. Gennaro de' Poveri. They form a long series of corridors and chambers, arranged in three stories communicating with one another by flights of steps. In one place is a church with three arches, supported by columns cut out of the tufa rock, with an altar, episcopal choir, and baptistery of stone; in another place the excavation has broached a fountain which may, of course, have been used for baptisms. Along the walls of the chambers are numerous *loculi*, in some of which may still be seen skeletons, and rude delineations of the olive-branch, dove, fish, and other usual early Christian symbols, with here and there a Greek inscription. These *loculi* were firmly closed by slabs of marble, many fragments of which, having inscriptions, form part of the pavement of the Church of S. Gennaro. These catacombs have not been fully explored; their extent is said to be very great. Burial in these catacombs and those of Sicily continued as late as the tenth century.

The Rev. C. F. Bellerman (1839) published good coloured plates of the fresco paintings of the Naples catacombs with text.* Their subjects include the usual peacocks, doves, and flowers, anchors, dolphins, a jewelled cross, another with $A\Omega$, and figures of St. Paul, St. Lawrence, St. Januarius, and oranti. There is an Adam and Eve beautifully drawn; a picture of three females building a wall, from the "Shepherd of Hermas;" a Christ with nimbus on one of the vaulted ceilings. Some notice of the catacombs at Alex-

---

* See also Garucci, "Storia della Arte Christiana," vol. ii. Plates 93-101; D'Agincourt, "Histoire de l'Art," Plates 11, 9.

andria * will be found at p. 185; and of the cemetery at S. Generosa in Garucci's great work mentioned in the note.† At Cyrene are subterranean sepulchral chambers with an architectural façade like those of the Scipios and the Nasos of Rome.

* In December, 1892, Professor Botti, in excavating near Pompey's Pillar, penetrated into the catacombs and found several sarcophagi.
† See footnote, p. 128.

CHAPTER IX.

TOMBS AND MONUMENTS.

Tombs and monuments at Rome, Jerusalem, and elsewhere—Christian tombs: of Constantia, Helena—Syrian tombs at Kerbet Hass, Hass, Kokanaya—Subterranean chamber at Mondjéléia—Twin columns at Sermeda, Dana, Bechindelayah—Pillar stones in Britain—Tombs used for funeral rites—Primitive regard for the dead—Funeral feasts—*Confessio* of the martyrs; in the catacombs; above ground—Story of Theodotus of Ancyra—Basilica of SS. John and Paul, Rome—St. Alban, his *martyrion*—Early tombs represented in the paintings and sculptures of the Raising of Lazarus—Abyssinian tomb—Visits to tombs, and names scratched on them—Prayers to the saints.

BEFORE we apply ourselves to the study of the wall-paintings and the sculptured sarcophagi which the catacombs have preserved beneath the soil for all these centuries, there is something to be said about the tombs and monuments and funeral buildings which once studded the areas of the cemeteries above ground, but of which very few remain.

Some tombs which immediately preceded the Christian age ought to be mentioned because they formed the model of those which the Christians subsequently constructed for themselves. First, those in the neighbourhood of Rome. The monument of Cæcilia Metella, the wife of the consul Crassus, is the earliest of these tombs of ascertained date, and is the largest example of a very numerous type of these monuments. It consists of a square first story, surmounted by a circular second story with a frieze and cornice, and is supposed to have been finished with a conical roof. We find the same type at Pompeii, at Jerusalem, in North Africa, in Gaul, and in Syria. The white marble pyramid of Caius Cestius, containing a small chamber, the sides and ceilings of which were covered with arabesque paintings, is an example of another common type. The Tomb of Augustus was a reproduction of one of the most ancient and universal types of the tomb of a great man, an earthen mound; but in this instance the lower part of the mound was encased with a wall of white marble adorned with columns which supported a cornice and frieze, the upper part of the mound was planted with evergreens, and it terminated in a bronze statue of the emperor. At Madracen, in Algeria, is a mound surrounded by a wall and Doric peristyle, like that of Augustus, and probably imitated from it, by Juba, the *protégé* of the great emperor.* At Jerusalem, the so-called Tomb of Zacharias is a mass of the native rock *in situ*, cut into a cube, ornamented at the sides with Ionic

---

* Lucian, the satirist, alludes to these monuments and tombs in the " Menippus ; or, Oracles of the Devil : " " Tell me, Menippus, they who possess these costly and lofty tombs upon the earth, and monumental slabs, and pictures and inscriptions," etc.

columns and pilasters, and surmounted by a pyramid. The Tomb of Absalom is formed in the same way out of the native rock, adorned with Ionic columns and pilasters carrying a frieze; the upper part, built of masonry, is circular, with projecting cable mouldings, and is finished with a concave-curved pyramid, terminating in a finial of palm leaves.*

Another very common type of monument is a pillar, of which the columns of Trajan and Antoninus are the noblest examples known to us. There are three small tombs of this period still remaining in Gaul—a pillar at Cussi, near Beaune, an obelisk at Igel, near Trèves,† and the elegant Tomb of St. Remi.‡

There are similar monuments in North Africa, *e.g.* at Kasrin, Tunisia,§ and at Thugga.

The Street of the Tombs at Pompeii outside the Herculanean Gate gives the most complete existing example of the custom. The tombs are in a continuous line on each side of the road, of various types: the little temple with a portico of Corinthian columns, the square base with round upper story, the cubical cyphus; the pillar, and the headstone. A common form of headstone has the upper part rounded into the outline of a head, and while the front is nothing but the flat surface of the stone the back is sculptured in imitation of hair. It reminds us of the common modern Turkish headstone whose top is carved into

---

* Fergusson's "History of Architecture," vol. i. p. 357.
† Ibid., p. 350.   ‡ Ibid., p. 349.
§ "Transactions of the Royal Institute of British Architects for 1880," Plate XX. 41.

the representation of a turban, and suggests another meaning for the name of headstone than the common one that they are placed at the head of the grave.

Of Christian tombs the best known are those of the daughter of Constantine, now the church of Costanza, and the tomb of his mother, the Empress Helena. The Tomb of the Empress Helena is now

The Tomb of the Empress Helena.

only a ruin of massive brickwork, with a central chamber in which are eight circular recesses; it seems to have been originally of the common type of a square basement with a round upper story, roofed with a dome or conical cap. The Tomb of Constantia is a circular building, 100 feet in external diameter;

within that a smaller circle (35 feet) of twenty-four pillars, carry a domed roof. In a square niche opposite the door stood a costly sarcophagus of porphyry, which is now in the Vatican Museum. The roof of the aisle is adorned with mosaics of the vintage and scenes of rural life, like many of the pagan tombs; the vine may or may not have been

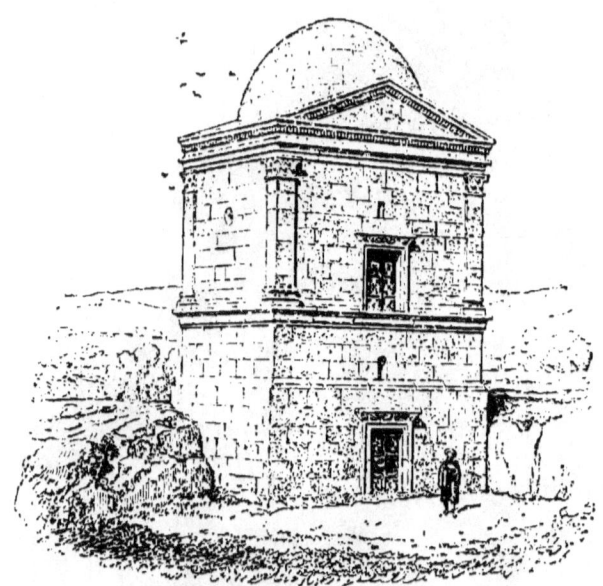

Tomb at Hass, Central Syria.

intended to have a Christian symbolism. There is a small portico in front of the entrance.

The cemeteries attached to the deserted cities of Central Syria contain a large number of monuments and tombs, ranging from the third to the seventh centuries, some like those we have seen elsewhere, others supplying types which are otherwise lost.

The illustration ("Syrie Centrale," Plate LXXII.) is a tomb at Hass, restored from the existing remains and by comparison with other tombs. It is of two stories; the ground floor is divided into two compartments with recesses for sarcophagi. The upper stage is constructed with great solidity, three recesses being left in the solid masonry for sarcophagi. Enough remains to restore the angle columns and the pediment, but it is only a conjecture derived from similar tombs that this was finished by a cupola. Another* at Kerbet Hass has a façade like a little temple. Another at Hass, adorned with columns round its sides, has an inscription in large Greek characters in the hollow mouldings; only fragments remain of those of the upper story; the lower story still retains part of a quotation from Ps. cxlviii. 26, 27; it has also a Christian monogram on the door. De Vogüé attributes it to the year A.D. 377.

There do not appear to be any extensive catacombs about these Syrian cities, but subterranean sepulchral chambers are very common. The simplest form is that of a grave dug down into the rock and enlarged to right and left into a crypt which would contain several bodies; the opening of the grave being covered by a massive stone ridged like a roof, with antæ at the corner, in imitation of the corner tiles of a classical roof. The idea clearly was that the chamber was the last narrow house of the dead. The same kind of ridged cover is used for the sarcophagus lid, and was very common in the fourth, fifth, and sixth

* De Vogüé's "Syrie Centrale," Plate LXXXIV.

centuries. An example of it at Kokanaya is the more interesting because it has an inscription giving the name of the person interred in it and the date of his death—

+ Εὐσεβίῳ + Χριστιανῳ +
Δόξα πατρὶ καὶ υἱῷ καὶ ἀγίῳ πνεύματι
Ἔτου ζιύ μηνὶ λώο κζʹ.

"To Eusebius, a Christian. Glory be to the Father, and to the Son, and to the Holy Spirit. Year 417 the 27 loiis."

The era 417 of Antioch is equal to A.D. 368–369

There are whole cemeteries still crowded with stone coffins with covers of this type. There is one near Julia Concordia nel Veneto, of which a photograph is given in De Rossi's "Bullettino," 2nd series, anno 5; in several places in Syria;* and at Arles, in France; and scattered examples are to be found on the sites of Roman cities throughout the empire. They are the types from which our Saxon and mediæval "stone coffins" were derived.

Several of the Syrian sepulchres are constructed in the same way as the tombs of the Nasos and Scipios, and the earlier chambers of the Cemetery of Domitilla, at Rome: a sloping road has been excavated down into the rocky soil until the scarped rock in front was sufficiently high for its purpose; then a door has been cut through the front, and a sepulchral chamber, or series of chambers, excavated out of the hill beyond; finally, the scarped front of the rock has been faced with an architectural design.

The illustration ("Syrie Centrale," Pl. LXXXVIII.)

* De Vogüé's "Syrie Centrale."

represents a sepulchral chamber at Mondéjélia hewn in the rock with three recesses for sarcophagi, approached by a sloping way, the entrance ornamented by a portico partly formed of the rock, partly built of stone projecting above the level of the rock. It is probably of the fifth century.

Over or near to the sepulchral chamber was frequently erected a monument, and these monuments

Subterranean Sepulchre at Mondjéléia, Central Syria.

are of various types. One of the earliest, at Sermeda, consists of two tall columns with Corinthian capitals, united at the base by a common plinth, by a cornice at the top, and by an ornamented stone at about three-fifths of their height. De Vogüé thinks it certain that they supported a statue; we may suggest further that an equestrian statute would alone fill the cornice and be in due proportion to the rest of the composition. It has an inscription, but unfortunately nothing is legible except the artist's name and the date, which corresponds with April 6, A.D. 132. At Dana there are two tall rectangular pillars similarly coupled, which bear an inscription to one Isidorus and the date October 9, A.D. 222. At Bechindelayah is a single tall rectangular pillar, with a panel towards the summit containing the bas-relief of a man; an inscription is cut in the face of the pillar beneath this panel, commemorating Tiberius Claudius Sosandros, who died A.D. 134. This pillar adjoins and belongs to an underground sepulchral chamber cut in the rock, with an architectural façade.

The accompanying woodcut from Professor Ramsay's "Church in the Roman Empire," represents, as the inscription declares, the "Memorion" of Abirkios (Avircius), son of Porphyrios, a deacon at Prymnessos, in Phrygia, and Theuprepia his wife, and their children. If the open declaration that Avircius was a deacon did not point to a date after the Peace of the Church, Professor Ramsay would, from the style of art, assign it to the third, rather than the fourth century. We venture to think that since the Church built public churches and had its special cemeteries in the third century, and its clergy were known to everybody, there was no reason why the sepulchral inscriptions of its clergy should not record their status. The central figure on the monument, Professor Ramsay takes, with great probability, to represent our Lord, and the heads to represent Avircius and Theuprepia. In the latter head the Professor says

A Christian monument at Prymnessos, Phrygia.

there is an individuality which the engraving inadequately represents, and which carries with it the conviction that it is a portrait; and he can hardly imagine it to be the work of a fourth-century artist. But it is certain that fourth-century sarcophagi not infrequently have sculptured portraits of the deceased; and on the whole we incline to assign this interesting monument to that period.

Short unadorned pillar-stones with an inscription are common everywhere. Of these we have some examples in the Celtic portions of our own island. At St. Just, Penrith, is one inscribed with the monogram XP and an inscription "SENILIS IC IACET." Two others in Cornwall have the monogram XP, one at St. Helen's Chapel, the other at Phillack. One in Wales, in Permachno Church, Carnarvonshire, has an inscription, "CARAUSIUS HIC JACET IN HOC CONGERIES LAPIDUM." In Scotland, in the old burying-ground of Kirk-madrine in the parish of Stoneykirk, are two stones inscribed with the monogram XP and AΩ, and inscriptions—on one, "HIC JACENT SCI ET PRÆCIPII SACERDOTES ID EST VIVENTIUS ET MAVORIUS; of the other inscription only the name "SC FLORENTIUS" remains.

The idea that the tomb is the house of the deceased is a very common one. Even cinerary urns are commonly found in Central Italy, and elsewhere, made in the shape of a house, and afford a curious evidence of the general outline of the houses of the period at which they were made. Many of these early Christian tombs are like houses, and their chambers are so commodious and so handsomely painted, and look so habitable, as even to have suggested to a recent writer * the idea that they were actually inhabited. It is highly probable that the clergy who fled to the catacombs for refuge in times of persecution, really sojourned in these habitable tombs, and retreated into the mazes of the galleries with which they communicated only in case of a hostile visit to the tomb. Thus St. Cyprian, when his life was first threatened, is said to have concealed himself in the tomb of his family. The Acts of Paul and Thekla, though apocryphal, may be accepted as evidence of the customs of the early age of Christianity. It says that when the apostle was expelled from Iconium, he and the family of Onesiphorus, with whom he had been lodging in the city, spent many days in a tomb on the road which leads to Daphne. That the tombs were frequently visited is certain, and the commodious chambers were intended for these visitations. The heathen, we know, had elaborate funeral rites and were very solicitous for their due performance; a striking witness to their instinctive belief in a life after death. There was a funeral feast on the occasion of the funeral, which took place in the sepulchral chamber or some chamber adjoining it. The tomb was visited again on every anniversary of death, and on the ferialia when everybody visited the tombs of their relatives; so that the visits paid to a family tomb in the course of the year would be

* In J. H. Parker's "Archæology of Rome."

numerous enough to make it very desirable to have a convenient chamber for these meetings.

Christians continued these ancestral customs with clearer faith and a higher intention. The vague instinctive belief of the heathen in a life after death became in these early Christians the profoundest conviction of the continuity of life, and a more vivid realization of the unseen world than is common even with ourselves. The result was that the dead occupied a larger space in religion, and were regarded with a somewhat different shade of feeling. The Church then really knew no more than we do of the details of the condition of the departed, but it drew larger deductions from what it did know; it was more keenly alive to the truth that the faithful still militant in this life, and the faithful departed resting after their labours in Paradise, were not beyond the reach of one another's sympathies and prayers—that they still formed one Church and had mystical communion one with another in Christ. Christians therefore regarded the bodies of their brethren with reverence, and laid them in their tombs with abundant honours and solemn services, and held a great funeral feast, at which they entertained large numbers of the poor; and returned again to the tomb at the month's end, and again on their anniversaries, with a firmer persuasion that they were keeping up a real communion with the departed than the heathen could possibly have, and than we in these days commonly possess.

Happily in our times a new impulse has been

given to a more vivid realization of our abiding relations with our loved ones who have gone before to Paradise by the example of her Majesty Queen Victoria, who, following the instincts of the religion of the heart, has revived the celebration of annual commemorative religious services. To her Majesty also we owe the encouragement of those accessory funeral services by means of which a whole nation in all its churches may assist at the funeral honours paid to its great men, so that the funeral of a Colonial Premier may be virtually celebrated in Westminister Abbey.*

There is an example of the funeral feast in the case of Pammachius the senator, the friend of Jerome. When his wife Paulina died in 397, he caused it to be proclaimed by sound of trumpet throughout Rome that on the occasion of the funeral a funeral feast, followed by a distribution of money, would be made to the poor in the Church of St. Peter. Crowds assembled. Pammachius himself presided. The long tables spread in the church were filled again and again with guests. As they departed Pammachius gave to each a new robe and a considerable alms. Jerome, in narrating the incident, remarks, "Some husbands assuage their grief by scattering upon the tombs of their wives, roses, lilies, and purple flowers; Pammachius bedews this holy dust with the balm of charity." Pammachius became a monk. It is a valuable illustration of the times which is placed before us when we are told that he took his place

* In the case of Lord Macdonald.

in the senate in his brown monk's tunic amidst the laughter of his pagan colleagues.

This reverence for the dead gave rise to a class of buildings which became very common in the cemeteries of the early Christians, chapels built in honour of the saints and martyrs.

The ages of persecution we have left sixteen centuries behind, and in the long perspective of history "the noble army of Martyrs" seems to us to stand side by side with "the glorious company of the Apostles" and "the goodly fellowship of the Prophets," three bands of blessed ones, dimly perceived through the halo of glory which surrounds them, far removed from the experiences and sympathies of our daily life.

But in the three centuries of the Church's gradual growth, through misrepresentation and contempt, through suspicion and opposition, through constant danger of injustice and punishment, through liability to local outbreaks of persecution involving torture and death, through occasional general persecutions, the martyrs and confessors of the Faith were very real persons. They had relations and friends who took a personal interest in their fate. Their relations and friends in the flesh were proud of the distinguished position they had won in the great crusade of Christ against the world; their descendants were proud of it, as we are of the fame of an ancestor who won the nation's gratitude by some great deed in which he lost life in maintaining his country's cause. Many of these sufferers were the bishops and clergy in whom their Churches felt a special interest. Their constancy under torture and death were so many victories of the faith, so many glorious testimonies to the ever-present succour of Him who was seen by the first martyr " standing at the right hand of God."

The Diocletian persecution especially, so general, prolonged, and horrible, made a great impression on the mind of the Church. The people perhaps hardly realized the grandeur and glory of the strife while they were engaged in it. It was only when the last great effort of the emperors to crush the Christian name out of existence had failed, and when the greatest of the emperors had himself embraced the Christian faith, that all men fully realized the magnitude and conclusiveness of the victory. Then the martyrs shone forth as the heroes and champions of the great campaign, who, like their Lord, had conquered by dying. The subject is curiously illustrated by a comparison between a monument which Diocletian had erected in Spain with the inscription " RELIGIO CHRISTIANORUM DELETA," and the dying exclamation of Julian, " O GALILEE, VICISTI ! "

The whole Christian community felt a personal interest in these illustrious members of the Church, and delighted to do honour to their memories. Their names were recorded in the diptychs and mentioned at the celebration of the Holy Communion; their relics (as in the case of Ignatius, *c.* A.D. 116) were reverently treasured; and the whole Church visited their tombs, adorned them with evergreens and

L

flowers, and took part in the commemorative services on the anniversary of what, with a beautiful euphemism, was called their birthday—into the higher life. Monumental chapels were constructed in connection with these visits. Sometimes, as we have already seen (p. 123), a space was cleared away around the burial-place of the saint by removing the neighbouring blocks of tufa, and a miniature basilica was built in the catacomb itself. Sometimes a chapel was built above ground, over or near the place where the body of the saint rested in the catacomb beneath, and probably in such cases a communication existed or was made between the chapel above ground and the sepulchre below. Such a building was called in Greek μαρτύριον, and in Latin *confessio*. Bishop Fabian (236-251) is said to have erected a number of such buildings in the cemeteries of Rome; and certain little churches scattered over the Campagna, which cover entrances to the catacombs, have recently attracted attention, and are now believed to be examples of these chapels. Northcote and Brownlow give woodcuts of two of these, one in the Cemetery of St. Sixtus and St. Cæcilia,* the other in that of St. Soter; each is a rather lofty and very plain building, square in plan with an apse on each of its three sides. The woodcut gives a plan of the first of these, showing the stairs by which it communicated with the catacomb beneath. It has an interesting history. The decree of Valerian in the middle of 258 ordered bishops, priests, and deacons

* Compare Lanciani.

to be summarily executed; persons of rank to loss of dignity and goods, and on their refusal to renounce Christianity, with death; imperial officials to labour in chains. Xystus or Sixtus was surprised by the soldiers seated on his episcopal chair, surrounded by his deacons and others, in the Cemetery of Prætextatus on the Appian Way, and, according to some of the accounts, he was beheaded on the spot, and the two deacons Agapetus and Felicissimus and others with him. The bishop was taken for burial to the episcopal sepulchral chamber in the Cemetery of Callistus, the others were buried in the cemetery in which they were slain. Lanciani asserts that Sixtus and his flock were assembled in this spot, which was then a schola open to the air, or sheltered by a wooden roof, and that the upper walls and vaulted roof were added at a later period when the building was converted into a chapel. When De Rossi discovered it it was used as a wine cellar. It has again become the property of the Church, and divine service was recommenced in it in April, 1891.

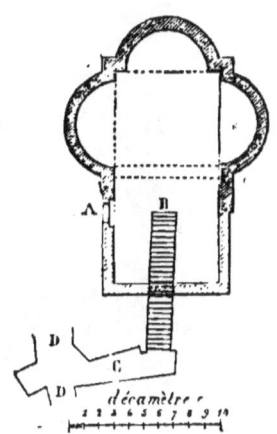

Plan of chapel in the cemetery in Via Ardentian, Rome.

It is curious to see how ancient forms survive in out-of-the-way places among unprogressive communities: here is a modern Abyssinian tomb * of the

* *Illustrated London News*, March, 1893.

Abouna Kyrilos (Bishop Cyril) at Adowa, on the model of the tombs of the fourth and fifth centuries.

There is a very interesting story in the "Acts of Theodotus and the Seven Virgins," * which illustrates

Tomb at Adowa, Abyssinia.

many features of the Christian life of the East in the beginning of the fourth century, and among others the existence and uses of these chapels.

In the beginning of the Diocletian persecution Theodotus, fleeing from the persecution at Ancyra, the capital of Galatia, retired to a place near the village of Malus, about forty miles distant, and there found some other fugitive Christians of Ancyra whom he knew, living in a cave whence the river Halys flowed. "They reclined on the grass, for there was much grass there, surrounded by both fruit-bearing and forest trees, adorned with all kinds of sweet-smelling flowers, enlivened by the chirping of cicadæ and the song of nightingales and of all various birds, and, in short, supplied with everything with which Nature can

* Ruinart's "Acta Primorum Martyrium," Amsterdam, p. 338.

adorn a solitude." During the repast Theodotus smilingly suggested to the priest of the neighbouring village, Fronto by name, who had joined them after he had said the office of the sixth hour, what a charming place it was for the erection of a *martyrion*, and asked why he did not set about it. "Do you supply me," Fronto replied, "with an occasion to set about such a work and you shall not have to blame me for tardiness; it is necessary first to have the relics, and then to think about building an edifice." "It is my affair," rejoined Theodotus, "or rather God's, to find you the relics, yours diligently to prepare the sacred house; therefore I pray you not further to delay the work, for as soon as you have finished it the relics will speedily come to you;" and, taking off a ring from his finger, he gave it to the priest, saying, "God be witness between me and thee, that you shall shortly be provided with relics." Theodotus returns to Ancyra, and ultimately meets with a martyr's death. The village priest, Fronto, happens to come to the city that day to sell the wine of his vineyard; he rescues the body, carries it away secretly, and buries it in the spot which Theodotus had suggested, and a chapel is ultimately erected over it. In the course of Theodotus's adventures in the neighbourhood of Ancyra, we read of his going by night to the Confession of the Patriarchs to pray, but finding it blocked up (*obstructam*) * by the unbelievers, he prostrated him-

---

* Probably with thorns. Gregory of Tours (ii. 25) says that Euric, the Arian Visigothic king (*c.* A.D. 600), blocked up the doors of the

self in prayer outside near the apse (*juxta concham*), and then went to the Confession of the Fathers and found that also blocked up, and prayed there also.

There is a unique example of a basilica built within the City of Rome over the tomb of a martyr, in the Church of SS. John and Paul in Rome. John and Paul were chamberlains of Constantia, the daughter of Constantine the Great, who on the accession of Julian were killed by his order, and buried in the basement of their own house. Julian's successor directed Pammachius (already mentioned at p. 143) to build a basilica over the place of their martyrdom and burial. The architect seems to have pulled down the upper part of the house to the level of the ground, filled in all the chambers except the scene of the martyrdom, and built the basilica over the site. The lower portions of the present church are part of the work of Pammachius, and recent excavations have disclosed what remains of the house of the chamberlains.

We have already had occasion to notice that sometimes a simple sepulchral chamber of a catacomb, in which some popular saint had been buried, was

---

Catholic churches of Auvergne with thorns. St. Eligius (588-659) is said to have threatened St. Columb to close the door of his church with thorns so that no one should thenceforth come to render homage to him ("Études Historiques," by C. Barthélemy, p. 380). Bishop Ralph of Chichester, in the time of Henry I. ("Diocesan Histories, Chichester," S.P.C.K.), closed the churches of his diocese, barring the doorways with thorns. The custom is alluded to in the "Ayenbite of Inwit" (*c.* A.D. 1340), "Stoppe thine earen mid thornes and ne hyer not the queade tongen," "Stop thine ears with thorns and hearken not to the evil tongue."

enlarged into a subterranean chapel. Sometimes—perhaps usually—the ground was cut away so that the walls of the building should enclose the grave. Such is the origin of the greatest sanctuaries of Christian Rome ; the churches of St. Peter on the Via Cornelia, St. Paul on the Via Ostiensis, St. Sebastian on the Via Appia, St. Petronilla on the Via Ardentina, St. Valentine on the Via Flaminia, St. Hermas on the Via Salaria, St. Agnes on the Via Nomentana, St. Lorenzo on the Via Tiburtina, and fifty others. When these graves were not very deep the floor of the basilica was almost level with the ground, as in the case of St. Peter's, St. Paul's, St. Valentine's ; in other cases it was sunk so deep in the heart of the hill that only the roof and upper tier of windows were seen above the ground, as in the basilicas of St. Lorenzo, St. Petronilla, etc. There are two or three basilicas built, or rather excavated, entirely underground ; the best specimen is that of St. Hermas on the old Via Salaria. The damage done to the catacombs by these sunken basilicas is incalculable.

The violation of the cemeteries of Rome by the Lombards led the Popes, as we have seen, to cause the bodies of the saints to be removed into the city and placed in the churches. The example was followed elsewhere ; and this removal of the bodies of martyrs and saints from the cemeteries into the churches was the beginning of the fashion, which in time became a law, that every church should have the relics of a saint beneath its altar, and of the desire to add sacredness to the church by obtaining relics of as many saints as possible; and this led to the forgery of relics; and so threw doubt upon the genuineness of any of them, and ended in a natural revulsion of the educated Christian mind against the whole system.

We Britons have our one martyr of the Diocletian persecution to boast in St. Alban, whose interesting story is told by Bede. What concerns us is that here, as in other countries, when the Church had peace the Christians of Verulam built a martyrion or basilica over the place of the martyrdom on the hill outside the city. When St. Germanus of Auxerre attended the Synod of the British Church at Verulam A.D. 429, he visited the martyr's tomb, and enriched it with relics of the apostles and other saints.* A later and less trustworthy, but still probable legend, says that on the approach of the barbarians (Saxons) the relics were placed in a wooden box and hidden underground. Offa (A.D. 793) discovered the site and the relics, and built a monastery there. The Roman bricks and Saxon balluster shafts of the present church are genuine monuments of these most ancient incidents in the history of our Church.

A very interesting illustration of these sepulchral chapels is found in the representations of the subject of the raising of Lazarus, which are so very frequent in the paintings in the catacombs, the sculptures on the sarcophagi, the mosaics in churches, the gilded glass

* Constantius's "Life of St. Germanus."

vessels, the illuminations in manuscripts, and, in short, in Christian art generally down to the end of the Middle Ages. It must be borne in mind that in the art of those times there was no attempt at antiquarian accuracy in the accessories of a subject ; for example, there was no attempt to ascertain what kind of tomb Lazarus was really buried in, or what was the tomb of his period : but his tomb was represented by one of the period at which the subject was executed. Only this other principle of ancient design must also be borne in mind, that the conventional representation of all scriptural subjects tended to the retention of ancient forms long after they had become obsolete. Bearing these two principles in mind, we have no hesitation in saying that the representations of the raising of Lazarus in ancient art preserve to us illustrations of the sepulchral chapels of primitive Christianity.

Lazarus is almost always represented, and the examples are very numerous, as folded in grave-clothes and swathed in bandages, almost like a mummy, standing at the door of a little building. This building is of two stories in height, with a stair leading to the door of the upper story at which Lazarus stands ; the door is in the gabled end of the building, and is often flanked by pillars with ornamental capitals and bases ; frequently the building has windows in the upper story, and, rarely, in the lower story also. One of the most perfect representations of this chapel which we have observed is in an arcosolium in the Roman catacombs, figured in vol. ii. Plate 57 of Garucci's " Storia della Arte Christiana;" another, equally interesting, is in another arcosolium of the catacombs, figured in the same volume at Plate 76. Two other examples, from sarcophagi in the Lateran, are given by Garucci, vol. v. Plate 313; two still more clearly defined examples at Plate 339, from a sarcophagus from the sepulchral chapel of the counts of Tolosa at the cathedral of that place, and there is one equally defined from a tomb at Lucq-de-Béarn, photographed in Le Blant's "Sarcophages de la Gaul," Plate 37.

The raising of Lazarus. From a painting of an arcosolium.

They might be rough sketches of some of the actually existing buildings figured in De Vogüé's "Syrie Centrale;" they clearly are sketches from memory of the sepulchral chapels with which the artists of the paintings and sculptures were familiar.

There are some rare but interesting and instructive varieties in the treatment. In the representation of the subject in the valuable manuscript at Corpus Christi College, Cambridge, of the end of the sixth century, which is probably one of the manuscripts which Gregory the Great sent to Augustine of Canterbury, the tomb is of two stories, the lower story square and the upper circular, covered with a dome, like the Tomb of Helena and other earliest types of Christian tombs. In the Church of S. Celso at Milan the tomb of our Lord is represented as circular, with a conical roof, a reminiscence of the holy Sepulchre at Jerusalem.* In the mosaics in the Tomb of Galla Placidia, Ravenna, is an example in which, within the sepulchral chapel, a sarcophagus is seen, out of which Lazarus has risen.

We have seen how it became the custom to remove the relics of a saint from the suburban cemeteries to the great church in the neighbouring city; and how at length no church was considered to be fully furnished unless some relics were treasured beneath its altar. We see the permanent influence of these early institutions in the customs of the Church for many centuries afterwards. The remarkable crypts at Ripon and Hexham, which are of Saxon date, and in all probability the work of Wilfrid, resemble a cubicula with the adjoining galleries of a catacomb, and were very possibly copied from the chamber in the Cemetery of Callistus, in which the bodies of St. Peter and St. Paul were at that time visited by pilgrims. The crypt under the original church at Canterbury is expressly said by Edwin the Chanter (quoted by Gervase in his account of the fire which partially destroyed the church in A.D. 1067) to have been copied from the Confession of St. Peter, "ad

* Garucci, vol. v. Plate 315.

instar confessionis Sti. Petri fabricata." The crypts under our great churches generally are probably a reminiscence of the catacombs; and the little chapels attached to their aisles are the descendants of the martyrions and family tombs of which we have been speaking. Saints' days we still keep—at least in our calendars; and the Welsh have retained the ancient custom of visiting the graves of their departed and decorating their tombs once a year on All Souls' Day.

St. Jerome has recorded how the burial-places of the saints in the catacombs became places of pious pilgrimage, which attracted visitors numerous in proportion to the celebrity of the saint. These visitors have left their own historical record in the scribblings ("*graffiti*") which abound upon the walls in the neighbourhood of all the famous graves in the catacombs. These pilgrimages were not mere results of that natural sentiment of interest with which we visit the birthplaces, the haunts, the graves of celebrated people; and the names which the pilgrims scratched on the rock are not mere records of their visit. There were religious motives for the visit, and for the record of it. The first motive of the visit was to do honour to the saint, and the second was to ask his or her intercession; the name written near the tomb was not only an historical record, but was intended to keep the writer under the notice of the saint. The illustration is from a wall painting near the tomb of St. Cornelius, who was buried by Lucina in the Cemetery of the Cornelii on the

Appian Way in 253. The painting is of much later date, almost Byzantine in style. It is given to illustrate the *graffiti* of the pilgrims to his tomb. In the majority of cases the name alone was held sufficient, like leaving a visiting card; in some cases the intention was expressed at full length by the addition of the words " pray for me." We are not defending the practice, but it is our business to record and appreciate it. Very likely their eschatology was not very different from ours, but whereas we have learnt by the experience of the past the danger of allowing sentiment and conjecture to run into superstition and abuse, they frankly

Wall-painting of St. Cornelius, Bishop of Rome. From the Cemetery of Callistus, Rome, with the names of pilgrims scribbled over it.

indulged sentiment and acted upon mere conjecture. Nobody really knows whether the departed have any knowledge of what passes in this life or not. We, because no one can prove it, refuse to act upon the possibility that they have; they, since nobody had thought of denying it, assumed it to be true, and acted upon it.

In after times the practice developed into strange superstitions; as when King Chilperic laid a letter to St. Martin on his tomb at Tours with a blank sheet of paper for the saint's answer; or when, to this day, Italians—and probably others—write letters and place them on the saints' tombs, especially on their commemoration day, stating their wishes and asking for the saints' intercession.

CHAPTER X.

PAINTINGS.

Classical paintings at Rome and Pompeii—Christian paintings in the sepulchral chambers and catacombs—In churches—Wider range of Scripture subjects introduced in the fourth century—Canons of Illiberis—Churches at Nola—Pictures of martyrdoms—St. Nilus—Painting in English churches: at Wearmouth and Jarrow—Scripture subjects in the decoration of houses; testimony of Asterius, Palace of Constantine; House of SS. John and Paul, Rome—Subjects of paintings at different periods: Symbolical, historical, apocalyptic, Passion subjects, Madonnas—Style of the early Christian school of painting; of the Byzantine school—Repetition of a narrow cycle of subjects—Originated in the East—The ΙΧΘΥΣ; the ΧΡ; the ΑΩ—The origin of the emblems: lamb, dove, etc.—Conventional treatment of subjects—The "Guide to Painting"—Came from the East—Clement of Alexandria—The Apostolical Constitutions—St. Ephrem; St. Gregory of Nyssa; St. Cyril—Paintings in North Africa; in Alexandria.

HE catacombs are interesting in themselves, with their labyrinths of passages, and their sepulchral chambers and chapels, but their interest and value is increased a hundredfold by the treasures which they contained —fresco paintings on the walls, sculptures on the sarcophagi in the chambers, inscriptions on the graves, and utensils and ornaments of many kinds.

We consider first in this chapter the fresco paintings.

Of the paintings of classical art, none have come down to us, except a few which were by accident buried in the earth, and so preserved from the wear and tear of time, and again by accident discovered in recent times. The best known examples are the wall-paintings of the so-called house of Livia, which was a part of the palace of the Cæsars, of the houses of Pompeii, of the Baths of Titus, and of some of the early sepulchral chambers at Rome.

There are among these no great serious "high-art" pictures; they are all merely "decorative" paintings. But they are of a very high class of decorative design, clearly belonging to a time of great refinement and appreciation of art. Slight and elegant in style, they produce the decorative effect which was their motive, with a minimum of expenditure of labour. The walls and ceilings are divided into panels and spaces with wonderful ingenuity, and an inexhaustible and graceful fancy; these panels and spaces afford the ground for little sketches of landscapes, pastoral scenes, and subjects from the poets; well drawn, charmingly coloured, subdued in tone. They give the impression of being the work of a school of art which had produced much grander things, and perhaps was still capable of producing grander things when they were called for, but which had, at the call of its patrons, bestowed great powers upon mere decoration. The walls and ceilings of some of the earliest chambers of the catacombs * of Rome are ornamented in this school of decoration, and in some cases are good examples of the school. The wood-

Painted ceiling of one of the chambers of the Cemetery of St. Callistus.

cut represents the ceiling of one of the chambers of the catacomb of St. Callistus. In the middle is the Orpheus symbol of our Lord; this is surrounded by

* For a description of the paintings of some of the pagan sepulchral chambers, see p. 265.

M

eight panels containing Scripture subjects alternately with pastoral scenes; the subjects are the striking the Rock, Daniel, the raising of Lazarus, and (perhaps) David with his sling. The angles of the ceiling are filled in with doves bearing olive branches. In this early period there was also a richer method of wall decoration in use, in which the ornamental forms are executed in low relief in stucco and then coloured. Some examples of it exist in the painted tombs in the Appian Way, and there are also some examples in the earliest chambers of the Cemetery of Domitilla.

But by far the larger number of the fresco paintings in the catacombs are of later date, and in a very inferior style. We cannot compare these with contemporary secular work, because all other paintings from the second century down to the eighth have perished; the impression which they make is partly that the art of painting had deteriorated, but especially that we have here only the work of inferior artists.* These rude frescoes have nevertheless a great interest for us, because of the light which they throw upon the history of the early Church.

The principal part of the painting of the sepulchral chambers now to be found is on the ceiling, which is usually divided by circles and other geometrical lines into panels of various shapes, and these panels are

* The paintings discovered in the Baths of Constantine (erected A.D. 326), which consist of some historical subjects in the portico and a ceiling, are in a better style of art than any work of the same period in the catacombs; the figure-drawing is very good, the vine-branches with their cupids are elegant, but no doubt the best artists of the time were engaged upon the work (D'Agincourt, "Painting," Plate IV.).

occupied by symbols and Scripture subjects; it will be convenient to describe some of these ceilings more fully when we endeavour to systematize and explain their subjects. It seems probable from the analogy of domestic painting that the walls of the chamber would be divided into a dado below, and

Ceiling. From the catacombs (Bottari, Plate III. 23).

panels above; but we do not find any complete examples of such an arrangement. The arcosolia gave occasion for special decorative treatment. Subjects are often painted on the *lunette*, the semi-circular space at the back of the recess, on the *soffit*, the underside of the arch of the recess, and less frequently on the wall space around at the sides and in front of the arcosolium. There is sometimes a painted frame around a loculus, and sometimes an ornament or symbol on the slab which closes it. Other subjects are placed irregularly on the walls.

The first conclusion to which we are led by a general survey of the series of paintings before us, is that the early Church had no theological objection to painting, whether used for decoration, or for the representation of scriptural subjects and religious ideas. We are so used to the bare walls of our churches, that we are almost unconscious of their cold and unfinished effect ; but with the early Christians it was not so. The Christian congregations were accustomed, in the Upper chambers or the Atria of well-to-do converts in which they assembled for worship, to arcades of marble columns with gilded capitals, painted walls and ceilings, and tesselated pavements ; and in passing through the sepulchral chambers of the same "princes of the congregation" to the narrower galleries beyond, they were accustomed to see them decorated, like the rooms of a house, in the elegant taste of the time. When they built basilicas of their own for their worship, and when they prepared sepulchral chambers for their own dead, it was natural that they should continue to use the fashions to which they were accustomed ; only, from the first, subjects which were morally objectionable, or belonged to the heathen mythology, were excluded. People were not indeed in the latter respect puritanically precise ; and they made no scruple to continue the use of certain subjects which had come to have a merely symbolical meaning. They introduced Oceanus and the Tritons to indicate the sea, and river gods to indicate rivers, the bow of Iris, winged genii, and perhaps other like conventions of pagan art.

The question at what period paintings of Scripture subjects and sacred persons were first used in churches has been much discussed, and is not free from difficulty. The Council of Illiberis, in Spain (A.D. 301), made a canon which appears to forbid the introduction of pictures into churches: "Pictures ought not to be placed in churches, nor that which we worship or adore to be painted on the walls," from which we do not necessarily conclude that the walls and ceilings of churches before that time were not painted with the common decorations which we find in the chambers of the catacombs, or the usual cycle of symbols and symbolical pictures; but that there was an objection to the introduction of the figure of our Lord or the saints in any way which would be likely to attract a superstitious reverence. The free introduction of these symbolical subjects in the catacombs leads to the confident conclusion that they were not forbidden in the churches; while the objection to the introduction into churches of the figure of our Lord, in such a way as to attract devotion to it, is illustrated by the way in which such representations are avoided in the catacombs. The earliest notice of the introduction of a wider cycle of Scripture historical subjects is in the description which Paulinus, Bishop of Nola (*circa* 395), gives of the paintings with which he had adorned his new church over the tomb of St. Felix, and the old basilica of the town, and the basilica at Funda. Among the subjects in the first were the creation, the offering of Isaac, the continence of Joseph, the overthrow of Pharaoh, the separation of Ruth and Orpah. In the second he introduced "the two Testaments;" in the apse of the third he placed the symbol of the Passion in the form of a white Lamb crowned beneath a red cross. He explains that his reason for this unusual practice (*raro more*) was to interest and instruct the rude multitudes who came to the saint's festival.

Pictures of martyrdoms were not infrequent, especially no doubt in the chapels and basilicas erected over the graves and dedicated to the memory of the martyrs. Gregory of Nyssa (*circa* 400) describes a picture of the martyrdom of Theodorus, one of the victims of the Diocletian persecution, which seems to have been painted on the wall of the church which contained the saint's relics. The artist, he says, had depicted in glowing colours the heroic acts of the martyr, his struggles, his pains, the brutal forms of his persecutors, their insults, the flaming furnace, the blessed consummation of the soldier of Christ. A painting, he adds, though silent can speak upon the wall and greatly profit.* Olympiodorus (*circa* 430)

* Other examples are the martyrdom of St. Cassian (Prudentius Perist., ix. 5); of St. Hippolytus (ibid., xi. 126); of St. Felix (Paullinius, Poem xxv. 20); St. Euphemia (Asterius, ep. 7, Syn. Act. 4, p. 617).

consulted St. Nilus about the decoration of a church erected in honour of the martyrs; he contemplated covering the walls with hunting scenes and the like. Nilus advised him to place one single cross at the east of the temple, and to fill the holy sanctuary (τὸν ναὸν τὸν ἅγιον) with histories of the Old and New Testaments by the hand of a skilful artist, in order that those who are unable to read the Divine Scriptures may, by looking at the paintings, call to mind the courage of men who have served the true God, and be stirred to emulation of their heroic exploits. Augustine bears witness to the custom of painting "Christ and His Apostles" on the church walls in his time, and remarks on the existence of the growing abuse of paying veneration to them.

There are for four or five centuries no pictures of the Passion, no picture of the sacrifice of the cross, no picture of the cross itself; the Christ to be adored is only hinted at by the Good Shepherd, or the Lamb standing on the mount, or later by the cross enthroned.* In short, the mind of the primitive Church seems to have been the same as the mind of the English Church at this day, that the representation of sacred subjects and sacred persons in church is lawful and may be usefully introduced, but that outward reverence to these representations is unlawful, and is to be guarded against.

There is an interesting notice of paintings in the early English Church in Bede's "Lives of the Holy

* See p. 201.

Abbots." He relates that when Benedict Biscop returned from his third voyage to Rome in A.D. 675, "He brought with him pictures of sacred representations to adorn the Church of St. Peter which he had built (at Monkwearmouth), viz. pictures of the Virgin Mary and of the Twelve Apostles, with which he intended to adorn the central nave, on boarding placed from one wall to the other; also some figures from Gospel history to adorn the south wall; others from the Revelation of St. John for the north wall; so that every one who entered the Church even if they could not read, wherever they turned their eyes might have before them the loving countenance of Christ and his Saints, though it were but in a picture, and with watchful minds might meditate upon the benefits of the Lord's Incarnation, and having before their eyes the perils of the Last Judgment, might examine their hearts more strictly on that account."

On a fifth journey, about A.D. 685, Benedict brought back, for the church dedicated to the Virgin Mary (in addition to the great church dedicated to St. Peter) in the monastery in Wearmouth, pictures enough of the Divine history to go round the church. For the church of St. Paul at Jarrow he brought pictures arranged in type and antitype, viz. one pair of Isaac carrying the wood for the sacrifice and of our Lord carrying His cross; another pair of the brazen serpent and of our Lord on the cross.

Another interesting question is as to the use of

Scripture subjects in domestic decoration. We know that the pagan people of those early times used painting very largely in the decoration of the walls and ceilings of their rooms, and that besides ornamental patterns, landscapes, pastoral scenes, and the like, they also introduced subjects from their poets, and historical and mythological subjects.

We may be quite sure that people did not altogether cease to have their rooms decorated with paintings when they became Christian; the question is whether they did or did not introduce Christian subjects into their paintings. Now, the pagan sepulchral chambers of the age were commonly painted with the same subjects as the chambers of their houses. The early Christians probably followed the same fashion. Since then we find Christian sepulchral chambers painted with the old kind of ornamental patterns, only with Christian symbols and symbolical pictures in place of the old figure-subjects, we should infer that the rooms of their houses were painted on the same principles, with the usual ornamental patterns and Christian emblems, and symbolical pictures. Again, from the fact that the early Christians used Christian symbols and pictures on their garments and all kinds of utensils and objects of personal and domestic use, as we shall see in future chapters, we should conclude that they would use the same class of subjects in the painting of their houses.

The conjecture is not entirely unsupported by positive evidence.* Over the grand entrance to the

* See quotation from Asterius, p. 327.

Imperial Palace at Constantinople, Constantine caused to be painted, in encaustic painting (a method used by the ancients, in which the pigments were mixed with wax to enable them to resist the rain), an allegorical picture, half religious, half political, which Eusebius describes and explains in detail. Constantine himself was represented, surrounded by his children, as a kind of St. Michael, with the cross over his head, and beneath his feet the enemy of mankind, "who, through the agency of impious tyrants, had assailed the Church of Christ, in the figure of a serpent, pierced through with darts and drowned in the depth of the sea; pointing out in this manner the Emperor's victory over the enemies of Christ and His Church as due to the force and potency of that salutary trophy which was placed above his head."

The paintings in the newly discovered house of SS. John and Paul, under the basilica of that name in Rome, confirm the conjecture that in the decoration of Christian houses the subjects usual in the chambers of the catacombs were adopted in place of the old mythological subjects. We have seen, at p. 150, that Pammachius took down the house to a certain level and built the basilica upon it, leaving the bodies of the saints in the chamber where they were, which thus became their *confessio*. Some of the original rooms of the lower portion of the house remain, apparently in their original condition, with the ornamental painting still upon walls and ceiling. The walls of the tablinum have a dado, painted in imitation of marble, and, above that, a frieze of bold scroll-work; the spandrels of the vaulting with sprays of vines, and the ceiling of the converging panels, which make frames for some of the usual early cycle of subjects: Moses taking off his shoes, sheep and goats, etc. Similar symbolical subjects are on the remaining wall of the atrium, and in other parts of the house.*

When we analyze the subjects of Christian art in the catacombs and basilicas, we find that they may be divided, according to the order of time, into three classes, which reveal the prevalence of different phases of thought and feeling at different periods of the Church's history.

1. In the first period, extending from the earliest paintings in the catacombs down to the end of the classical tradition of art, the same narrow cycle of subjects is in general use. The central figure of the cycle is the Saviour; at first in the character of the Good Shepherd, and later as the Healer of the sick and Raiser of the dead, and still later as the Head of the Church, sitting on the mount whence the rivers of Paradise flow, surrounded by His Apostles.

2. It was probably about the beginning of the fifth century that a new fashion arose in the choice of subjects for mural pictures; the cycle of symbolical Scripture subjects gave way to a new cycle of historical Scripture subjects, intended to put before the eyes of the people the principal events of sacred history and the principal facts of our re-

* The Rev. S. Baring-Gould, *Newbery House Magazine*, i. 175.

demption. St. Paulinus of Nola (*circa* 400) is always quoted as having been among the earliest to introduce pictures into his Church of St. Felix, with the motive, which he himself declares, of giving the ignorant people subjects for instruction and meditation during vigils and festivals, when no special service was going on in church.

3. Contemporary with the introduction of Byzantine art, comes in a new choice of subjects. The usual subject of the mosaics which adorn the semi-dome of the apse of the churches of this style is a colossal figure of the Lord seated on a throne, surrounded by a rainbow, accompanied by the four Living Creatures, the four and twenty Elders, and all the grand symbolism of St. John's vision in Patmos. It may be that the mind of the Church was then full of the triumphs of Christ—His triumph over the classical heathenism, over the philosophies which succeeded it in the minds of the better classes, over the rude paganism of the barbarian races which had conquered the West—of the vast extension of the Church over the further East beyond the bounds of the empire, in Armenia and Persia, into India and China. Later the widely spread opinion that the world would end with the tenth century had set men to the study of St. John's prophecies, and saturated their minds with the mysterious imagery of his language. And these things together may have led to the predominance of the representation of these apocalyptic subjects.

Though it carries us for a moment beyond the

limits of our present plan, it is worth while briefly to complete this view of the characteristics of Christian art by stating that in a later period the subjects of the Passion of the Lord were the characteristic subjects. Christ upon the cross was the central figure of its pictorial representations. Was it that the idea of the Divine self-sacrifice, as the noblest feature of the life of the Son of man, had taken hold of the mind of the Church? In this period also the walls of the church are covered with historical subjects from the Old and New Testaments, and legendary subjects from the lives of saints; and a terrifying dramatic representation of the Doom—the last Judgment—is painted on a large scale, in some conspicuous situation.

About the fifteenth century the Madonna became the favourite subject of Christian art—the representation of the mystery of the Incarnation of Deity.

In all these phases of the Church's thought and feeling, it is Christ who is foremost and uppermost in the mind and heart of the Church. Whichever symbol was for the time predominant, it included all the others. The Good Shepherd, of a higher order of being than the sheep, is the Incarnate Son of God, who laid down His life for the sheep; and it was because He was thus obedient to death, even the death of the cross, that God had given Him a Name which is above every name, and had very highly exalted Him. Thus the Incarnation, the Passion, the Majesty, are all included in the idea of the Good Shepherd. The eternal Sonship might be symbolized by the beardless youth of the representation; the lamb upon His shoulders symbolized at the same time the lost human race which He redeemed, the

Fresco painting. From the Cemetery of Callistus.

Church which was peculiarly His own, and the individual soul of every sheep of His flock.

To return to the study of the paintings of the catacombs. The sentiment of the subjects of the earliest is peaceful and serene. Vines and flowers, with children and genii sporting among them, landscapes and pastoral subjects, harvest scenes of corn and vine and olive, all of which, though continuations of the old decorative subjects, are now perhaps used as symbolical of great truths. In the figure-subjects the faces are calm and expressionless, the attitudes are simple and natural, without vehement life or movement; there is no attempt to affect the senses by impressive representation, no endeavour to idealize the persons represented. The subjects are treated with a view to their symbolical meaning rather than with an aim at dramatic representation of the history.

As we get down to the beginning of the new school of Christian art which succeeded this classical style, we do begin to find that the artists endeavour to elaborate facial expression, to idealize the faces of sacred persons, to give distinguishing individual character to Apostles, to impress the senses by a skilful use of the resources of art. The characteristics of the two schools are illustrated by the difference between the simple expressionless figure of a Good Shepherd on a ceiling of the catacombs, and the grand, awful, colossal representation of the Lord in Glory, in the semi-dome of a Byzantine basilica.

Two facts in regard to the selection of the subjects and their representation will at once be apparent to every one who glances through the subjects of this early art. A narrow cycle of subjects is repeated over and over again, all over Christendom; the subjects are always represented in so strictly conventional a manner that the rudest sketch is sufficient to identify the subject; even a fragment is enough to enable one who has studied them to pronounce with certainty to which of the subjects it belongs. First as to the selection of subjects. In the selection of subjects from the Old and New Testaments, the first thing which strikes us is that out of the immense number of subjects which were open to the painter's choice, and which find a place in the art of later ages, very few are selected; and that those which are selected are not those which we should have been disposed to expect. The subjects of Moses striking the rock, Daniel in the lions' den, Jonah, and the raising of Lazarus, are repeated with great frequency; then, but at a considerable distance, Noah in the ark, the sacrifice of Isaac, the three children in Nebuchadnezzar's furnace, and the healing of the paralytic. It may be said of all the rest that they are comparatively rare.[*]

We submit that the origin of the whole series of subjects is to be sought in the East. And first as to the mere emblems. Clement of Alexandria mentions the fish, anchor, lyre, ship, and recommends them for use as Christian symbols. But perhaps the most conclusive evidence that their symbolism originated in the East is to be found in the two which were the most frequently used, the fish and the XP monogram.

The significance of the fish is very largely due to

[*] Brownlow Maitland.

the fact that the Greek word which signifies "fish" (ΙΧΘΥΣ) forms the anagram of the words ΙΗΣΟΥΣ ΧΡΙΣΤΟΣ, ΘΗΟΥ ΥΙΟΣ, ΣΩΤΗΡ, "Jesus Christ, the Son of God, the Saviour." The allusion in the fish to the waters of baptism materially assisted the symbolical significance, but it may be doubted whether that was sufficiently striking to have made the symbol so popular among people who only knew it by its Latin name of *Piscis*. When Greek ceased to be the ecclesiastical language of the Roman Church, the fish symbol disappeared from its monuments.

Northcote and Brownlow observe that it is by no means improbable that the schools of Alexandria originated this symbol. The Church of that city was gathered largely out of the Jews, who formed so large and important a portion of its population; it was a very common practice for the Jews to coin names for their great men by means of a combination of names or by the initials of a legend or a motto which had reference to them. The name of Judas Maccabæus, for example, is made up of the initials of the Hebrew text, "Who is like unto Thee among the strong, O Lord?"

The monogram XP also is Greek; it consists of the first two letters of the name of Christ (ΧΡΙΣΤΟΣ). Its appearance on the labarum under which Constantine conquered, gave it great acceptance throughout the whole world, and it has been used in all the Churches ever since; but it was a known symbol in the Church before Constantine adopted it, and it is necessarily of Greek origin.

The AΩ emblem, taken from our Lord's words in the first chapter of the Revelation, may properly be mentioned here, as implying a general familiarity with Greek culture in the early Churches to which the book was addressed.

Who made the selection of the symbolical Scripture subjects; and how did it commend itself to general acceptance? It already existed at the date of the earliest literary notices in the East and of the earliest monuments in the West. In the absence of any direct evidence, we hazard the conjecture that it grew gradually in the earliest years of Christianity, and was crystallized by the frequent use of certain symbols and subjects as illustrative commonplaces by the popular teachers of the second century.

John the Baptist began it by making "the Lamb of God" the emblem of the sacrificial aspect of Christ's work for our redemption. The Baptism of our Lord fixed for ever the Dove as the emblem of the Holy Spirit's descent upon mankind. Our Lord Himself established the Good Shepherd as the type of His relation to His Church, and pointed to Jonah as the type of His resurrection. St. Paul's metaphor had made an Anchor the emblem of faith. St. Peter had quoted Noah as a type of the safety of those who would be in the Ark of the Church at the end of the world. Justin Martyr (a native of Palestine, *circa* A.D. 139) adduced the Ship with its mast and sails as an emblem of the Cross.* And so very possibly one

---

* Justin names other emblems of the Cross, as a spade, the figure of a man with outstretched arms (Holman Hunt's "Shadow of the

emblem was added after another, and one Scripture subject was suggested and then another; and the most authoritative and the most striking were at length selected, grouped, systematized, generally adopted into the popular teaching, and so accepted by the artists as the subjects of their art.

Next, as to the conventional treatment of the subjects.

This conventional treatment of subjects is one of the characteristics of all ancient art. To limit ourselves to Greek art, from which Christian art was derived. The art of Greece had from an early period settled types of the paintings and statues of its deities, and its conventional representation of the principal subjects of its mythology. Quintilian says of Parrhasius that "he was called the Lawgiver, because the types which he had handed down of gods and heroes were followed of necessity by all other artists." We recognize a statue of Jupiter, Mercury, Apollo, Hercules, as if they were portraits; a fragment of them is often enough—to a proverb (*ex pede Herculem*)—for their identification. The general composition of the great subjects of mythological story was equally traditional; it is a curious illustration of this fact that the discovery of an ancient gem engraved with the group of the Laocoon afforded an authority for the restoration of the missing portions of the famous marble group in the

Cross"), the face of a man with its nose and brows; an illustration of the way in which the imagination of the time was seeking for such emblems.

Vatican which had baffled some of the greatest modern sculptors and critics.

It is not meant that artists slavishly copied—made mere replicas—of the works of their predecessors; they adhered to established types of god or hero, followed the conventional composition of a mythological group, but treated them with a certain freedom. "The artists of those times," says Goethe,* "considered themselves as original enough when they felt themselves possessed of sufficient power and dexterity to grasp the original thought of another, and to reproduce it again after their own version." From time to time an artist of more originality would introduce a new passage in the conventional treatment, and if it met with general approval it was followed. At intervals of centuries some great genius would introduce a totally new treatment, with the result that the progressive half of the artistic world would adopt the new type, while the conservative half would adhere to the old ways.

This is the history of the conventionalism of Christian art also. At a very early period, earlier than any of the works which have come down to us, the types of the Good Shepherd, the Daniel in the lions' den, the Moses striking the rock, the raising of Lazarus, the healing of the paralytic, and the rest of the usual subjects, had been established; and they were adhered to, with a certain freedom of treatment, and occasional bold variations, down to the end of the period of classical art with which we have espe-

* Quoted by Rev. C. King, "Antique Gems and Rings."

cially to do; then the Byzantine artists introduced new subjects and new treatment; but a school of artists in the Eastern Church continued to reproduce the old types down to the present day.*

Who was the Parrhasius—the art lawgiver—of these Christian types we do not know, but we submit that this Christian art began in the East. The fact that the vast majority of the examples known to us are in the West, and especially in Rome, is calculated to mislead us into the conclusion that this art had its origin in Rome. The Churches of Palestine, Syria, Asia Minor, Macedonia, and Greece had been founded before St. Paul and St. Peter had settled the organization of the Church in Rome; and when the Church was planted in Rome it was for a couple of centuries not an indigenous Church, racy of the soil, but a Greek-speaking colony, deriving its religious ideas from the East. North Africa was the true source of Latin Christianity.

It is true that we have no actual remaining examples of Christian art in the East earlier than those which the catacombs have preserved for us in the West, but there is literary evidence that the usual

* M. Didron found in actual use at Mount Athos a sixteenth-century manuscript copy of a "Guide to Painting," supposed to have been compiled from an original compiled by Dionisius the monk, who had studied the famous paintings of Pauselinos. Additions have been made to it from time to time, and it is still in use as a manual of fresco-painting in the churches of Greece. M. Didron published it under the title of "Manuel d'Iconographie Chrétienne Greque et Latin." It contains descriptions how the usual subjects are to be treated, and how they are to be distributed in the different parts of the church, but does not give sketches of the subjects. Some such traditional unwritten guide to painting must have existed from a very early age.

cycle of Christian subjects was early known in the East, and that the subjects were treated in the conventional way which we know so well; and "without controversy" in all the early history of Christianity, the East did not derive its religious ideas from the West, but the West from the East.

St. Clement of Alexandria (A.D. 192),* in a passage which will be more conveniently quoted in connection with another branch of the subject,† is the earliest authority on the use of Christian emblems; he recommends a usage already existing in the second century.

The "Apostolical Constitutions," a book which, the Chevalier de Bunsen said, places us in the midst of the (Eastern) Church life of the second and third centuries, has a passage grouping together a number of subjects in a way which indicates that the Eastern cycle of subjects was the same as that which we find in the West.

V. 7. "He that made Adam out of the earth will raise up the bodies of the rest, etc. . . . Besides these arguments we believe there is to be a resurrection also from the resurrection of our Lord. For it is He that raised Lazarus when he had been in the grave four days, and Jairus' daughter, and the widow's son. It is He that raised Himself by the command of the Father in the space of three days, who is the pledge of our resurrection. For, says He, I am the Resur-

---

* Egypt belonged to the Eastern Church, as North Africa did to the Western.
† See p. 344.

rection and the Life. Now He that brought Jonas in the space of three days alive and unhurt out of the belly of the whale, and the three children out of the furnace of Babylon, and Daniel out of the mouth of the lions, does not want power to raise us up also. . . . He that raised Himself from the dead will also raise again all that are laid down. He who raises wheat out of the ground with many stalks from one grain, He who makes the tree that is cut down send forth branches, He that made Aaron's dry rod put forth buds, will raise us up in glory; He that raised him up that had the palsy whole, and healed him that had the withered hand, He that supplied a defective part to him that was born blind from clay and spittle, will raise us up; He that satisfied five thousand men with five loaves and two fishes, and caused a remainder of twelve baskets, and out of water made wine, and sent a piece of money out of a fish's mouth by one Peter to those that demanded tribute, will raise the dead."

St. Gregory of Nyssa, in the middle of the fourth century, describes the conventional treatment of the sacrifice of Isaac with great clearness: "Often have I seen in paintings the representation of the sacrifice of Isaac, and I could not contemplate it without tears, so truthfully did art present the scene. Isaac is placed beneath his father near the altar, he is kneeling and his hands are tied behind him. Behind, Abraham places his foot upon the side of his son, with his left hand he turns back the head of Isaac and hangs over his countenance, which regards him with an expression full of sadness. The right hand is armed with the knife; he is about to strike, and the point of the steel already touches the flesh, when the Divine voice is heard which arrests the stroke." *

St. Cyril, in the early part of the fifth century, also describes paintings which show the various scenes of this same history in one picture: "Here Abraham seated on the ass and leading his son and followed by the servants; there the ass remains below with the servants, Abraham carrying the knife and the fire, lays the wood upon Isaac; in another place is Abraham laying hold of his son and preparing to strike." †

The earliest painting known to us still existing in the East is in Cyrenaica.‡ It is a Good Shepherd of the usual type: the Shepherd is young and beardless, clad in a short tunic without sleeves, tied by a girdle, with naked legs, and feet in sandals. He carries a sheep on his shoulders, holding its feet with both hands; he holds a short staff in the left hand. There are six sheep about him and trees indicate the country. There is one feature which differs from the ordinary type—the head wears a garland of leaves. Around the subject are seven large and carefully drawn fishes.

In the same region, near Aphrodisias, is a sepulchral chamber with a fresco painting of less ancient date

---

* St. Gregory of Nyssa, " De Deitate, Fil. et Sp. Sanct.," vol. iii. p. 572 (Migne).

† St. Cyril's letter to Acacius, Labbe, " Concilia," vii. p. 204.

‡ Pacho, " Relation d'un voyage dans la Marmique, la Cyrenaique," etc., 1827, 1829. Garucci quotes it, vol. vi. 105*c*.

than the above. It is a branch of a vine loaded with grapes, with geometrical ornaments, one medallion encloses a fish, another a cross; on another a serpent twined around a cross recalls without doubt the brazen serpent.

The paintings in the catacomb at Alexandria include the miracle of Cana and the miracle of the loaves united in one design and treated more freely than usual.

CHAPTER XI.

THE LIKENESSES OF CHRIST AND HIS APOSTLES.

The earliest representations conventional — The statuary group at Paneas; the likenesses by St. Luke; the Veronica legend; Eusebius on the subject; Publius Lentulus's description — The two types of likeness, the classical and the Byzantine — St. Peter and St. Paul — The four evangelists.

SOME of our readers will probably wish to learn what is known on the subject of authentic early likenesses of our Lord and of the Apostles; and it may be a disappointment to learn that no such likenesses exist.

The earliest representations of our Lord—and they are very numerous in these centuries with which we are specially concerned, in fresco-painting and sculpture—are entirely conventional, there is no attempt at portraiture, or at the invention of an ideal face. The statues of the Good Shepherd, for example, offered a special opportunity for portraiture, or at least for the attempt to idealize, but a glance at them is enough to convince the spectator that

there was no such intention in the sculptor's mind.*
And the same thing may be said of the many representations which occur in the gospel scenes introduced into the ornamentation of the sarcophagi.

The first allusion to the existence of such likenesses seems to be of the fourth century. When the Empress Helena sent to Eusebius of Cæsarea to send her a likeness (εἰκών) of Christ, we may conclude that she had heard of their existence. Eusebius replied, that if she meant an image of the frail and mortal flesh which He bore before His Ascension, such images are forbidden in the Mosaic Law; they are nowhere to be found in churches, and it is notorious that with us alone they are forbidden. "Some poor woman," he goes on to say, "brought me two painted figures, like philosophers, and ventured to say that they represented Paul and the Saviour; I do not know on what ground. But, to save her and others from offence, I took them from her and kept them by me, not thinking it right in any case that she should exhibit them further, that we may not seem like idolaters to carry our God about in an image." The bishop's answer implies that pious credulity was beginning to invent apocryphal likenesses of Christ and His Apostles, but that no authentic likenesses were known to exist.

The story that the woman who was healed of her infirmity by touching the hem of our Lord's garment was a wealthy person, and that she caused a bronze

* See frontispiece.

group of the subject to be made as a memorial of her gratitude, and erected at Paneas, where she lived, is probably a mere story invented to explain a group of statuary existing at that place in the time of Eusebius; it is an ingenious conjecture that the monument may have commemorated the gratitude of a province or town to its governor, represented as a suppliant female kneeling at his feet.

The story of the likeness which St. Luke sent to Abgarus, the King of Edessa, is one of a family of stories of likenesses by St. Luke, the painter, and they are all alike unsupported by evidence.

The legend of St. Veronica—that when our Lord was on His way to Calvary she lent Him her head-veil with which to wipe the sweat of suffering from His face, and that when He returned it to her a portrait of the sacred features was found to have been miraculously impressed upon it—is very beautiful, but entirely without foundation. It gave rise to, or it arose out of, the existence of a number of faces painted upon linen or similar material, of which examples still remain at the Vatican, at Genoa, and elsewhere, which seem to be of the period of art which was tending towards the Byzantine school. Copies of some of them may be found in Mr. Heaphy's "The Likeness of Christ," Plates II., III., IV., V.*

There is a famous description of the personal

---

* For further information on the subject the reader is referred to Mrs. Jameson's "Likeness of Christ." We mention Mr. Heaphy's "The Likeness of Christ" only to show that it has not been overlooked; it is worth consulting for copies of pictures in Rome and elsewhere, which are not otherwise accessible to the student.

appearance of our Lord, which professes to have been written by Publius Lentulus, a friend of Pilate, which runs thus: "At this time appeared a man who lives till now, a man endowed with great powers. Men call him a great Prophet; his own disciples call him the Son of God. His name is Jesus Christ. He restores the dead to life, and cures the sick of all manner of diseases. This man is of noble and well-proportioned stature, with a face full of kindness and yet firmness, so that the beholders both love and fear him. His hair is the colour of wine [probably yellow] and golden at the root—straight, and without lustre, but from the level of the ears curling and glossy, and divided down the middle after the fashion of the Nazarenes [*i.e.* Nazarites]. His forehead is even and smooth, his face without blemish, and enhanced by a tempered bloom. His countenance ingenuous and kind. Nose and mouth no way faulty. His beard is full, of the same colour as his hair, and forked in form; his eyes blue and extremely brilliant. In rebuke and reproof he is formidable; in exhortation and teaching, gentle and amiable of tongue. None have seen him to laugh, but many, on the contrary, to weep. His person is tall, his hands beautiful and straight. In speaking he is deliberate and grave and little given to loquacity. In beauty surpassing most men." It is probable that this was written about the beginning of the fourth century, just when there was arising a general interest on the subject of our Lord's personal appearance, and when artists were beginning to aim at an ideal representation of the Great Subject.

It is, in short, one of the fancy portraits of the period done in words instead of pigments.

There is one striking fact in the early representations, namely, that there are two conventional types to be found in them. One is a youthful, unbearded, cheerful face, with crisp curled hair, the conventional classical face of a young man, which is the earlier type; the other is a long, grave, mature, bearded face, which appears in monuments of later date. The two are illustrations of two lines of conjecture, when men began to interest themselves in trying to form an ideal of the sacred countenance.

One school based their ideal upon the consideration that our Lord, being the Perfect Man, must have been the type of human beauty in person and feature as well as in mind and soul. They found support for their theory in such Scripture texts as, "Thou art fairer than the children of men; full of grace are Thy lips, because God hath blessed Thee for ever" (Ps. xlv. 2); "My beloved is white and ruddy, the chiefest among ten thousand . . . he is altogether lovely" (Cant. v. 10, 16); "Thine eyes shall see the King in His beauty" (Isa. xxxiii. 17).

The other school based their ascetic ideal upon the consideration of the suffering Messiah, and supported it by such texts as, "He hath no form nor comeliness; and when we shall see Him, there is no beauty that we should desire Him. . . . He was despised, and we esteemed Him not" (Isa. liii. 2, 3).*

* Consult a note at p. 253 of the translation of Tertullian, in the Oxford Library of the Fathers, for a collection of passages from the Fathers on the personal appearance of our Lord.

It was not, as we have already had occasion to say,* until the fifth century or later that artists began to give individual character to the chief persons of the Scripture histories which it was their business to portray. The face in the Cemetery of SS. Nereus and Achilleus, of the beginning of the fourth century, which De Rossi quotes as an early fresco of Christ, is considered by Roller to be a portrait of the deceased person there buried. The other famous "portraits of Christ" in the Cemetery of St. Pontianus and the crypt of Sta. Cæcilia are the one of the seventh to ninth century and the other of the ninth century at the earliest. The Byzantine artists at length developed an ideal Christ which appears in most of the mosaic pictures—a grave, solemn, awful face, with dark hair and beard, which partook more of the ascetic than of the lovely type, and which continued to be the accepted type of the Christ of art for many centuries.

We may add briefly, in order to complete the subject, that the Italian painters of the Renaissance introduced a new type, in which they endeavoured to add to the perfect Humanity some shadowing forth of the Divinity within. They adopted the fair type, which is not the prevalent type of Eastern physiognomy, but which is highly valued when it does appear among them. David was of this exceptional type, "ruddy and of a beautiful countenance" † and "fair of eyes" (marginal reading), that is, with fair complexion, golden hair, and blue eyes.

* Page 175.   † See 1 Sam. xvi. 12, 18; xvii. 42.

The illustration of our Lord holding a book with a basket of volumes on each side of Him, is from Bosio's "Roma Sotteranea," p. 475 ; the painting is not earlier than the fifth century.

There was an early tradition about the personal characteristics of St. Peter and St. Paul, which the artists adopted when they began to endeavour to give individual character to their subjects. It is seen especially in some of the gilded glass vessels, and in the bronzes, which are described hereinafter. St. Peter is represented by tradition, and in the art which follows it, as an elderly man of robust form, with strong, sensible features, crisp curling hair, bald at the crown ; St. Paul as a slight person, with a thin eager face, bald from the forehead backwards. Of the personal appearance of the other Apostles there were no traditions, except that St. John was the youngest of the Twelve. The artists of the earlier centuries represented them by conventional figures. The artists of the Renaissance showed their skill in inventing various types of feature, such as might be supposed to have belonged to the various types of character of those whom the Lord chose as the foundation stones of a world-wide Church. Perhaps this skill of the Christian artist reached its highest point in Leonardo's "Last Supper," at Milan.

The Four Evangelists are represented in the early classical school of art ; symbolically, by the four rivers of Paradise which flow forth from the mount on which stands the sacred Lamb ; personally, by conventional

Our Lord as the Giver of the Divine Word. Fifth century.

(frequently half-length) figures in classical costume accompanied by one or other of the four living creatures of Ezekiel and the Revelation which were taken to be their symbols; the angel for St. Matthew, the lion for St. Mark, the ox for St. Luke, and the eagle for St. John;* in the mosaics of Byzantine art the four living creatures of the Revelation are depicted on a large scale surrounding our Lord in glory.

* The symbolical creatures are not invariably thus assigned.

CHAPTER XII.

SYMBOLISM.

Emblems: the cross; the crucifix; the "Graffito Blasfemo;" the monogram—Symbolical subjects: the shepherd; the lamb; the fish; a fisherman; the ship; anchor; amphora; vine; olive; palm; doves; sheep; goats; peacock; phœnix; Orpheus; ox and ass; mount with four streams; stag drinking; hand; nimbus; aureole—Symbolical subjects from the Old and New Testaments: their meaning; Daniel; the Three Children; Jonah; Lazarus; Noah; sacrifice of Isaac; healing the paralytic; the infirm woman; the blind man; the passage of the Red Sea; giving the Law; the burning bush; gathering manna (?); seizure of Moses (?); striking the rock; Job; creation of Eve; fall of man; Adam and Eve clothed; Abel and Cain; translation of Elijah; baptism of Christ; entry into Jerusalem; arrest of Christ—Eucharistic symbols: feeding the multitude; miracle of Cana; manna; table with fish and bread; fish and bread—List of subjects on sarcophagi in the Lateran and Vatican collections—Groups of subjects: on ceilings, gilded glass, arcosolia.

FOR the purpose of a detailed consideration of the subjects of early Christian art it will be convenient to include both the paintings and sculptures in one view, to divide them into various classes irrespective of their date, and to introduce as may be convenient the few observations which may be needed on their chronology. We may divide the subjects into the following classes:

1. Pure emblems, as the anchor, lyre, etc. 2. Symbolical subjects, as the Shepherd, Orpheus, harts drinking at a stream, birds drinking from a fountain, etc. 3. Subjects from the Old Testament history; and from the Gospel history. 4. Representations of the deceased. 5. Personal symbols. Each of these classes requires separate consideration.

1. Emblems.

The CROSS was in constant use by the early Christians as a manual sign. Tertullian ("De Corona," § 3) says, "In all our travels and movements, in all our coming in and going out, in putting on our shoes, at the bath, at the table, in lighting our candles, in lying down, in sitting down, whatever employment occupies us, we mark our forehead with the sign of the cross;" and St. Ambrose[*] says that it was still the custom in his time: "Christians, at every act, sign the cross on their foreheads." They were quick to see the sacred symbol. Justin Martyr sees it in a ship's mast and sail, a plough, a spade, a man with outstretched arms, in the nose and brows of the human face, in the banners and trophies of the armies, in the statues of the emperors and gods (whose models were of clay built up on a stake and crossbar), in the four quarters of the heavens (Apol. 55). Tertullian also in birds with outstretched wings.[†]

St. Cyril explains at length that the symbol was used as a memorial of the mercies and duties of the cross.[‡]

---

[*] 1 Apol. 12 and 16; and De Orat. xi. 28.
[†] Migne's edit. vol. iii. 327.
[‡] De Cor. c. 3; Ad. Uxor. ii. 5.

It was not used upon their monuments until a late period; to the pagan mind the cross was associated only with ideas of ignominy, as the gallows is with us; it was "unto the Jews a stumbling-block, and

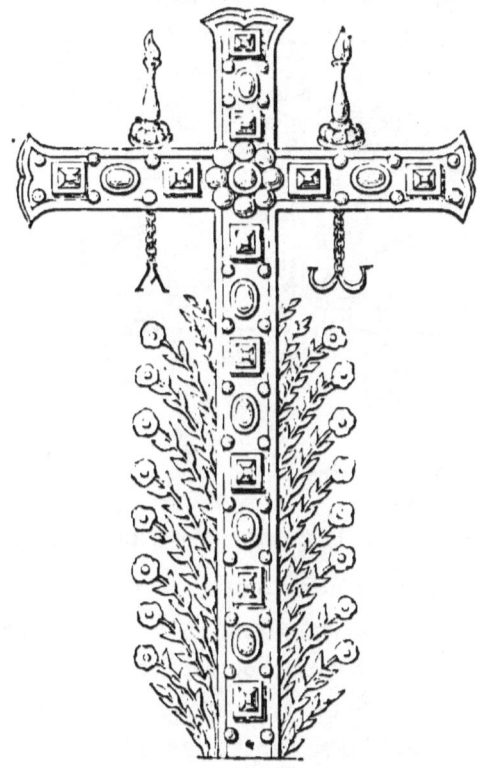

Wall-painting, from the Cemetery of Pontianus, Rome.

to Gentiles foolishness," and to exhibit it as a religious emblem was to provoke ridicule and insult.

It first appears, in the form of a plain Greek cross, in an epitaph on the monumental stone of Xene, the wife of Basileo, in St. Lawrence's, Verona (A.D. 407).

In later sarcophagi * and mosaics it appears, as an emblem of Christ's Person, in a central position, gemmed, crowned, surrounded by a laurel wreath, placed upon a throne. Similar gemmed and foliated crosses are painted in the catacombs. The accompanying woodcuts represent one on the wall over the

Wall-painting, from the Church of the Nativity, Bethlehem.

baptistery in the Catacomb of St. Callistus, mentioned at p. 92, and another somewhat similar from the Church of the Nativity at Bethlehem.†

A representation of the actual cross of Calvary appears first on the sarcophagus of Anicius Probus (A.D. 395), p. 271, and the historical subject of Christ led to execution on a sarcophagus of the fourth or fifth century in the Lateran Museum, engraved on p. 273. On the late sarcophagi, where SS. Peter and Paul stand on either side of our Lord, Peter is often represented carrying a cross over his shoulder similar

* See p. 274.   † De Vogüé, "Églises de la Terre Sainte," p. 72.

to that above mentioned; it is, perhaps, an allusion to the fact that Peter "glorified God" by crucifixion.

A lamb standing in front of a cross, or bearing a cross, is the earliest adumbration of the Crucifixion.

The earliest representation of the Crucifixion is in the curious caricature here given. It is one of a number of rude scribblings recently disclosed on an

Scribbling on the wall, Palatine Hill, Rome.

ancient wall adjoining the palace of the Cæsars on the Palatine Hill at Rome.

The habit of scratching writings and caricatures on the plaster of walls was exceedingly common in those early times, and these *graffiti* often afford very valuable insight into manners and customs. In the year 1857 some of the walls of the ancient palace on the Palatine Hill, called the *Domus Gelotiana*, were uncovered and a number of graffiti were brought to light, which introduce us into the intimacy of court servants of the higher class. It appears from them that after the murder of Caligula the house of Gelotius, which had belonged to that emperor, was used as a residence and training-school for court pages, and the pages practised the usual amusement of scribbling on the walls. One of the rough sketches represents a donkey turning a mill, and the schoolboy legend says, "Work, little donkey, as I have worked, and you will profit from it:" LABORA ASELLE QUOMODO EGO LABORAVI ET PRODERIT. The caricature represents a man with the hand lifted in adoration of a crucified figure with an ass's head;* the inscription explains it: ΑΛΕΧΑΜΕΝΟΣ ΣΕΒΕΤΕ ΘΕΟΝ (Alexamenos worships his God). Alexamenos was doubtless one of these court pages, whose Christian faith is thus ridiculed by his companions.† The name "Alexamenos the Faithful" is repeated thrice, showing that the Christianity of

---

* Tertullian (1 Apol. xvi., 198 A.D.) mentions a picture put forth by a certain apostate Jew, with the title "The God of the Christians conceived of an ass;" which represented "a creature with ass's ears, with a hoof on one foot, carrying a book, and wearing a gown." Tertullian himself explains the origin of this strange notion. Tacitus, he says, in the fifth of his Histories, had related that the Jews in the wilderness of Sinai were saved from dying of thirst by following certain wild asses to the springs which they frequented, for which service they consecrated the image of the ass; "and so, I suppose, it was thence presumed that we, as bordering on the Jewish religion, were thought to worship such a figure."

† It is photographed by Garucci and Lanciani.

Alexamenos was a favourite subject for jesting. Among other names, that of LIBANIUS occurs, and beneath it, in another hand, EPISCOPUS, a jest, perhaps, on another Christian page whom his comrades had nicknamed "the Bishop."

The full representation of the sacred subject was very slowly approached. In the first four, or perhaps five, centuries, there is absolutely nothing to indicate that the crucifix was ever used. On one of the oil-vessels sent by Gregory to Theodelinda (590–604) there are all the usual accessories of the Crucifixion—the sun and moon above, two angels at the sides, St. Mary and St. John below; but the principal figure is entirely left to the beholder's imagination. The picture on p. 202, from the Syriac Gospels of Rabula (A.D. 586), is usually quoted as the earliest complete representation of the scene. The lower part of the picture contains three subjects: in the centre the glory of the rising Lord strikes the Roman soldiers to the ground; on the left the angel appears at the tomb to the holy women; on the right the Lord appears to the women. Pope John VII., at the beginning of the eighth century, first represented the Crucifixion in a church, viz. in the mosaics of the ancient basilica of St. Paul at Rome. In the early Crucifixions Christ is clothed, and stands with arms horizontally extended, without any attempt at naturalistic representation.

The MONOGRAM XP, formed out of the first letters of the word ΧΡΙΣΤΟΣ, is one of the most common of the Christian emblems in the fourth and following centuries, and has continued in use to the present day. It was the vision of Constantine, and his adoption of the emblem on the standards of his legions

Miniature painting, from the MS. Syrian Gospels, by Rabula.

and the helmets of his soldiers at the decisive battle of the Milvian Bridge, which gave it a world-wide popularity. It is probable that it was in use among Christians before Constantine's adoption of it, but in spite of diligent search, only a few and ambiguous traces of it can be found.* A coin of Decius, in which it is used in an ambiguous manner, is noticed at p. 337. There is a sepulchral stone at Sivaux, in Gaul, on which it appears, together with an epitaph,

Monumental inscription at Sivaux, France.

Monumental inscription in the Roman catacombs. "Roma Sotteranea," ii. p. 323.

which De Rossi thinks to be of the date A.D. 298; but Le Blant, the great epigraphist of Gaul, assigns it to the fifth century.

The A Ω of the magnificent declaration, "I am A and Ω, the Beginning and the Ending, saith the Lord, which is, and which was, and which is to come, the Almighty" (Rev. i. 18), was a favourite emblem. It was used generally together with other emblems, especially with the cross; for example, the two letters were frequently suspended by chains from the arms of the gemmed and foliated cross of the sixth and later centuries.

* Justin Martyr quotes Plato, where he says in the Timæus that God placed His Son in the universe after the manner of the letter X. "Apol.," lix., lx.

2. OF SYMBOLICAL SUBJECTS.

The SHEPHERD occurs, probably, twice as often as any other subject, and occurs most frequently in the earliest times; in marble statues, on the most skilful of the wall-paintings of sepulchral chambers, in bas-reliefs on the sarcophagi, and in rude outlines and mere scratchings on the humbler graves. It is beyond doubt that the most popular idea of the Lord Jesus Christ in the early Church, that which had touched most deeply the souls of the converts from Judaism and heathenism, was that presentation which the Lord gave of Himself to His disciples as the Good Shepherd. In the earliest representations of the subject He is represented as carrying on His shoulders the sheep which had been lost, which He had come down from heaven into the wilderness of this world to find, and bring back to the fold amidst the rejoicings of the angels. Sometimes the Shepherd is represented with His sheep standing around Him; sometimes as a single figure, with staff and scrip and pipes, without any attempt to idealize its rustic simplicity.

Another allegorical representation of our Lord is as the LAMB, sometimes standing on a mount and surrounded by twelve other lambs, representing the Apostles; but this occurs seldom, and in later times, when the mystic imagery of the Revelation was beginning to take hold of the mind of the Church. There is a remarkable instance of this symbol on the tomb of Junius Bassus (p. 269), where a lamb is represented as performing the miracles of the Old Testament and of the New.

The Quini-Sext Council, A.D. 691, decreed that whereas the traditional manner of representing our Lord was under the figure of a lamb, for the future the Lamb which took away the sins of the world should be represented in the human figure which He wore in the flesh, in order that the people might have their thoughts turned to His passion and saving death, and through His humiliation might learn His glory.

Of this class of emblems the most remarkable and, perhaps, the most frequently used in one form or other, is the FISH. And it has a double meaning. First it means the Christian people. When the Lord called His earliest Apostles, He promised them that they should become fishers of men; in the two miracles in which He bids them cast their nets, He showed them that they should fill the net of the Church. The symbol conveyed an allusion to Baptism, in whose waters men become the fish of the Church. Secondly, it was a very recondite symbol of Christ Himself. It was a sign, understood only by the instructed, of a sacred acrostic; for the Greek word ΙΧΘΥΣ ("fish") is made up of the initial letters of the words ΙΗΣΟΥΣ ΧΡΙΣΤΟΣ, ΘΕΟΥ ΥΙΟΣ, ΣΩΤΗΡ, "Jesus Christ, the Son of God, the Saviour." * The fish is found less frequently after the first two centuries; even in the first half of the third century it is

---

* Tertullian (about A.D. 196) says, "We poor fishes, following after one ΙΧΘΥΣ, Jesus Christ, are born in water, nor are we safe except by abiding in the water " ("De Baptismo," c. 1).

noticeably going out of use, and is extremely rare by the middle of the fourth century. The *dolphin* occurs frequently after the third century.

Very often, instead of a fish naturally drawn, was substituted a mere hieroglyphic, a pointed oval, which was supposed to be the shape of the bladder of a fish (*vesica piscis*), and this *vesica* became a symbolical form in art, widely used and continued to the present day.

A multitude of little fish have been found in the catacombs, in crystal, ivory, mother-of-pearl, enamel, and precious stones, some of them pierced with holes so that they might be worn by a cord round the neck.

A FISHERMAN is an emblem of our Lord. The oldest of all uninspired Christian hymns, the Στόμιον πώλων ἀδαῶν, "Bridle of the steeds untamed," attached to the *Pædagogue* of Clement of Alexandria (A.D. 170–220), speaks of our Lord as the Shepherd and also as the Fisher of Souls. It may also represent an Apostle according to our Lord's saying (Matt. iv. 19).

The SHIP is very frequently found painted on the walls, scratched on sepulchral stones, or sculptured on sarcophagi. Justin Martyr (A.D. 139) adduces it as a Christian emblem, on the ground that its mast and sailyard make a figure of the cross. But the ship is usually the emblem of the Church. The meaning is derived partly from the ship of Noah, in which mankind was saved from the first great destruction of the ungodly, and partly from the ship

---

* Ecclesiastical and episcopal seals are usually in this form.

which so often contained Christ and His Apostles sailing over the Sea of Galilee. In this sense it is mentioned by St. Clement, in the passage already alluded to.* Ambrose speaks of a bishop as sitting at the stern of the ship and steering; indeed, it is one of the commonplaces of the Christian writers.† On a sarcophagus is a ship with a figure kneeling in prayer, and a hand stretching down from above which represents the protecting providence of God. The ship of Jonah, which is so frequently represented, very probably conveyed this general symbolical meaning.

An ANCHOR was a very common symbol, painted on graves, engraved on rings, moulded on lamps, etc. Its stock, or cross-piece, gave it an obscure likeness to a cross; and it is remarkable that it was the only exhibition of the cross which appears for almost three centuries, though Christians were continually using the manual sign of the cross on all sorts of occasions. The symbol was probably derived from "the anchor of the soul, sure and steadfast, which entereth into that within the veil," and symbolized the Christian's hope fastened upon the immutable promise (Heb. vi. 19).

An AMPHORA is often incised beside the inscription upon a gravestone. It may mean, perhaps, the body out of which the soul has departed, and be equivalent to the epitaph, "Here lies the mortal part of So-and-so; his soul has departed."

The VINE, which so frequently occurs, and might pass as a mere ornament, was no doubt intended

---

* See p. 345.   † See Eusebius's "Sermon at Tyre," p. 44.

to be significant, first of Christ the true Vine, and then of the Sacrament. There are often figures like little genii or cupids among its branches, and birds pecking at its clusters; these may represent Christian people, with a sacramental allusion. The branches, with their leaves and fruit spreading over a ceiling or the wall of a sepulchral chamber, may represent the bliss of Paradise;* in this case the genii and birds will mean the departed who now enjoy rest and peace.

The OLIVE appears on the walls of a chamber in the Crypt of St. Janarius in a series of harvest scenes, the others representing the vintage and wheat harvest. We can only suggest that there is an allusion to the ingathering of ripe souls.

The PALM BRANCH, borrowed from classical symbolism, is of frequent occurrence, probably with the classical meaning of victory. When found upon a loculus it does not necessarily indicate the grave of a martyr, but of a Christian whose death — like his Master's — is a victory over sin and death. Palm trees occur often as adjuncts to Scripture subjects, and sometimes on

Glass vessel embedded in the mortar of a loculus, with palm branch ("Boldetti," p. 149).

---

* Cyprian says (Ep. lxxiii. 9), "The Church expressing the likeness of Paradise, encloses within her walls fruit-bearing trees, which she waters with four rivers," etc.

each side of a single figure of Christ, or an Apostle, or an orante, where they may be emblematic of victory or of Paradise.

BIRDS, probably intended for DOVES, are frequently introduced, as above, pecking at the clusters of the growing vine or at baskets of grape-clusters. Two birds perched on opposite sides of a fountain, or cup, and drinking from its contents, is an ancient classical device, adopted by Christian Art with the symbolical meaning of believers partaking of the water of life or of the wine of the Sacrament. Cyprian, "On the Unity of the Church," v. 8, alludes to the "doves of Christ" meaning Christian people. These doves seem sometimes to represent the departed souls of Christians; "the names of two or three [departed] Christians so often stand in juxtaposition with the same number of lambs or doves, that it cannot be doubted that the one was intended to stand for the other" (Brownlow Maitland).

SHEEP frequently occur, especially in conjunction with the Shepherd, and obviously represent "the sheep of His pasture."

GOATS sometimes occur where we should rather expect sheep, apparently not with any sinister meaning.

The PEACOCK was borrowed from pagan symbolism. It was let loose from the funeral pyre of an empress, and signified her apotheosis, and so came to be a symbol of immortality.

The PHŒNIX was also a pagan symbol of renewed life. St. Clement, in the first century,* mentions the

---

* First Epistle, ch. xxv.

P

phœnix as an emblem of the resurrection, and tells the story which is more fully given below. Tertullian also gives it,* and others of the Fathers. A passage in the Apostolical Constitutions, on the subject of the resurrection of the dead, tells the curious myth thus: "The heathen can show a resemblance of the resurrection; for they say that there is a bird, single in its kind, which they say is without a mate, and the only one in creation. They call it a phœnix, and relate that every four hundred years it comes into Egypt, to that which is called the altar of the sun,† and brings with it a great quantity of cinnamon and cassia and balsam-wood, and, standing towards the east, as they say, and praying to the sun, of its own accord is burnt and becomes dust; but that a worm arises again out of those ashes, and that when the same is warmed it is formed into a new phœnix; and when it is able to fly it goes to Arabia, which is beyond the Egyptian countries."

The ORPHEUS occurs very early in the ornamental ceiling of a chamber in the Cemetery of Domitilla.‡ It occurs in three other paintings in the catacombs, on two sarcophagi and on a gem. Lanciani ("Pagan and Christian Rome," ii. 23) gives an engraving of the painting most recently found in 1888 in the catacombs of Priscilla. He is seated on a rock, playing the lyre, surrounded by wild beasts and

---

* "De Resurrectione," § 13.
† On, Heliopolis, is perhaps the city where Joseph dwelt, and where Joseph and Mary and the Divine Child are said by tradition to have sojourned.
‡ See p. 49.

serpents. The special points of his history which made him regarded as a type of Christ are probably his taming the wild beasts, and moving the very rocks and trees with the music of his lyre—an obvious allegory of Christ taming the passions and moving the rugged hearts of men; his alleged abode

Orpheus.   From the Cemetery of Domitilla, Rome.

in Thrace, where he civilized and gave religion and law to its wild inhabitants; and especially his descent to and return from Hades. It is a curious adoption into Christian use of a Greek myth; but the story of Orpheus was very popular, and we know that this Christian application of it was familiar, because it is alluded to by several of the early writers of the Church.

The introduction of the OX AND THE ASS in the rare and late representations of the Nativity is not merely a picturesque accessory in the artist's conception of the subject. It arose out of Isaiah i. 3, "The ox knoweth his owner and the ass his master's crib," and still more directly out of Hab. iii. 2, which in the Septuagint ran, "Between two living creatures (or two lives, according to the accentuation of ζωων) thou shalt be made known;" and in the old italic version was rendered, "Between two animals thou shalt be recognized." The strong feeling of the early ages that everything which had been foretold of Christ in the Old Testament had been fulfilled, induced a tendency to amplify the details of the gospel narrative so as to include every supposed prophecy. So we find the pseudo-Gospel of St. Matthew (ch. xiv.) stating that "Mary laid the Child in the manger, and the ass and ox adored Him."

A MOUNT WITH FOUR STREAMS issuing from it represents Paradise with its four rivers; it is a very usual subject in the later sarcophagi and the mosaics. Frequently our Lord stands upon the mount or is seated on a throne which is placed upon it, or a lamb stands upon it, or a cross stands or is throned upon it, and the Apostles are ranged on each side. It is perhaps not possible to determine whether this was intended to symbolize the paradise of the redeemed in the intermediate state, where the saints are "with Christ, which is far better" (Phil. i. 3); or the heaven to which Christ has ascended, and of which He said, "I will that they whom Thou hast given Me be with Me where I am, that they may behold My glory" (John xvii. 24).

The STAG DRINKING at a river is an allegory no doubt derived from the forty-first Psalm, "Like as the hart desireth the water-brooks," and conveyed to the instructed beholder the idea of the spiritual hungering and thirsting after God, on which the Lord pronounced His benediction on the mount: "they shall be filled." It is late and rare.

A HAND is an emblem of power (Exod. xv. 16; Ps. xvii. 7; xx. 6; xl. 3; Acts iv. 28, 30; John x. 28, 29, etc.), and is used as a symbol of God, *e.g.* in the subject of Moses at the burning bush, and reaching down from heaven at the baptism of our Lord, and later at the Crucifixion. In later times the hand is surrounded by a nimbus.

The NIMBUS is a halo of light, usually round the head of a figure; it is represented by a circular disc, or by a line which is supposed to define the margin of the halo; in later paintings the line and the disc are of gold. In pagan pictures the heads of deities are sometimes surrounded by a halo, as in wall-paintings at Pompeii. Christian artists did not begin to distinguish their sacred figures with the nimbus until the fifth century, and it is not universally used as the symbol of a saint till the eleventh century.

In the ninth century a rectangular nimbus is sometimes used about the head of a living person of great distinction, as in the case of Pope Leo and Charles the Great in the Vatican mosaic; of Pope Pascal in the mosaic at St. Cæcilia, Rome; of Gregory IV. in the mosaic at St. Mark. Divine Persons are distinguished by a cruciferous nimbus; since the Second Person is far the most frequently represented, it gives the false impression that this form of nimbus is exclusively appropriated to Christ. The First Person sometimes is distinguished by a triangular nimbus.

The AUREOLE, a large nimbus of pointed oval shape, enclosing not the head only, but the whole figure, was introduced later than the nimbus; it is especially used about our Lord in pictures of the Ascension,* and of our Lord in glory. Roller (Plate LXXXIV.) gives a plate of representations of Christ distinguished by a nimbus, probably none of them earlier than the fifth century; but there is no example in the catacombs, either in fresco or sculpture, of a Virgin Mary with the nimbus.

3. Symbolical Subjects from the Old and New Testaments.

Subjects are taken about equally from the Old and the New Testaments, indicating an equal familiarity with their contents. In three or four cases out of many hundreds a subject is taken from apocryphal books of the Old Testament, and in two or three cases a treatment of a subject is suggested by an apocryphal Gospel. We very soon recognize that the subjects of the Old Testament are not presented as historical incidents, but only in their symbolical meaning; and the absence of the great subjects of the gospel history leads us to realize still more strongly that even the New Testament subjects which occur are only given as symbols of truths, and must be regarded in that light if we desire to understand their meaning in this early period of Christian art. Just as the shepherd, the vine, the fish, the Orpheus, the peacock, and the phœnix are used for the purpose

---
* See p. 315.

of representing certain ideas, so the Moses striking the rock, the raising of Lazarus, the paralytic carrying his bed, and the rest are used, not for their own sake, but entirely for their allusive meaning.

Every inquiring mind at once eagerly undertakes the task of studying the exact symbolical meaning with which the oft-recurring subjects are used, and of interpreting the meaning, as a whole, of the connected groups of subjects which so frequently occur, for example, on the painted ceiling of a catacomb chamber or on the sculptured front of a sarcophagus. Unhappily, the meaning of many of the subjects is so recondite that the numerous archæologists who have applied their minds to the study of them fail to agree as to the meaning of the definite symbols, and equally fail to show that the groups of subjects are the expression of a definite and connected line of thought. Unhindered by the general failure, every one who undertakes to treat at all of this subject of early Christian art seems bound to attempt the explanation of its teaching; and we shall venture to make some remarks upon it.

The first step to be taken seems to be to get a well-reasoned meaning for each of the individual subjects, and then to study them in their groupings. We shall only trouble the reader with our attempt to assign meanings to those subjects which most frequently occur, and those which are combined in several of the groups.

DANIEL in the lions' den, nearly always in the attitude of prayer. When we call to mind that **he** was cast into the lions' den for persisting in praying to his God in violation of the law, we can hardly err in thinking that the subject is used as a type of providential deliverance in persecution. In some of the later representations is introduced an incident from the apocryphal book of Bel and the Dragon, which says that an angel lifted Habakkuk the prophet by the hair, and transported him to the den to convey food to Daniel; in which we suggest that there may be an allusion to the well-known practice of the Christians to convey food and comfort to the confessors in prison.

In the representations of the THREE CHILDREN in the fiery furnace we see a similar meaning. In some cases the history is given in two scenes. In the first, the Hebrew youths are refusing to worship the golden image. The image is represented by a bust set upon a short column; and we suggest that it may be a reminiscence of the image of Cæsar, before which the martyrs and confessors were required to burn incense.

The history of JONAH is of very frequent occurrence. It is usually given in several scenes.* We call to mind that our Lord twice gave it as a sign of His own Resurrection, which might suffice to account for its being a favourite subject. But a little further consideration brings to mind that Jonah was in other particulars a type of Christ. The incident of the disgorging upon the dry land is the type of the Resurrection, but the incident of the casting into

---

* See p. 275.

the sea is a type of Christ voluntarily giving Himself to death for the salvation of those who were in the ship (read Jonah ii. 11, 12); the incident of his reclining under the shade of the gourd, which is so frequently added that it is plain it formed an important part of the symbolism, we take to be a type of the repose of Paradise. What was intended by the introduction of the incident of the withering of the gourd we are unable to conjecture. The form of the sea-monster is often borrowed from the classical representations of the deliverance of Andromeda, the scene of which fable is laid at Joppa,* the port from which Jonah sailed.

The RAISING OF LAZARUS (there are only one or two examples of the raising of Jairus's daughter or of the widow's son) must be a type of our resurrection. Two brief extracts from St. John's narrative indicate the depth of its teaching: "Thy brother shall live again," for "I am the Resurrection and the Life, saith the Lord." Lazarus is always represented as standing, wrapped in grave-clothes, at the door of a tomb, which gives us a very interesting representation of a common type of tomb of the first centuries.†

NOAH IN THE ARK, with the dove bearing the olive branch, is a complex symbol. Justin Martyr says,‡ "For Christ, being the Firstborn of every creature, was made again the beginning of a new race, which is regenerated by Him through water and

---

* St. Cyril of Jerusalem speaks of the "whale of death."
† See p. 154.
‡ "Dial. cum Trypho," c. 138.

faith and word." Tertullian says,* "As after the waters of the Deluge, in which the old iniquity was purged away, as after that baptism (so to call it) of the old world, a dove sent out of the ark and returning with an olive branch, was the herald to announce to the world peace and the cessation of the wrath of Heaven; so by a similar disposition, with reference to matters spiritual, the dove of the Holy Spirit sent forth from heaven flies to the earth, *i.e.* to our flesh, as it comes out of the bath of regeneration after its old sins, and brings to us the peace of God; where the Church is prefigured by the ark." So Noah in the ark is a type of Christ, the beginning of a new race of redeemed mankind, and of the water of Baptism, and of the ark of the Church, and the dove of the Holy Spirit, bringing the olive branch of peace to those who are in the Church. St. Cyprian says, "The ark of Noah was a sacrament of the Church of Christ." † St. Ambrose caused this subject to be painted in his church at Milan, and beneath it these verses—

> "Arca Noe nostri typus est, et Spiritus ales,
> Qui pacem populis ramo prætendit olivæ."

It is remarkable that the ark is always represented, not as a ship or boat of any kind, but as a square chest with a lid, within which stands the single figure of Noah, or the two figures of Noah and his wife. A coin of the city of Apamea, on the Euphrates, of the reign of Septimus Severus (see p. 337), has the head of the emperor on the obverse; and on the reverse,

---

* "De Baptismo," vii.   † Ep. lxxv. 16.

just such a square chest, with a single standing figure, and on the front of the chest the letters Nω, *i.e.* Noah. There was a local tradition that the ark had rested at this city. It would be obvious to conclude that the Christian representation of the subject was taken from this coin, but that De Rossi maintains that the paintings of the subject in the catacombs (*e.g.* in that of Domitilla) extend back to a period a hundred years before the date of the coin. This curious form of the ark remains to be accounted for.

The sacrifice of Isaac is so striking a type of the love of the Father in giving His only begotten Son, and of the Son in voluntarily submitting Himself a Sacrifice for sin, "that whosoever believeth on Him should not perish, but should have everlasting life," that we can only account for its infrequency by the general reticence of early art on the subjects of the Passion.

Among the many miracles of healing, three are specially selected—the healing of the paralytic, of the woman who touched the hem of our Lord's garment, and of the blind. The frequency of the use of the healing of the paralytic is probably explained by its being the symbol of the great doctrine of the forgiveness of sin. The man is usually represented as carrying away his bed, which directs us to the words of the Gospel, that it was in order that they might know that the Son of man hath power on earth to forgive sins, that He said to the sick of the palsy, "Arise, take up thy bed, and go unto thine house" (Matt. ix. 6). His carrying away his couch was the visible expression of the article of the Creed, " I believe in the forgiveness of sins."

The special significance of the HEALING OF THE INFIRM WOMAN lies in the fact that it was by touching the hem of His garment that "virtue went out of Him," and she was made whole. "Now, His raiment is His Church," says St. Augustine, in connection with this miracle; "and in a garment, the border is the last and lowest part." * And again, in another place,† "the absence of His body and presence of His power" is illustrated in the miracle. And St. Ephrem, the Syrian, says, "Thy garment, Lord, is a fountain of medicine; in Thy visible vesture there dwelleth a hidden power." ‡ We gather that the miracle was adopted as a symbol that though Christ is absent, His power dwells in His Church, and that those who come to Christ by faith, in the Church and its ordinances, will find His grace in them.

The BLIND MAN is probably the one whose eyes our Lord anointed with clay, and then bade him "go to the Pool of Siloam and wash" (John ix. 7); and it is perhaps a symbol of Baptism, which was in primitive times known by the name of Illumination, "I am the Light of the world."

Moses appears both in the paintings and bas-reliefs in several scenes. The incident of striking the rock appears on almost all the sarcophagi of Italy and Gaul; other scenes appear more rarely, and perhaps only in the later examples, as the passage

* " Serm.," xxviii. 78*B*.   † " Serm.," xii. 62*B*.
‡ " Rhythm," x.

of the Red Sea, the giving of the Law, the gathering of the manna, and a doubtful seizure of Moses by the rebels.

The PASSAGE OF THE RED SEA we have St. Paul's authority (1 Cor. x. 1, 2) for taking as a symbol of Baptism. When we observe in some of the bas-reliefs that the destruction of the Egyptians is rendered with considerable force and detail, we are led to conjecture that it may also have been intended as a symbol of God's deliverance of His people from oppression, and the destruction of the oppressors; and we are reminded of the tremendous effect which the deaths of the imperial persecutors and the misfortunes of their families, at the end of the third and commencement of the fourth centuries, had upon the minds both of Christians and heathens, as is set forth at length in the " De Mortibus Persecutorum " of Lactantius.

In the GIVING OF THE LAW Moses is an obvious type of Christ, the Giver of the New Dispensation.

In the incident of the BURNING BUSH, God is sometimes represented in human form, sometimes as a hand. In all cases, Moses is in the attitude of removing his shoes. We might take it as an allusion to our Lord's mission from the Father; but several of the ancient writers, *e.g.* Gregory Nazianzen and Augustine, assuming the Rock-scene to allude to Baptism, take this as alluding to the renunciations preceding Baptism, the putting away of sins.

The GATHERING OF THE MANNA. There are several subjects in which a figure points with a rod, or touches with a rod, a number of baskets before him, which are filled with what at first sight appear to be round loaves, and the scene has been usually taken to be a representation of the miracle of the loaves; but it has been suggested that it really represents Moses pointing to the manna, and in that case it might be taken as one of the symbols of the Eucharist.

The SEIZURE OF MOSES BY THE REBELS is a doubtful explanation of a scene which is frequently represented in connection with the striking of the rock. Two men, sometimes wearing a peculiar flat-topped cap, hold a man between them by the arms, as if in the act of arresting him; and these two men, identified by the peculiar cap, in the subsequent scene, are eagerly drinking at the stream of water as it gushes from the rock. It is difficult to recognize in it any scene in the sacred narrative, and equally difficult to conjecture its meaning. See below on the arrest of Christ.

The STRIKING OF THE ROCK at first sight seems easy of interpretation, but we confess ourselves baffled in the endeavour to arrive at a satisfactory explanation of what the Christians of those days understood it to symbolize. Its introduction as a single subject in the paintings, and in nearly every group of bas-reliefs on the sarcophagi, shows that it was a very favourite symbol and one of the greatest importance. In considering it, it is necessary to bear in mind that in some of the later examples Peter is represented as the agent in the miracle; in one instance, on a gilded glass vessel, his name

PETRVS is written over his head. We must also bear in mind that in the great majority of examples this subject is closely associated with the raising of Lazarus. Another curious version of the subject is on the sarcophagus of Junius Bassus (p. 269), where Christ, represented as a lamb, is not only performing several miracles of the New Testament, *e.g.* raising Lazarus, multiplying the loaves, but also, as the prototype of Moses, receiving the Law and striking the rock. What was it intended to represent? We call to mind our Lord's words, in connection with this miracle, at the Feast of Tabernacles: "If any man thirst, let him come unto Me, and drink. . . . This spake He of the Spirit, which they that believe on Him should receive: for the Holy Ghost was not yet given; because that Jesus was not yet glorified" (John vii. 37, 38). Again, we have St. Paul's Eucharistic interpretation: "They all drank of that spiritual Rock that followed them: and that Rock was Christ" (1 Cor. x. 4). And we cannot overlook its striking symbolism of the piercing of our Lord's side upon the cross, whence flowed blood and water (John xix. 34). On the whole we are disposed to regard the subject as the most popular symbol of Baptism?* Then the

* Tertullian says ("De Bapt.," viii. 9), "If Christ be the Rock, the water in the Rock is Christ, and therein we see that baptism is blest." Cyprian says, "The Rock is Christ, and the water from it symbolizes baptism" (Ep. lxiii. 5). Jerome says (on Isa. xlviii.), "There is no peace for the wicked who have not merited to drink of the Rock, whose side, wounded with the lance, flowed with water and blood, declaring to us baptism and martyrdom." Against its meaning Baptism is the fact that in all the baptisteries, including that in the Catacomb of Pontianus, the Baptism of our Lord is always adopted as the appropriate symbol.

introduction of Peter as the agent would allude to his bidding the first converts among the Jews to " repent and be baptized" (Acts ii. 38), and to his being the first to admit the Gentiles to Baptism : " Can any man forbid water, that these should not be baptized ? " (Acts x. 47, 48).

JOB is represented in paintings in the cemeteries of Domitilla, Callistus, and others, on the Tomb of Junius Bassus, and on several Gallic sarcophagi. Martigny says that it is because he was the prophet of the Resurrection—" I know that my Redeemer liveth," etc. (Job xix. 25)—and notes that his prophecy occurs in the most ancient manuscripts of the Antiphonary of Gregory the Great, on the Tomb of Bishop Flavian (*c.* 550), and in inscriptions at Naples and Rimini.*

Other subjects which are not so difficult of interpretation are—

The CREATION OF EVE out of the side of Adam, a symbol of the creation of the Church out of the side of Christ.

The FALL OF MAN represented by a tree with a serpent coiled round it (often with a human head), with Adam and Eve standing on each side.

The new covenant with man is typified by Adam and Eve being clothed with the skins of the first sacrifices, and therefore reconciled to God in Christ Jesus. Adam is often represented holding a spade, and Eve a spindle, symbolical of the new life of labour to which they were sentenced.

* Martigny, "Dictionaire des Antiquités Chrétiennes:" Job.

The SACRIFICE OF ABEL AND CAIN, a type of the sacrifice of Christ; and a symbol of the worship of the Church and of the heathen.

The TRANSLATION OF ELIJAH, a type of Christ's Ascension.

The BAPTISM OF OUR LORD is a common subject, and its meaning obvious; it is the one subject represented in painting or mosaic in all the baptisteries, and the dedication of all the baptisteries is to St. John of the Fonts.

The TRIUMPHAL ENTRY INTO JERUSALEM is not infrequently found, the symbol of Christ's entry into heaven with all His saints after the judgment.

The ARREST OF CHRIST. The subject of two men holding a third between them by the wrists as if arresting him, has already been noticed as occurring in connection with Moses striking the rock. It is also found on some sarcophagi in connection with the denial of Peter, and in Leofric's Missal at Rouen, in connection with the betrayal of Judas. This plainly indicates that the subject is the arrest of Christ in the garden; and this identification is confirmed by a picture in the Book of Kells, which illustrates Matt. xxvi. 30.

We remark the absence from this list of the subjects of our Lord's Passion, and we do not know how to account for it. The narrative of them fills a very large space in all the Gospels, and their pictorial representation occupies the prominent place which seems natural to us in the ecclesiastical art of a later period; but in the art of these early ages these subjects are "conspicuous by their absence." We call to mind that in the preaching of the Apostles, recorded in the Acts of the Apostles, there is a similar reserve; the subjects of those preachings are the Resurrection and Ascension of the Lord and the gift of the Holy Ghost, and the fulfilment in these great events of ancient type and prophecy; and in the Epistles, which are addressed to Christian people, though there are many allusions to our Lord's Passion and death, there is no detailed presentation of the moving incidents so fully described in the Gospels, by way of appeal to their affections. This unemotional preaching of the early ages is in harmony with the fact which we have noted in the cycle of subjects treated in early Christian art. Neither do the historical series of the events of our Lord's life—except the Adoration of the Magi—find the place we should expect in early art: the Nativity, the Baptism, Christ before Pilate, are rarely found and on late sarcophagi.

There are numerous symbols of the Eucharist, and they are of very frequent occurrence. The most common are the miraculous bread and fish of the FEEDING OF THE FIVE THOUSAND, and the miraculous wine of the MARRIAGE FEAST AT CANA. Another, which seldom occurs, is the Old Testament miracle of the MANNA. There are one or two other subjects which may be Eucharistic: A small THREE-LEGGED TABLE WITH FISH AND BREAD upon it; in one example a man stands on one side the table as if blessing the bread, and a female in the attitude of prayer on the other side. A FISH BEARING A

BASKET OF BREAD on his back, and De Rossi says that in the middle of the basket is an indication of a glass vessel of red wine. A phrase of Jerome affords a curious illustration of the picture ; speaking of Exuperius, Bishop of Toulouse, he observes, "Nothing can be richer than one who carries the Body of Christ in a basket made of twigs, and the Blood of Christ in a chalice of glass."

Wall-painting, Cemetery of St. Callistus, Rome.

The late Dean Burgon, in his interesting letters from Rome, took the pains to compile a list of the subjects which appear on the sarcophagi in the Lateran Museum, and to record the number of times they appear. Professor Westwood has added the number of times the same subjects appear on those in the Vatican collection. The following list gives both these enumerations in the order of their frequency :—

1. History of Jonah, various incidents, 23 in Lateran, 11 Bosio.*

2. Moses, occasionally Peter [?], striking the rock, 21, 16.

3. The miracle of loaves and fishes, 20, 14.

4. Apprehension of St. Peter [? of Moses], 20, 14 ; soldiers or Jews in peculiar flat caps.

5. The cure of the blind, 19, 11.

* Bosio's plates, as given by Northcote and Brownlow, are from forty-eight sarcophagi, thirty of which were found in the crypts of the Vatican.

6. Miracle of Cana, 16, 8.

7. Raising of Lazarus—a mummy-like figure, "bound hand and foot in grave-clothes," standing at the door of an ædicula or chapel-tomb, 16, 14.

8. Christ with the cock [and St. Peter, the warning of Peter], 14, 8.

9. Daniel in the lions' den, sometimes with Habakkuk bringing food (Bel and the Dragon), 14, 7.

10. Cure of the paralytic, generally bearing a kind of sofa-bed, 12, 7.

11. Creation of Eve, 11, 2.

12. Sacrifice of Isaac, 11, 9.

13. Adoration of the Magi, 11, 8.

14. The temptation and fall, often a tree and serpent, often Adam with a sheaf of wheat and Eve with a fleece ("When Adam delved and Eve span"), 10, 14.

15. The woman with the bloody flux, 8, 9.

16. The Good Shepherd, 6, 9.

17. The entry into Jerusalem.

18. Noah in his square chest, or *arca*, with the dove, 5, 6.

19. Our Lord before Pilate, the latter generally washing his hands; a second figure is sometimes present who may be Herod.

20. Adam and Eve receiving the wheat-sheaf and lamb from (?) the Second Person of the Trinity, 4. See also No. 14 in this list.

21. Moses receiving the Law, 4, 6.

22. The "Three Children" with Phrygian caps, 4, 3.

23. Christ bearing His cross. Three times in the Lateran.

24. Moses at the burning bush, 2, 2.
25. Translation of Elijah, 2, 3.
26. The Nativity, with ox and ass, 1, 4.

Other rarely represented or highly interesting subjects are—

a. Our Lord on the holy mount, whence issues the four rivers of Paradise, attended by His disciples. Not infrequent.

b. "Thou shalt go on the lion and adder." Youthful Christ on a sarcophagus, at St. Niccolo, Ravenna.

c. A feast—semicircular table, with crossed cakes of bread ; (?) an allusion to the Holy Eucharist, or the Marriage Supper of the Lamb, or a funeral feast. Parker's photos, 2928, 2930.

d. The vision of Ezekiel on two or three photos, 2921. The Saviour standing in the act of raising small (apparently shrivelled) dead figures.

e. Daniel and the dragon (Parker's photo, 2920).

f. Susannah and the elders—doubtful.

g. Pharaoh and his host in the Red Sea (photo 2933).

h. Offerings of Cain and Abel (photos 2908, 2910).

i. The woman of Samaria (Bottari, pl. 137 ; Aringhi, i. 297 ; Dagincourt Sculpt., Plate VIII. Fig. 9).

j. The Baptism of our Lord (Parker, 2677, 2919 ; Bottari, Plate 193).

k. The daughter of Jairus raised from a sarcophagus (Parker, 2919, 2920 ; Bottari, Plate 193).

Our next task is to study these individual subjects in their groupings, and to endeavour to discover some scheme of symbolism, some connected lines of thought, in the various groups.

One of the most elaborate of these groupings of Old Testament symbols is in the painted ceiling of a chamber in the Cemetery of St. Callistus, of the third or fourth century. It is geometrically divided by a combination of circle and octagon, into many panels, which form concentric circles. In the centre is a Good Shepherd. The first circle of subjects is an ornamental row of couples of birds pecking grapes out of eight baskets; the next circle consists of Old and New Testament subjects which surround the Good Shepherd. They are: The paralytic carrying his bed; the miracle at Cana; the raising of Lazarus; Daniel in the lions' den; Jonah swallowed by the sea-monster; Jonah cast ashore by the monster; Moses striking the rock; Noah in the Ark, with the dove.

Why this cycle of subjects? why these eight out of all the Old and New Testaments? Why in this order? As to the order, since they are arranged in a circle, any one may be first in the series, except that the two incidents in the history of Jonah must be taken in historical sequence.

There are five Old Testament subjects and only three New Testament, and we find nothing like the juxtaposition of type and antitype of which the artists were so fond in a later age. If we take them in the order in which we should read the inscription of a medal, beginning at the bottom and going round by the left hand we get Jonah (our Lord's Resurrection); the stricken rock (Baptism); Noah (the Church); the Paralytic (forgiveness of sins); Cana (the Eucharist); Lazarus (the resurrection of the dead); Daniel (deliverance in persecution). There does not appear to be any natural sequence of thought in this—or any other—order.

In another circular ceiling given by Garucci (ii. 24), of a cubiculum in the Cemetery of St. Cæcilia, Christ sits in the centre, with five Apostles, a casket of manuscript *Volumina* at His feet. Around this centre are five larger and five smaller radiating panels. The larger panels contain these subjects: The stricken rock; Moses pointing to the Manna; sacrifice of Isaac; Three Children in the furnace; Noah in the Ark. On the smaller panels, elegant foliage, with peacocks. Again we fail to see any scheme of selection or grouping.

Some of the gilded glass vessels found in the catacombs,* have their ornamentation arranged in a manner which resembles the designs of some of these ceilings, and afford additional groups for study. One in the private collection of Mr. Wilshere has in the centre the portrait of a man and his wife, with the usual inscription PIE, ZHSES ("Drink, long life"), surrounded by the following Scripture subjects: Adam and Eve (creation); sacrifice of Isaac (redemption); Paralytic (forgiveness); Lazarus (resurrection).

Another in the same collection has St. Peter and St. Paul in the centre, surrounded by the following subjects in six radiating compartments: The Three

* Page 309.

Children; a man standing in front of a symbolic figure of the sun (Isa. lx. 20); a woman in the attitude of prayer; Isaiah being sawn in two; the brazen serpent; the stricken rock.

The arcosolia present numerous examples of smaller groups of subjects arranged in the lunette at the back of the recess, on the soffit of the arch of the recess, and on the wall beneath, which is really the front of the tomb itself. Perhaps the motive of the selection of the subjects in these groups may, in some cases at least, be more easily conjectured. We briefly indicate the subjects of several of the groups, and their arrangement.

1. In the lunette, a portrait of the deceased; on the soffit, three subjects—a Good Shepherd in the middle, between Daniel and the stricken Rock.

2. In the lunette, Jonah reclining under the gourd; on the soffit, a Good Shepherd between two oranti.

3. In the lunette, three figures — man, woman, and child—probably representations of the deceased buried there; the soffit divided into three compartments—in the centre a Good Shepherd between the usual four scenes of the Jonah subject, on the left the Three Children refusing to worship the golden image, on the right the Adoration of the Magi.

4. In the lunette, the Good Shepherd; on the soffit, an orante between Jonah and the stricken Rock.

5. In the lunette, Jonah disgorged; on the soffit, the stricken rock, between Jonah sitting under the gourd, and Jonah reclining under the gourd.

6. In the lunette, an inscription; on the soffit, the

Good Shepherd, between Daniel and the Three Children.

7. The lunette is divided into three vertical compartments—in the middle an orante, on the left a feast with five persons present, on the right the five Wise Virgins; on the soffit, the Good Shepherd between Adam and Eve and Daniel. The front of this tomb is also painted in three vertical compartments—in the middle an orante, between the Three Children and Jonah in three scenes—swallowed, disgorged, and reclining.

8. Is a very elaborate arrangement. The lunette is divided into three vertical compartments by two trees—in the middle a Good Shepherd with two figures (probably the deceased) kneeling at His feet, between Lazarus and an orante. The soffit is divided into five compartments—in the centre Daniel, at the ends the three Magi before Herod and a male orante; the intermediate compartments have a subject within a subject—in one, the paralytic between Adam and Eve; in the other, Noah between two sitting figures.

These may suffice as examples; it is only in the simplest groups that we can venture to hope that we understand the motive for the selection of the subjects.

There is the same difficulty in understanding the grouping of the subjects sculptured on the sarcophagi, but it will be more convenient to reserve the few additional sentences which we have to say about them until we have the subjects more immediately before us in a later chapter.

CHAPTER XIII.

SYMBOLISM—*continued.*

The representation of individual persons—Representations of deceased; oranti; oranti with saints—The so-called Madonna of the Cemetery of Priscilla; the so-called Madonna of St. Agnes—Funeral feasts—Personal emblems: fossors; sculptor; painter, etc.—Punning emblems: a dragon for Dracontius, etc.—Instruments of martyrdom (?).

THE REPRESENTATION OF INDIVIDUAL PERSONS is the fourth class into which we have divided these subjects of early Christian art. Some are conventional figures of the men, women, and children there buried, who are sometimes identified by the inscription of their names. Some of the later figures seem to make an attempt at portraiture.

In these representations of deceased persons there is a remarkable omission, considering the actual life of the Church during those ages, of all allusion to the sufferings of the faithful at the hands of the persecutors. We know from other sources of information that the Church took the profoundest interest in the

SYMBOLISM. 235

conflicts and triumphs of its martyrs and confessors. At a very early period the *acta* of the martyrs were carefully recorded in the fullest detail; the relics of martyrs were eagerly collected and treasured; their burial-places were honoured; their memory was kept fresh in the mind of the Church by the record of their names in the diptychs, and by annual celebrations of their birthdays, *i.e.* the days of their birth into the new life; but we find no attempt to represent their martyrdoms on their graves,* no record of them in inscriptions. Was the omission in the same spirit in which St. Peter, speaking to Jews (Acts iii. 17), apologized for the acts of their rulers who killed the Prince of Life: " I wot that through ignorance ye did it, as did also your rulers," and omitted all allusion to the agency of Pilate in his address to the Roman Cornelius and his friends?

In this class we have no hesitation in placing the vast majority of figures standing with outstretched arms, to which the Roman antiquaries have given the convenient title of *oranti*— praying people. They are found in great numbers painted on the walls of the catacombs, sculptured on

Wall-painting, Cemetery of St. Marcellinus. An orante clad in chasuble.

---

* The common subjects of the Three Children in Nebuchadnezzar's furnace and of Daniel in the lions' den may be allusions to them.

the sarcophagi, in mosaics as at Salonica, on the gilded glass vessels; lastly, on every page of the *Menologia*; and have been the subject of much controversy.

Wall-painting, Cemetery of St. Soter, Rome.

The example on p. 235 is a male orante of early date clad in the chasuble, which afterwards, when it

Inscription on marble.

went out of lay use, was retained as a clerical vestment. It is from a wall-painting in the Cemetery of St. Marcellinus.*

* Bosio, p. 377.

SYMBOLISM.

The next, from the Cemetery of St. Soter, Rome, is one of four persons in a garden full of flowers and

Wall-painting, Cemetery of St. Cæcilia, Rome.

fruits, in the midst of which are birds of various kinds, representing Paradise. It is of the third century.*

The third is an interesting design on a marble slab published by Boldetti, p. 329.

* De Rossi, "Roma Sotteranea," ii. 9.

The fourth is a wall-painting of Byzantine style, from the Cemetery of St. Cæcilia, Rome.

The attitude was that of prayer among Jews and Gentiles.* The early Christians continued to use the same attitude. Tertullian describes it, "looking up, with hands spread open, and head uncovered," and further remarks that the position of the praying Christian represents Christ upon the cross.† The attitude among the early Christians was as universally the posture of prayer as kneeling with joined hands is among ourselves.‡

We find male and female oranti, separately, together as man and wife, and sometimes children associated with them in a family group; not infrequently their names are inscribed over their heads or by their sides.§ Thus on the lunette of an arcosolium at Naples is a half-length male orante between two candlesticks with lighted candles, and the inscription "HIC REQVIESET PROCVLVS;" ‖ and a group of man, woman, and child, inscribed "ILARIS VIX AN.XLV. THEOTECNVS VIX AN.L. NONNOSA VIX AN.II.MX," in the lunette of an arcosolium in the Upper Cemetery of San Gennaro, at Naples.¶ There can be no doubt that

---

* The hands of Moses were extended in prayer during the battle of Amalek (Exod. xvii. 12). See Ps. xxviii. 2; xliv. 20; cxliii. 6. Æneas is described by Virgil, *Duplices tendens ad sidera palmas.*

† 1 Apol., xxx.

‡ It has been suggested that the puzzling word πεπλασατε at the commencement of the anaphora in the Διδαχή is a direction to the faithful to spread out their arms in this striking attitude; it is immediately followed by the further direction, "Lift up your hearts."

§ Roller, Plate XLVIII.

‖ Garucci, vol. i. Plate 101.

¶ Appell, "Monuments of Early Christian Art," p. 67.

in these cases we have representations of deceased persons in the attitude of prayer, just as in the case of the mediæval effigies lying with joined hands

Painting from the Upper Cemetery of St. Gennaro, Naples.

upon their altar-tombs, or, at a later period, kneeling at a prayer-desk.

Figures in this attitude of prayer are not uncommon in early Celtic art. See curious examples at Llanhamllech, and at Llanfrynach, Brecknockshire.*

Some of the female oranti are represented in such a way as to have given ground for the theory that they represent the Blessed Virgin Mary, or the Church.

In the Chapel of Sta. Felicitas, at the Baths of Titus, is a colossal female figure †—with hands outstretched over smaller figures on each side of her, and over her a head of Christ amid clouds—which certainly looks

* Engraved in "Early Christian Symbolism," J. Romilly Allen, p. 128.
† Garucci, "Storia della Arte," vol. iii. Plate 154.

very much like a Blessed Virgin interceding with the Divine Son for the votaries around her; but the inscription shows that the figure is intended for Sta. Felicitas, in whose name the chapel is dedicated, and the smaller figures are contemporary saints, whose names are inscribed over their heads.

There are several examples of a female figure occupying the central place in the sculptured front of a sarcophagus, with Apostles on each side of her, or standing between St. Peter and St. Paul. That this is not the Virgin Mary, but a figure of the deceased person whose remains were laid in the sarcophagus, is established by two pieces of evidence. In some cases the name of the orante is inscribed over her head, as "FLORA" between SS. Peter and Paul on a Spanish sarcophagus, figured by Roller;* in other cases,† the face of the orante has been left unfinished, exactly as in the case of the medallion portraits mentioned at p. 264, and for the same reason —that the portrait of the deceased might be added after the purchase of the sarcophagus.

This fashion of placing the effigy of a deceased person among saints or between two Apostles is easily explained. The effigy was not so much a portrait of the person during lifetime, as a representation of the spirit after death. To sculpture it in the midst of the saints was a striking way of conveying, in the language of art, the common epitaph, *cum sanctis*, "So-and-so is with the saints." To place this departed spirit between SS. Peter and Paul was to

---

* "Catacombes de Rome," vol. ii. Plate XLI. † Ibid.

represent the Princes of the Apostles as introducing it into Paradise, just as in the mosaics at SS. Cosmas and Damian and other churches, SS. Peter and Paul are presenting the founder of the church, or the donor of the mosaic, to our Lord in glory. That the disembodied spirit was represented in early art by a human figure is shown in the martyrdom of St. Stephen in the sculptures of the great doorway at Arles, and in that of St. Lawrence, on the medal at p. 343, where the dying martyr is breathing forth his spirit in this form. So in mediæval pictures of the Crucifixion, the painters often represented the souls of the dying robbers. This idea of the apotheosis of a departed Christian is found in mediæval times in the modified form of two angels bearing upward the soul—in the form of a small nude human figure—in the hollow lap of a long sheet.

Among the gilded glass medallions are some in which there is a female orante between two men, and all three have their names inscribed over them—"PETER, MARIA, PAVLVS;" but that does not imply any peculiar distinction of the Blessed Virgin Mary over all other saints, since there are similar groups on other medallions, inscribed "PETER, PAUL, AGNES," and "CHRISTOS, AGNES, LAWRENCE;" on another medallion are two female saints, inscribed "ANNE (= AGNES), MARIA;" there are several of Agnes alone.

In short, there is not in the art of the first five centuries an example of a representation of the Virgin Mary, except as a necessary figure in the representation of the Annunciation, the Nativity, and the Adoration of the Magi. She is never put forward prominently, as the Apostles, for example, are constantly put forward, as persons of special distinction in the Church. Still less is she put forward as concentrating the spectator's attention upon her personality, and implying some special cult. There are many indications that in the fourth century St. Agnes, the virgin martyr of the Diocletian persecution, was the popular saint—her name is still retained in our English Prayer-book; the real claims of the Blessed Virgin to special reverence were hardly recognized until the discussions which terminated in the decision of the Council of Ephesus (A.D. 431) called attention to them.

There are two or three examples which seem to contradict the assertion in the preceding sentence. In the Cemetery of Priscilla, in an inconspicuous position among other subjects, over an arcosolium,* there is a picture of the Virgin holding the Child in her arms; in front of her is a male figure, pointing to a star above and between them; De Rossi suggests that it is a pictorial allusion to the prophecies of the Nativity. In De Rossi's "Bulletino di Archæologia Christiana" for 1844-45, is a photographic representation of a recently discovered fragment of a sculptural group, with woodcuts of De Rossi's conjectural restoration of it. The principal portion of the subject is a female figure, seated with a child on her lap, facing to the (spectator's) left—no doubt, the

* Roller, Plate XV.

Blessed Virgin and the Divine Child. There are plain indications on the (spectator's) left of an angel looking towards the Virgin. On the right, behind the Virgin, are indistinct traces of a standing figure; and above

Wall-painting, Cemetery of St. Callistus, Rome.

the Virgin's head is a hand pointing upwards: De Rossi's conjectural restoration combines these into a male figure pointing to a star. The sculptured subject may be fairly compared with the wall-painting noticed above, and may be interpreted as an allegorical representation which combines the conventional "Annunciation" with the conventional allusion to the prophecy of the "Star," presented in the wall-painting. The so-called "Madonna of St. Agnes" is an orante and her child painted in the lunette of an arcosolium.* In the Cemetery of St. Valentine, on the Flaminian Way, there is an undoubted "Madonna"

* See Roller, Plate LXXV.

of the mediæval type; both the Virgin and the Child are nimbed, and there is an inscription, "SAC DEI GENETRIX," but it is of late date.* In the famous

Orante and child, the so-called Madonna of the Cemetery of St. Agnes.

Rabula manuscript † is a representation of an Ascension (see p. 315), in which a female figure ‡ occupies the centre, with an angel on each side of her, each addressing a group of six Apostles, who fill up the picture. In the same manuscript is a representation of the Day of Pentecost, in which again the Virgin occupies a central and conspicuous place; and this rendering of the two subjects continued in use throughout the Middle Ages. One of the earliest representations of the Madonna is in the Early Church (crypt) of St. Clement at Rome, where is also an assumption of the Blessed Virgin, but these decorations are of the eighth century.

In the mosaics in St. Agnes in Rome, is the earliest (*circa* A.D. 630) instance of the patron saint occupying the central place in the apse instead of that of our Lord; and in the Church of St. Maria in

---

* Garucci, vol. ii. Plate 84, 1.   † Ibid., vol. iii. Plates 139, 140.
‡ In the West the Blessed Virgin Mary was seldom represented in the attitude of an orante; in the East she was, and is, frequently.

Dominica (A.D. 820), for the first time the Blessed Virgin occupies this prominent position.

The suggestion that some of these oranti represent the Church has, perhaps, still less evidence in its favour. It is not till we come to the fifth century that we find, in the basilica of Sta. Sabina, at Rome, an undoubted example of this symbolical representation of the Church; there are two female figures, each holding a book, one inscribed " Ecclesia ex Circumcisione," and the other " Ecclesia ex Gentibus." Eve, and Sarah (Gal. iv. 22–end), and the Bride of Rev. ix. 1, are obvious types of the Church, but the idea does not seem to have been included in the cycle of the early symbolism.

Another subject which occurs very frequently in the wall-paintings of the catacombs is A GROUP OF PERSONS SITTING OR RECLINING AT TABLE, which is usually of horseshoe shape, and upon it are a fish

Wall-painting, Cemetery of St. Callistus, Rome.

lying in a dish, and a few round loaves, which are usually marked with a cross. Three suggestions have been made as to the meaning of this subject: (1) That it represents the Last Supper; (2) the funeral feast; (3) the happiness of Paradise.

We incline to think that these pictures in the first instance represent the Funeral Feast. It needs some acquaintance with ancient manners to appreciate the importance of these funeral feasts. From very early times, we know from the "Iliad," the holding of a festival at the tomb was an indispensable part of the obsequies, and the custom continued in full force at the period of the introduction of the Christian religion; and Christians, while adopting burial in place of cremation, made little other alteration in the funeral customs of their time.

We have seen (p. 119) that the common existence of burial guilds afforded the Church facilities for obtaining and managing its cemeteries under sanction of the law. One of the customs of these funeral guilds was that all the members assisted at the funeral of a member, and attended the funeral feast, met again at his tomb at the expiration of a month, and held an annual commemoration of his death, the meeting always concluding with a feast. In the series of chambers of the most ancient part of the Cemetery of Lucina, this subject is repeated, with some minor variations of treatment, because (we suggest) those chambers were used for funeral feasts, and therefore the subject was an appropriate one for the decoration of their walls. In some examples of this subject the names of the guests at the feast are painted over their heads, leaving it beyond question that the painting is a record of an actual funeral feast of some person buried in the chamber on the wall of which the painting appears, or in the neighbouring gallery.

The festivals celebrated in honour of the saints enrolled in the calendar are funeral commemorations on a large scale. Sidonius describes the festival of Justus, the popular Gallic saint in the latter part of the fifth century. These funeral feasts were often abused. St. Augustine says, "In North Africa I know many who hold luxurious drinking-bouts over the dead, and, setting dainty meats before corpses, bury themselves [in intoxication] above the buried, and make their own voracity and drunkenness a matter of religious observance." St. Ambrose in Milan speaks of "drunken revels in the crypts," and exclaims against the folly of men who thought drunkenness could be a part of sacrifice. Canons were made to restrain the licence of the assemblies at the vigils and festivals of the saints. The custom continued throughout the subsequent ages, and has not even yet disappeared. The large attendance of relations and friends at a funeral in the northern counties; the attendance of the members of a benefit society at the funeral of one of their fellow-members; the custom of returning to the house after a funeral and partaking of refreshments ;—are survivals of the customs which we trace back to the prehistoric ages.

It is very possible that this subject had also, in the minds of people who were so accustomed to symbolism as the early Christians, a symbolical meaning, but we doubt whether that meaning was directly and primarily Eucharistic. The fish and loaves on the table are in accordance with such a meaning, but in mediæval representations of feasts of all kinds fish and bread are very often found as the only viands upon the table. There is in these pictures no hint of a central person distributing the food to those on each side of him. Eucharistic symbols abound, and we have noticed some of them, but these are not of them.

We commonly accept a representation of the Last Supper as having a Eucharistic meaning, but it is doubtful whether it was used in early and mediæval art with that intention. The *Cœna Domini* of the Middle Ages meant primarily the marriage supper of the king's son, *i.e.* the happiness of heaven.* At the close of the Nicene Council, when the assembled bishops, representatives of the whole Church, dined with Constantine, Eusebius says it was like an image of the kingdom of Christ. In the seventh-century Gospels of Corpus Christi College, Cambridge, is a representation of our Lord and eight of His Apostles sitting at table, and the picture is inscribed " CŒNA DNI." The paintings of "The Last Supper" by Leonard da Vinci and others are not on the reredos of the altar of the church, but on the wall behind the high table in the refectory. No doubt every Christian meal, consecrated with prayer, is quasi-sacramental, or at least symbolic of the Sacrament ; and very pos-

---

* The lunette of an arcosolium (figured by Roller, ii. Plate LXXXIII.) is painted with a representation of the subject of the Parable of the Ten Virgins. Our Lord stands in the middle ; on His left are the five foolish virgins at the closed door ; on His right the five wise virgins seated at a banquet at a semicircular table in the conventional manner.

sibly to minds so trained to see the mystic meaning of all things, the funeral feast suggested not only the feast of fat things, of wines on the lees, well refined, which the Lord will make in His holy mountain when He has swallowed up death in victory (Isa. xxv. 6), but also that anticipation and foretaste of it which He gives to His people here at His holy table ; but we think the primary intention of these paintings in the catacombs was to represent the funeral feast.

5. PERSONAL EMBLEMS.

The use of the characteristic instruments of a man's occupation as a symbol of the man must necessarily go back to primitive times and be of universal adoption; it is a kind of natural hieroglyphic language, and it largely survives among unlettered populations. It is to be found specially in two applications—as a sign outside a man's door to direct those who need his services, and means, here lives a baker, a blacksmith, or whatever he may be ; and on his gravestone to mark his resting-place—here lies a baker, or blacksmith, or what not, whose work is done. The sign of the Chequers indicated a house of public entertainment in Pompeii in the first century, just as it does now in Portsmouth in the nineteenth ; it was the mechanical help to cast up the reckoning. One of the most curious monuments of Rome is that of Eurysaces the Baker, which is partly built of the stone mortars in which bread was kneaded, and has a frieze of bas-reliefs representing the operations of the baker, from the carrying of corn to the mill to the final weighing and distribution of the bread.

So among the expedients adopted for identifying a particular loculus among the many which presented themselves along the walls of the galleries of the catacombs, numerous trade signs appear. Among the most interesting, perhaps, are those which relate to the catacombs themselves. In several of the catacombs are several paintings of *fossores*,* members of the guild of artisans whose business was the excavation of the catacombs; the effigy of the fossor is surrounded by the implements of his calling —the picks with which he worked at the rock, and the lamp by whose light he worked.

At Urbino is a sarcophagus † which represents a sculptor and his studio. It has an inscription: ΑΓΙΟC ΘΕΟCΕΒΕC ΕΥΤΡΟΠΙΟC ΕΝ ΙΡΗΝΗ (The holy pious Eutropius in peace). His men are represented at work upon a sarcophagus, and one of the methods of the ancient sculptor is shown in the use of the drill worked by a cord and bow. On another sarcophagus, on a panel between dolphins, is inscribed his own name ΕΥΤΡΟΠΙΟΣ. We recognize that the sculptor had designed his own tomb and had it executed in his lifetime, and had emphasized its *memento mori* by causing his name to be carved on the pictorial sarcophagus, ΕΥΤΡΟΠΙΟΣ.

In another catacomb ‡ is a painting which commemorates one of the decorative artists who painted

---

* Roller, Plate VI. † Garucci, vol. vi. Plate 488, fig. 25.
‡ Ibid., fig. 19.

the walls and ceilings of the sepulchral chambers, representing him as actually engaged in laying out the geometrical pattern of the ceiling of a chamber. The fossor lies at last in the gallery which he excavated, and the sculptor in the sarcophagus which he sculptured, and the painter under the ceiling which he himself designed.*

The emblems on the loculus of a painter are a pair of compasses, a crayon, and two paint-brushes. The forceps of a dentist are found on another. A case of surgical instruments (engraved by De Rossi, "Bulletino," 1864, p. 36) indicates a professor of the healing art. Among others are found the pincers and hammer which symbolize a blacksmith; a leather apron (a skin) is inscribed on the tomb of another who is described as FABER, a blacksmith; the saw, adze, and chisel of a carpenter, the comb and shears of a wool-comber, the carpenter's adze and the mason's plumb-line, occur on sarcophagi at Arles.

It is maintained that in some cases these tools are the instruments of martyrdom inscribed on the loculi of martyrs. Martigni, after reciting some of them, says, "We have not full confidence, sometimes in their authenticity, sometimes in the interpretation put upon them, but enough remains to establish the fact that it was customary to represent the instruments of their torture and death upon the tombs of martyrs in the primitive Church;" but this is very doubtful.

Another curious class of symbols of which a few examples occur are punning symbols, like the

* Garucci, "Storia," etc., vol. vi. Plate 488.

mediæval "canting heraldry." The tomb of one Dracontius has a dragon; that of Onager, an ass; that of one Leo, a lion; of Doliens, a cask (*dolium*); of Porcella, a pig; of Caprioles, a goat; of Jugas, a yoke.

There are evidences of representations of martyrdoms at the tombs of the martyrs. For example, the painting of the martyrdom of St. Theodorus mentioned by St. Gregory of Nyssa, and a sculptured representation of the beheading of St. Nereus found near his tomb; * but these were works of a later date when the tombs had become places of pilgrimage.

* See p. 166.

CHAPTER XIV.

SCULPTURE.

Classical sculpture—Christian statuary: the Good Shepherd, at Rome, Constantinople, and Athens; the St. Hippolytus; the St. Peter—Sarcophagi: Egyptian, Etruscan, Roman, Christian; kept ready made—The subjects sculptured on them—Sarcophagi of Empress Helena; Constantia; Petronius Probus; Junius Bassus; Anicius Probus, etc.—Sarcophagi in Gaul, Spain, etc.—Pagan sarcophagi used for burial of Christians—English examples—Survivals of style and subjects in stone crosses and fonts.

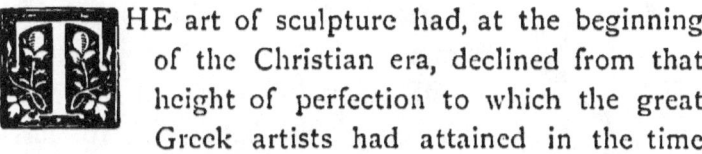HE art of sculpture had, at the beginning of the Christian era, declined from that height of perfection to which the great Greek artists had attained in the time of Phidias and Praxiteles years before; but Greece and all the countries to which the Greek civilization had extended were still full of noble examples of it. The Romans could appreciate these treasures, and victorious generals and plundering proconsuls brought them in great numbers to adorn the temples and public places and palaces of Rome; and it is probable that replicas of favourite ex-

amples were executed by Greek sculptors for Roman patrons.

In the time of Augustus there were sculptors, both Greek and Roman, capable of executing grand and noble designs; but after that splendid age the decline of the art set in. Its works seem soon to have been limited, as with us at the present day, to the execution of portrait statues and busts and the decoration of buildings. There was a temporary revival of the art in the period of the Antonines; after that no great works were executed —at least, none have come down to us. For seven or eight hundred years the art is represented by the bas-reliefs of the sarcophagi, ivory carvings, and a few bronze articles of furniture and ornament. In the thirteenth century the art revived and grew until it reached another climax of excellence at the Renaissance.

The Good Shepherd. Statue in the Lateran Museum.

Of works in the round which we can claim as belonging to early Christian art, the number is lamentably small, and they are not of any great account as works of art. The earliest and best of them is a small marble figure of the Good Shepherd, now in the Lateran Museum, probably of the second or early part of the third century, of which a photograph is given in the frontispiece. It is a standing figure, clad in a short tunic fastened round the waist, the legs below the knees in cross-banded stockings and boots, a scrip suspended from the right shoulder. The head is uncovered, the face youthful; there is no attempt to idealize it. The sheep lies on his shoulders, and its legs are held in front with both hands.* We only recognize it as a symbolical figure of the Good Shepherd from its likeness to the figures which are so frequent in the wall-paintings of the catacombs, and from the absence of any such subject in pagan art. Some writers, indeed, allude to mythological sheep and goat-bearing figures † as if they might have been the type from which the Christian symbolical figure was derived, but a glance at them is enough to show that the two have no relation to one another.

A naked Good Shepherd, which looks as if it had been suggested by one of these classic examples, occurs on a late Gallic sarcophagus,‡ at Vienne.

The heads are all conventional; so much so that in glancing through the hundreds of them which exist on the sarcophagi, a head with any "character" at once attracts attention. For example, Roller gives a photogravure of a finely designed sarcophagus § in which are several heads of our Lord strikingly like the modern type; but on inquiry it turns out that all these heads are the work of modern restoration.

---

* Engraved in Perkins's "Tuscan Sculptures," vol. i. Plate XLIII., and photographed in Parker's Series, 2901.
† The statue by Calamis, or of his time, called Hermes Criophorus, or the Ram-bearer. See it engraved in Seeman's "Götter und Heroen," *sub nomine*.
‡ Le Blant, p. 23.   § Plate LXXXI. fig. 3.

A second ancient statue of the Good Shepherd, of inferior workmanship, two feet high, is also in the Lateran Museum. The figure is young and beardless, clad in a short tunic girded round the waist, loose knitted stockings, and short boots. His left hand supports a long staff, and his right hand grasps the four feet of a sheep, which he bears on his shoulders.

A third statue of the same subject, of poor workmanship, is in the Kircherian Museum of the Collegio Romano.

Another, with the legs broken off short, of the end of the third or beginning of the fourth century, has been recently found near the Ostian Gate of Rome, and is photographed in De Rossi's "Bulletino" for 1887.

There is still another small example of the same subject at Seville, which is probably of the fourth century.

M. Bayet * mentions a damaged statuette in the Museum of St. Irene, at Constantinople, which is of the usual type of the Good Shepherd, and, he thinks, of about the third century. Also at Athens, among the fragments of sculpture in the museum of Patissia, is a portion of a marble statuette of the Good Shepherd, of inferior workmanship, which is not later than the fourth century. The resemblance between these two is striking. A bas-relief at Athens, which seems to be earlier than the fourth century, represents a shepherd of the type described above, but it has a

---

* C. Bayet, "Récherches pour servir à l'histoire de la peinture et de la sculpture."

nimbus round the head which does not occur on Christian monuments till later, and which does appear on pagan monuments of earlier date, *e.g.* in the paintings at Pompeii; behind, a second person,

From a sarcophagus in the cathedral, Tortona. Fourth century.

bent towards the earth, holds a sheep in his arms; beside him is a tree with a serpent coiled round it. Among the sculptures with which Constantine adorned the public places of his new capital Eusebius mentions

S

the Good Shepherd and Daniel with the lions, which were of bronze covered with plates of gold.

On the preceding page is a woodcut of a Good Shepherd in low relief from the end of a sarcophagus of the fourth century in Tortona Cathedral.

A portion of a marble bust, with locks of hair hanging down on each shoulder, probably intended for our Lord, found in 1888, is engraved in the "Melanges de l'École Française de Rome" (1888), Plate IX. It seems to be a work of the fourth century.

A life-size marble figure of St. Hippolytus seated in his episcopal chair, in the Lateran Museum, is a fairly good work of art. It is identified as that of Hippolytus by the fact that the "Pascal Canon" of which he was the author is inscribed on one side of the chair, and a list of his works on the other. The saintly bishop lived in the third century, and the chair and the lower part of the figure may be of that date, but the upper part of the figure is said to be a restoration of the sixth century. Roller suggests that an earlier work representing some philosopher has been appropriated and converted into a St. Hippolytus.

Statue of St. Hippolytus, Lateran Museum.

The famous bronze seated figure of St. Peter in St. Peter's at Rome, with the right hand raised in blessing, while the other holds the symbolical keys, is an imitation of the antique portrait statues. It is believed by some to be a statue of Jupiter taken from the Capitoline Temple furnished with a new head and hands. There is a tradition that Pope Leo I. had the Capitoline Jupiter recast into a St. Peter; this would make it a work of the middle of the fifth century. Signor Lanciani, who has had special opportunities of examining it, says with great decision that it is a complete and unaltered casting [Mr. J. H. Parker says in bell-metal], that "the head and hands are essential and genuine details of the original composition. The difficulty, and it is a great one, consists in stating its age;" the keys, he says, are of comparatively modern form. Roller's judgment is that, far from being an ex-Jupiter of the best period, it is a stiff and misshapen product of the seventh or eighth century.

The sculptured sarcophagi are by far the most numerous examples of the sculpture of these early centuries, and they are of the greater importance in the history of art because they are the only existing works, either pagan or Christian, which represent the art of sculpture for several centuries.

Some two hundred of them have been preserved, chiefly in Italy, the south of France, and Spain. By far the largest collection is that in the Vatican and the Lateran, of those found in the neighbourhood of Rome.

The custom of preserving the dead bodies of illustrious persons in sarcophagi is coeval with the earliest civilization. We are all familiar with the grand granite sarcophagi of the Egyptians, with their sides sculptured with hieroglyphic inscriptions, and the calm, solemn effigy of the deceased in high relief on the massive cover. The custom passed, together with the Egyptian civilization, into Eastern Europe. The Etruscans, whose power was dominant in North and Central Italy before the might of Rome supplanted them, used sarcophagi of stone and terra cotta, and placed them in sepulchral chambers hewn out of the rock and adorned with paintings. The Romans, or at least certain families of them of Etruscan descent, continued these ancestral usages. From the beginning of the third century pagan Rome began to disuse the practice of cremation, and by the end of the fourth it had almost entirely ceased; and as a consequence sarcophagi became more numerous. Christians from the first buried their dead unmutilated; but it was only Christians of wealth and station who used the costly sarcophagus, and consequently sarcophagi known to be Christian in the first three centuries are rare; indeed there is not one of the second century and hardly any of the third. Unless, indeed, some early Christians, like some of later times, were buried in pagan sarcophagi. This idea finds support in the fact that some sarcophagi have a strange mixture of pagan and Christian subjects. Martigny mentions one in the Villa Medici with a Cupid and Psyche and a Jonah; the

Psyche may be used as an emblem of the soul. Another in the Vatican, figured by Cancellari, has a Bacchanalian scene with a Christian inscription. Some of those which have only a central bust and strigillated panels may be the tombs of Christians.

The larger number of sarcophagi sculptured with bas-reliefs of Christian subjects belong to the fourth and fifth centuries, though they continued in use to the seventh century; after that the stone coffin was retained throughout the Middle Ages, but its shape and ornamentation were modified.

The most usual type of sarcophagus of the early centuries of our era is a rectangular stone chest, of not superfluous dimensions, covered with a single block of the same stone, which was usually ridged like the roof of a house.

The ornamentation was most commonly limited to the front of the coffin, but frequently extended to the ends, to the back, and to the lid. The most simple design was a medallion in the middle of the front, in which was sculptured the portrait of the deceased, while the rest of the front was covered with a strigillated pattern, *i.e.* a series of shallow parallel channels, diagonal in their general direction, with an O.G. curve; forming altogether a simple but elegant decoration. In some the front is divided into panels by shafts bearing round or straight-sided arches, each arch containing a figure or a subject. In others the subjects are all in one long panel without any division. But perhaps the most common design is that in which the front is divided by a horizontal line, and contains two series of subjects without any divisions between them.

It is well known that both the Greeks and Romans sought to accentuate the effect of sculpture by the application of colour; and there are indications that some of the sarcophagi have been thus treated.*

The artistic merit of the sculpture on these monuments varies greatly. The majority of them have this advantage that, having been hidden and preserved from the wear and tear of time and accident for so many centuries, they have come down to us in a perfect state of preservation, and represent the art of their time more fairly than the contemporary faded, battered, and sometimes restored frescoes. The great mass of those which are ornamented with Scripture subjects are not without merit; the general effect of the front covered with bas-reliefs is rich and pleasing; in the several subjects the story is told with *naïveté*, but with effect. One common defect is that the heads of the figures are disproportionately large; it arises probably from the comparative lowness of the panel into which a large number of figures had to be crowded, leading the artist to sacrifice the proportion of his figures to bringing out of his heads. In the subsequent style of art, by a natural reaction, the tendency is to make the figures disproportionately tall.

Some of the bas-reliefs are of very creditable workmanship, some even astonish us with unexpected excellence. On the next page are two subjects from the tomb of Junius Bassus, A.D. 359, carefully drawn

* Roller.

SCULPTURE.

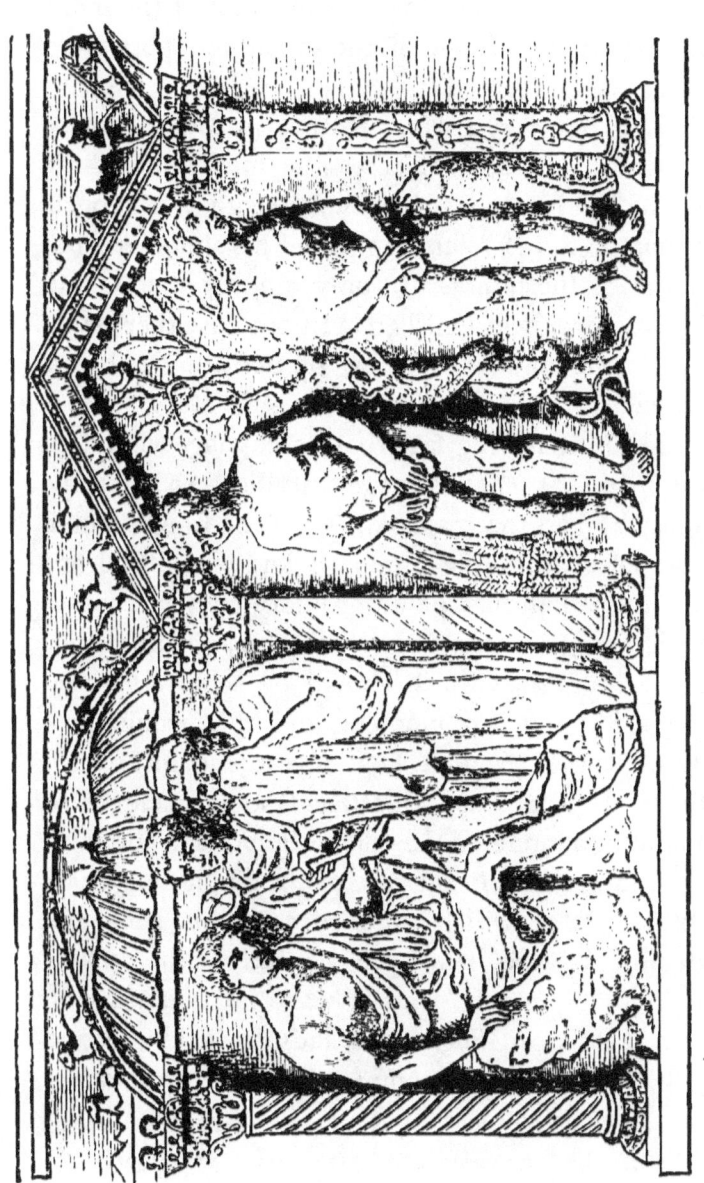

From the sarcophagus of Junius Bassus, A.D. 359 (see p. 268).

to a large scale in order to give some idea of the merit of the sculpture. Some of the medallion portraits * are very well executed.

There is one very curious feature in some of these monuments. In several cases the medallion in the centre of the front has the usual design of the busts of a man and wife, her arm round his shoulder; but the faces of the figures are only roughly shaped out, and have never been finished. In one case there is an orante in the middle of a row of Scripture subjects whose face is left in the same unfinished state. † This reveals the interesting fact that sarcophagi were kept ready made at the sculptors' studios, so that the person who had the management of the funeral could go and select from the number; and would find one with a medallion bust of an ordinary citizen, another of a dignitary in appropriate costume, needing only that the rough-hewn face should be sculptured into a portrait at the last moment, and this would probably be copied from a bust already sculptured in lifetime. In the cases mentioned some accident or oversight had hindered the completion of the portraits.

So in later times, in the case of the effigies engraved on brass plates, which were so common from the fourteenth to the sixteenth centuries, the plates were kept "in stock," and it was only necessary to order a brass of a knight, or a lady, or a knight and lady, with or without canopy; there was very rarely

---

* See photographs in the South Kensington Museum of sarcophagi in the Vatican, by Macpherson, 402 $\frac{A}{B}$ 71763, 71757, and 71761.

† See p. 240.

any attempt at portraiture in them; only the narrow fillet which carried the inscription and the shields of arms had to be engraved at the last moment. The brasses were sent down to the local stonemason, who cut the proper matrices in a slab of marble, and inserted the brasses in their places. We find brasses of which the costume had gone out of fashion, turned over and engraved with a more modern effigy on the other side. In the cases where these mediæval effigies were sculptured on the marble slab itself, we constantly find evidence of a freer handling and inferior skill in the design, because it was executed by a local artist.

The subjects painted on the walls of the pagan sepulchral chambers and sculptured on their tombs may be studied with a view to the motive of the pagan artists in their choice of funeral subjects, in the hope of obtaining a suggestion as to the motive of the Christian artists in the choice of their cycle of subjects. The burial-vaults of the Tarquinii are ornamented with symbolical paintings of a very interesting character. The soul is led away, lamenting, by dark yet beautiful figures, genii or Eumenides, its white guardian angels interceding; there are chariots of Day and Night, the Seasons, and various other serious symbols. But, on the other hand, the wall paintings of the famous tombs on the Latin Way are chiefly taken from the Trojan war, as the Judgment of Paris, Achilles at Scyros, Ulysses and Diomed with the Palladium, Philoctetes at Lemnos, Priam at the feet of Achilles, Jupiter and the Eagle, Centaurs hunting lions and panthers, etc.

Some of the subjects of the sculptures on pagan tombs probably have reference to the occupation or character of the deceased; a battle scene may allude to his vocation as a soldier, or to some particular battle in which he won reputation; scenes of the chase may indicate his favourite pursuit; a portrait of the deceased with a book in his hand accompanied by the Muses probably shows that he was an author. The Cavaliere Visconti * thinks that some of the mythological subjects, are symbolical; the subject of Pluto carrying away Proserpine, which occurs in many sarcophagi, of the death of a girl in the bloom of youth; the subject of Niobe, which occurs on several funeral urns, of the grief of parents bereft of their children; the Labours of Hercules he takes to be an allegory of the triumph of Virtue; the Seasons to be an allusion to the ages of human life; he even suggests that the Baccanalian scenes, which are, perhaps, more common than any others, indicate that the deceased had been initiated into the mysteries of Bacchus. But the majority of the subjects seem to be taken from the poets, as the fables of Adonis, of Phædra and Hippolytus, of Bacchus and Ariadne, etc.

We confidently conclude that, in the great majority of cases, the subjects painted on the walls of the pagan chambers and sculptured on the sarcophagi within them are such as were chosen for the decoration of the chambers of a house, and of its furniture, and had no funereal allusion or individual significance.

* J. H. Parker's "Archæology of Rome."

Perhaps the earliest Christian sarcophagus of ascertained date is that of Helena, the mother of Constantine, who died A.D. 328. It is of very large size, of red Egyptian porphyry, which has been repolished in modern times, to the enhancement of the splendour of the precious material, but probably to its deterioration as a work of art. We know that the empress-mother was a devotee, who, by her personal example, encouraged the fashion of pilgrimages to the Holy Land, and the cult of sacred relics, but the ornamentation of her stately sarcophagus has nothing distinctively Christian in it. The body of the sarcophagus is ornamented with warriors on horseback, driving captives before them, or triumphing over them, without any representation of ground, so that they appear to be marching in the air. On the front and back, at the upper angles, are busts of Helena and Constantine; and on the lower are lions reposing, wreaths, and winged genii. The tomb of Constantia,* the daughter of Constantine, has in front a heavy festoon within whose three convolutions are clumsy genii gathering grapes from a vine; at the ends, two vines enclose genii treading out grapes; the ends have Good Shepherds, vines, and genii. Another large sarcophagus, among the oldest examples known,† has women and genii gathering grapes; with three figures of the Good Shepherd (bearded) in the centre and at the corners.

In Sta. Maria Maggiore is a sarcophagus which is

* Photographed by Parker and drawn by Roller, Plate XLIV.
† South Kensington Photos, portf. 406, No. 37.

supposed to be that of Petronius Probus, who was consul in A.D. 341. It is an example of an extensive series in which the portrait busts of the deceased are introduced in the middle of the front ground within a scallop shell or a circle. In this two busts of men past middle life are enclosed in the central shell, the remainder of the front is divided into two rows of Scripture subjects. In the upper row are the raising of Lazarus; the denial of St. Peter; Moses receiving the Law; the sacrifice of Isaac; Pontius Pilate on the judgment seat about to wash his hands, and Herod with him. In the lower row, a subject which has not yet been deciphered; Daniel in the lions' den, and Habakkuk * bringing him food; another group, the principal figure of which is an aged man reading a scroll, not identified; healing the blind; and the blessing of the loaves and fishes.†

At S. Francisco Perugia is a fine sarcophagus with a youthful classic figure of Christ supposed to be about the middle of the fourth century.

In excavating the new crypt of St. Peter's was found the sarcophagus of Junius Bassus, which is usually considered one of the best works of Christian sculpture. Its date is given in its interesting inscription, which is thus translated—

"Junius Bassus, who lived forty-two years and two months, in the very year in which he was Prefect of the city went to God a neophyte, August 25, A.D. 359."

* See Bel and the Dragon, v. 34.
† No. 2900 of Parker's photographs.

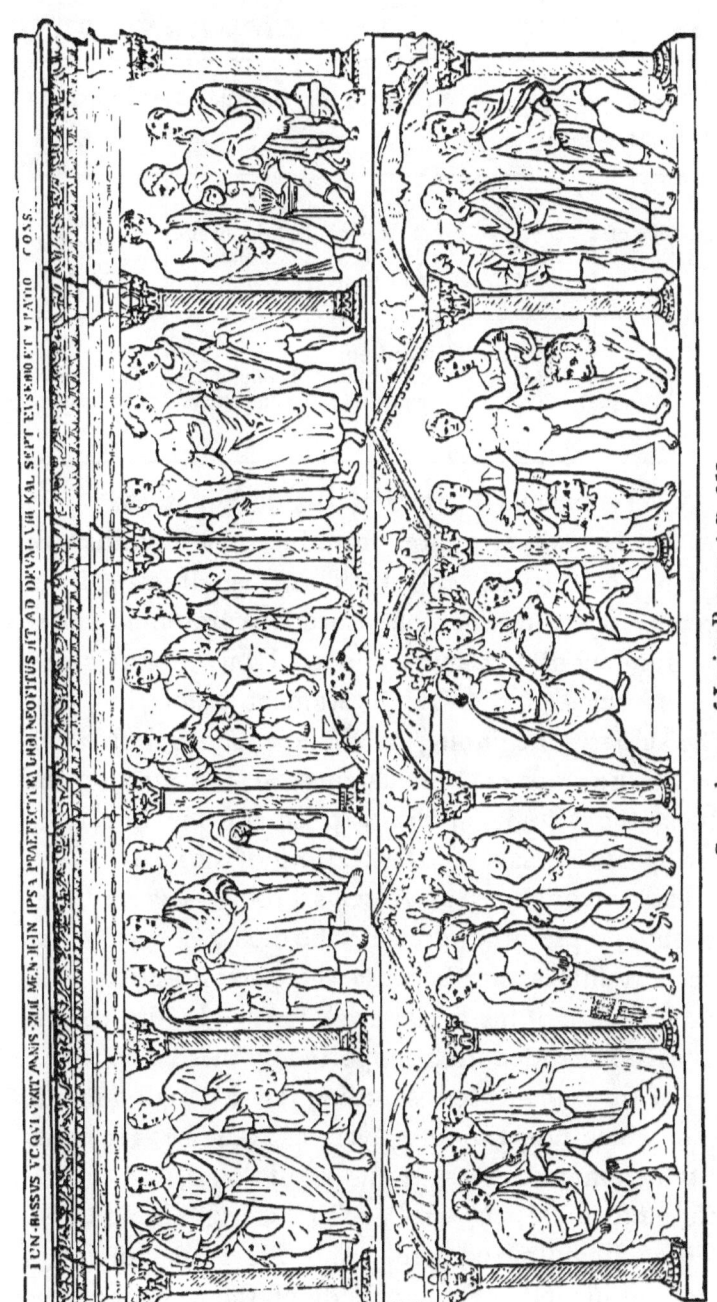

Sarcophagus of Junius Bassus; A.D. 359.

It has two rows of subjects in panels, arranged as follows :—

Sacrifice of Isaac.	Peter's denial (?).	Our Lord between SS. Peter and Paul.	Christ before Pilate.	Pilate washing his hands.
Job.	Adam and Eve.	Our Lord's triumphal entry into Jerusalem.	Daniel in the Lions' den.	The arrest of Moses (?).

A very curious feature of the design is that over the lower canopies are introduced a number of "vignettes," so to call them, of small size, in a sketchy style, in which our Lord is represented under the symbol of a Lamb; and to Him are attributed the miracles of the Old Testament as of the New. The subjects, beginning at the spectator's left hand, are the Furnace of Nebuchadnezzar, the Striking the Rock, the Manna (?), the Baptism of our Lord, the Giving of the Law (?), the Raising of Lazarus.

The sarcophagus of Anicius Probus, several times consul and pretorian prefect, who died A.D. 395, is also specially interesting because the person buried in it and the date of his burial are known. In the centre, beneath a rounded arch supported by twisted columns, Christ is represented standing on a small mound, from which flow the four rivers of Paradise; He holds a tall gemmed cross in his right hand, and in his left hand an open scroll. On his right stands St. Peter with upraised hand, and St. Paul holding a book on his left. On each side of the central arches

Sarcophagus of Anicius Probus, A.D. 395.

are two other arches, under each of which stand two Apostles. In the spandrels of the arches are birds picking grapes in baskets. Each end of the sarcophagus continues the design of the front, having three arches, under which are Apostles. On the back Probus and his wife are represented standing hand in hand (though his wife was buried elsewhere), a disciple stands on each side, and the intervening panels are of striated pattern.*

In the Lateran Museum is one of the most simple, and at the same time one of the most excellent in point of workmanship. The front is divided into seven compartments by eight beautifully carved columns upon which foliage and flowers are represented. In the centre is the youthful Christ seated between two disciples—probably Peter and Paul, beneath His feet is a youthful figure holding a large veil over His head, which is probably a symbolical representation of the sky. Four other disciples stand near. At the left end of the front is the sacrifice of Isaac; the two right-hand spaces are filled by Christ standing before Pilate, who is washing his hands. The figures are admirably designed and excellently sculptured in high relief. The two ends of the coffin are differently treated, so much so as to lead to the suspicion that they are of a different date or, at least, by a different hand. They are carved in very low relief; at one end is Christ predicting St. Peter's denial, at the

* Figured by Bosio, p. 49, etc.; Aringhi, i. 281, etc.; Bottari, i. Plate XVI., etc.; D'Agincourt, "Sculpture," Plate VI., Figs. 12-15; Appell, p. 12; Parker, photo. 451 B.

Sarcophagus in the Lateran Museum, late fourth or fifth century.

other the healing of the woman who touched the hem of Christ's garment, and they have an architectural background including a basilica and detached baptistery of great interest.

The largest sarcophagus in Rome recently found at the basilica of St. Paul-without-the-Walls has a portrait bust in a medallion. In the upper row, the Trinity creating woman; the fall and expulsion (angel giving Adam a spade, and Eve a fleece); Christ turning the water into wine; blessing the loaves and fishes; raising Lazarus. In the lower row, Adoration of Magi; healing blind; Daniel and Habakkuk; warning of Peter; Moses arrested (?); the stricken rock.

One of late fourth-century or early fifth-century date here given has several features of special interest. It has several Passion scenes, which are very rare at that period—Christ bearing His cross and crowned with thorns, in two panels on the left; on the right Christ before Pilate, and Pilate washing his hands; in the centre panel a symbolical Crucifixion, in which Christ is represented by the XP monogram surrounded by a garland. The stem of the P is lengthened to form the upright staff of a cross, on either side of which are St. Mary and St. John.[*]

Another sarcophagus in the Lateran Museum presents great originality of treatment. The principal subject is Jonah in three scenes—cast into the sea, disgorged, and under the gourd. The face of the stone is filled in with other usual subjects—the Raising of Lazarus, the Striking the Rock, three figures in

---

[*] Photo at South Kensington, portf. 406, No. 33. Compare p. 324.

Sarcophagus in the Lateran Museum.

the usual attitude of the Magi, with two figures lying on the ground, perhaps gathering manna, a shepherd and sheep at the door of a building; in the lower part of the design, two men (subject unknown), Noah and the dove, and a fisher.

The sarcophagus represented on p. 277 from the Lateran Museum has only two subjects—the Adoration of the Magi and Daniel in the Lions' Den. In the latter subject Habakkuk is introduced bringing loaves; and the two men bearing rolls of parchment, here and in the same subject on the tomb of Junius Bassus, are supposed to be the accusers of Daniel.

There are numerous examples at Ravenna; in the Chapel Tomb of Galla Placidia are those of Constantine III., A.D. 421, Honorius, A.D. 423, and Galla Placidia herself, A.D. 420. It adds an interesting fact to our general knowledge of the subject when we learn that Theodoric summoned from Rome a certain Daniel, who was famous for his skill in sculpturing marble, and gave him the privilege of supplying sarcophagi to the people of Ravenna. The Ravenna designs belong to the rising school of the mosaic artists rather than to that of the sarcophagus sculptors of the previous centuries.

There are examples at other places in Italy, at Verona, Tortona (with a mixture of heathen and Christian symbols), and Milan, described by Dr. Appell, photographed in the South Kensington Museum, and engraved in numerous works. In Southern France there are considerable numbers; Arles is especially rich in them. It is to be noted

SCULPTURE.

Sarcophagus in the Lateran Museum.

that many of these seem to have been executed by native artists, and that in forming a judgment of their date it must be borne in mind that the fashions of Italian sepulchral subjects seem to have begun almost a century later in Gaul. The Gallic ex-

End of sarcophagus of Archbishop Theodorus, St. Apollinare in Classe, Ravenna, seventh century.

amples are engraved and photographed in Le Blant's great work, "Les Sarcophages de la Gaule" (1835). Others in various towns of Spain are described by Dr. Appell, in his "Monuments of Early Christian Art."

The necropolises of Salone have supplied a certain

number of inscriptions and of bas-reliefs. Among the latter a sarcophagus is ornamented with the subject of the passage of the Red Sea, with an orante on another of its sides. Another sarcophagus has in the centre a Good Shepherd of the bearded type; in another part of the decoration is a group of five persons, man, wife, and children, grouped around a door decorated with lions' heads. On the right and left of the Good Shepherd are two novel subjects; on one side twenty-eight figures, male and female, of different stature, are grouped around a person who holds a scroll in his hands; on the other side a group of small figures of more equal height and youthful countenances surround a female of ripe age. M. Bayet conjectures that they are a cleric—priest, deacon, or lector—and his deaconess-wife.

The classic school of figure sculpture in stone and marble died out on the continent of Europe with the discontinuance of these elaborate sarcophagi; the sculptor's skill was directed to the execution of smaller works, of which the carved ivories remain as the best examples of the art for several succeeding ages.

There are examples of pagan sarcophagi which have been used over again for the burial of Christians.

Recently, in digging in the crypts of the Vatican for the foundations of the new sacristy, was found a sarcophagus whose bas-relief represents a bachanalian scene, with an inscription stating that "this vessel of ancient workmanship had been used for the sepulchre of two Christians." The most striking anomaly, perhaps, is in a sarcophagus found in the Cemetery of St. Agnes, Rome, whose ornamentation is a Bacchus surrounded by little naked cupids and by the genii of the Seasons, whose inscription states that it was used for the burial of a young female, by name Aurelia Agapetella—"ancilla dei"—which probably means a Church virgin.

Two handsome sarcophagi, on one of which is represented the rare and curious subject of the Forge of Vulcan, enclosed the bodies of St. Victor and of St. Mauron, bishops of Marseilles. The body of St. Honorat, Bishop of Arles, was buried in an ancient Roman coffin. And, lastly, the sarcophagus in which rested the feet of the sitting body of dead Charlemagne in the crypt at Aix, is an ancient Roman coffin, ornamented with a bas-relief of the Rape of Proserpine. Roul-Rochette mentions several later examples.

There is an English example which shows how such things were likely to take place. When Etheldreda's body was translated into the church of Ely (A.D. 660), the monks made a voyage across the fens to find a stone large enough for a coffin; "and coming to a small abandoned [Roman] city called Grantchester [near Cambridge], they found near the city walls a white marble coffin most beautifully wrought and neatly covered with a lid of the same sort of stone, and having washed the virgin's body, and clothed it in new garments, they carried it into church and laid it in the coffin that had been brought, where it is held in great veneration to this day" Bede, "Ecclesiastical History," chap. xix.).

We have no examples in Britain of this sculptured type of Christian sarcophagus. And their absence is perhaps to be taken as one among other indications that while Britain was a province of the empire the Church included few members taken from the wealthier classes. One example of a Roman sarcophagus found in London and now preserved in the British Museum * has a medallion portrait of the deceased, and the rest of the panel striated, and at the end is a basket containing loaves or fruit. There is nothing to indicate that it was a pagan monument, and nothing to prove that it was Christian.

Fragments of another found at Barming, Kent, have patterns something like a combination of palm-branch and cross, roughly incised upon them. †

Another sarcophagus was found in 1869 in the ground outside the north of the nave of Westminster Abbey. On the front, enclosed in a panel with moon-shield shaped ornaments at each end, was the following inscription:—

"MEMORIAE . VALER . AMAN
DINI . VALERI . SVPERVEN
TOR . ET . MARCELLVS . PATRI . FECER."

The inscription and the panel are both conclusive of a Roman date, probably not later than the end of the third century. The cover was of the same kind of shelly oolite, which must have been brought from a distance; a cross is rudely sculptured on its whole length and width, with expanded upper limbs and

* C. R. Smith's "Roman London," Plate IV.
† C. R. Smith's "Collectanea Antiqua," i. p. 183.

the lower limb terminating in a fleur-de-lys; the design is of late character, perhaps as late as the twelfth or thirteenth century. The whole suggests the idea that a Roman sarcophagus has been re-used at a later period for Christian burial, and the original coped cover cut down to its present form.

When these sculptured scenes of Scripture History were no longer in use on the continent of Europe, we find them still surviving in Ireland on the high crosses, and in England on the tympana of church doors in the tenth and eleventh centuries. They are more rudely executed than in the examples of the fourth, fifth, and sixth centuries, but they are the same cycle of subjects treated in the same conventional manner. Some of these even appear on tympana and fonts of the eleventh and twelfth centuries.* For example, the cross of Muiredach at Monasterboice, has the following subjects: The Temptation and Expulsion of Adam and Eve; the Adoration of the Magi; Christ seized by the Jews; the Sacrifice of Isaac.

The cross of St. Patrick and Columba, at Kells, has the Sacrifice of Isaac, and the Three Children. The churchyard cross at Kells has the expulsion of Adam and Eve, the Baptism of Christ, and Noah. On the font at Lenton, Notts., are the Baptism of Christ, the Crucifixion, the raising of Lazarus, and the Maries at the Sepulchre.

* For these and other mediæval examples, see "Early Christian Symbolism," by J. Romilly Allen.

CHAPTER XV.

THE MOSAICS.*

History of mosaic decoration; its subjects—Examples: at Rome: St. Constantia; St. George Salonica; Sta. Maria Maggiore; Sta. Pudentiana; Vatican; SS. Cosmas and Damian; S. Praxedes, etc.—At Ravenna: tomb of Galla Placidia; the two baptisteries; St. Vitalis; St. Apollinare Nuovo; and in Classe—At Constantinople, etc.—At Aix-la-Chapelle; St. Mark's, Venice—Fragments in the Catacombs.

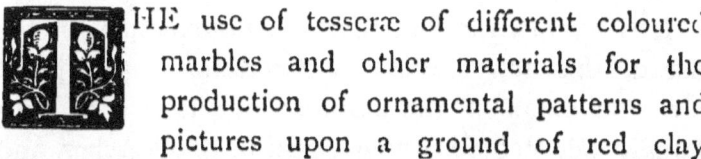HE use of tesseræ of different coloured marbles and other materials for the production of ornamental patterns and pictures upon a ground of red clay tesseræ, in the pavements of their houses and public buildings, had existed in Greece and Rome long before the Christian era. The same method of decoration, almost exclusively in ornamental patterns, had also been applied to small spaces, such as

* Garucci devotes vol. iv. of his "Storia della Arte Christiana" to the mosaics. J. H. Parker has published photographs of the principal mosaics of Rome and Ravenna; the Constantinople mosaics are in W. Von Salzenberg's Monograph. A complete list of mosaics and their subjects is published by the South Kensington Museum in its Universal Art inventory.

spandrels and niches in the walls of houses. Pliny describes a mosaic picture of two doves drinking from a vase, executed as early as 200 B.C.

In the course of the fifth century the art received a sudden impulse from an invention which placed a vast addition of new material in the hands of the artist. The old tesseræ were chiefly different coloured marbles, hard stones, and terra-cotta of different colours; the new invention was of cubes of vitreous pastes artificially coloured, which supplied the artist with every possible colour, in a material easily broken to any form which his design might require; at the same time gilt tesseræ were invented for the background of the pictures, composed of a film of gold leaf between two plates of glass, which were mounted on a tessera of earthenware, and the whole vitrified by heat into a solid cube.

It is remarkable that there are no examples of the use of this new method of decoration in the great civic buildings of the empire; but it was at once largely adopted for the decoration of churches, and accompanied a great change in the style of pictorial art; so that mosaic-painting may be considered a characteristic Christian mode of decoration. It came into use at a time when the artists were introducing a new choice of subjects. The mind of the Church had been directed to the mystic grandeur of the scenes of St. John's visions, narrated in the Book of the Revelation,* and the artists turned to them for their principal subjects. The usual subject for the

* See p. 172.

decoration of the semi-dome of the apse of a church became a solemn figure of superhuman size of the Lord seated upon a throne, or upon a rainbow, surrounded by a halo of glory, sometimes attended by apostles and angels. The patron saint of the church and its founder were sometimes added. On a lower band of decoration, round the base of the dome, it was very usual to represent the Lamb standing on the mount, from which issue the four rivers of Paradise, and on either side six sheep, types of the Apostles, and so of the whole body of believers. The wall space over the arch of the apse is usually filled with other scenes from the same Book—a jewelled cross placed upon a throne, the Lamb on an altar, the seven golden candlesticks, the Book with the seven seals placed on a throne, the four angels commanding the four winds, the four living creatures, and the four and twenty elders. On the side walls were often subjects from Scripture history, especially from the Old Testament.

The treatment of the series of mosaic paintings executed in the fifth century, leads to the supposition that, with the adoption of a new material and a new series of subjects, the artists sought an improved style, by going back to earlier works of classical art for their models. The works of a century later, the sixth, are still in the classical style, but inferior in conception and drawing. In another century, the seventh, the characteristics of the Byzantine style are fully developed, in the ninth it began to decline till the end of the tenth, and was partially revived in the twelfth.

The material lends itself to—almost necessitates—breadth of treatment. Its durability makes it a specially valuable method for the decoration of monumental buildings, it is "painting for eternity." The general effect of the mosaics is grand and solemn; a certain religious dignity is given to the figures by exaggerating their height, by posing them in statuesque attitudes, and by giving a severe gravity to the expression of the faces; the colouring is like that of a crimson and purple sunset; and the background of gold tesseræ, reflecting the light at all angles, gives to the whole the gorgeous brilliancy in which the taste of the time delighted.

There are some small works of this class in the catacombs, which have a special interest from their locality, but the most important examples are found in the churches of Rome and Ravenna, Constantinople and Thessalonica, and later examples in St. Mark's, Venice, the royal chapel at Palermo, and the cathedrals of Monreale and Cefalu in Sicily.

The earliest considerable example of the mosaic decoration of a sacred building is that of the Church of St. Constantia. The mosaic pictures decorate the bays of the roof of the circular aisle of the building. They are on a white ground, in the style of the early mural paintings; for example, one bay, a central half-length figure, which might be a portrait (*e.g.* of Constantine), but is probably a Good Shepherd, is surrounded by a flowing vine pattern, with naked genii and birds among the branches; at the four corners are vintage scenes, carrying the grapes in a cart drawn by two bullocks, treading out the grapes, etc.*

The cupola of the church of St. George at Salonica, (whose erection is assigned by Texier and Pullan to A.D. 323), is decorated with extensive mosaic pictures, which are probably not later than the middle of the fourth century; they consist of a series of representations of sacred edifices in a fantastical style of classical architecture, with figures of local saints introduced.

The mosaics in the vaults of the chapels of St. John the Baptist and St. John the Evangelist of the Lateran baptistery are of the fifth century, and still retain the feeling of the early school of Christian art.

The extensive series of mosaic pictures in Sta. Maria Maggiore are remarkable as being in a distinct style of art, different from that of the early Christian period which we have been studying, and equally different from the Byzantine style which succeeded it. They were executed by order of Sixtus III. (432–440), and his artists seem to have taken the sculptured bas-reliefs of an earlier and better art, especially those of the columns of Trajan and Antoninus, as their models. At the apex of the arch of the apse they placed some usual Christian symbols, the throned roll with seven seals; and over it a gemmed cross and crown, supported by St. Peter and St. Paul with the evangelistic symbols on each side; below are five rows of subjects from the

* There are full-size fac-similes of these mosaics in the South Kensington Museum.

New Testament. In one of the rows of subjects are introduced the conventional holy cities, Jerusalem and Bethlehem, and the sheep; on the north and south walls are double rows of pictures from the Old and New Testaments, but treated in a manner so different from the conventional method of the period that we have difficulty in identifying them.

The mosaic in the apse of the Church of Sta. Pudentiana at Rome is usually said to date from the first reconstruction of the church by Siricius, A.D. 390, but it seems to have been skilfully restored at a much later period. The principal subject is our Lord throned in the midst of His Apostles with an architectural background, designed with much freedom in the classical style of art; while the upper part of the semi-dome is occupied, with very incongruous effect, by the symbolical figures of the Byzantine school—a gemmed cross upon a mount, and large figures of the four living creatures, symbolizing the four Evangelists.

The example which we are able to give here is from the semi-dome of the apse of the ancient Vatican. The design is divided into three portions. In the principal portion the central figure is our Lord in glory, seated on the throne of heaven, holding the Book (of Revelation or of Life) in the left hand, the right hand raised in the attitude of benediction. The starry background represents heaven; and above, at the central point of the apse, is the hand of God, surrounded by rays of glory. On each side of the Saviour are the standing figures of St. Paul and St. Peter, the patron saints of the Roman Church. Their names are inscribed beside them in Greek and in Latin, . ΠΑΥΛΟC $\widehat{SCS}$ PAVLVS, and . ΠΕΤΡΟC $\widehat{SCS}$ PETRVS. The figures are flanked by two palm trees. Beneath the throne is the mount of Paradise with its four rivers, and the two stags drinking. Some other

Mosaics in the apse of the ancient Church of the Vatican.

figures on a small scale appear upon the same platform, the meaning of which it is difficult to determine, unless they represent the souls in Paradise. The second portion of the design consists of a broad band running round the lower part of the semi-dome. In the centre is an altar bearing a cross, and "in the midst of the altar a Lamb as it had been slain," according to the description of St. John in the Revelation. From the foot of the altar flow the rivers of Paradise, whose source we see above. Approaching the altar from each side are two processions of sheep, one of which issues from a building inscribed "Jerusalem," the other from a building inscribed "Bethlehem;" they represent the faithful of the old and new dispensations. The background is ornamented with trees; the figures on each side of the throned cross probably represent the bishop and the emperor of the time at which the mosaic was executed. The third portion of the design is a narrow border, which bears the inscription in Leonine verses—

"SUMMA PETRI SEDES EST HÆC SACRA PRINCIPIS ÆDES. MATER CUNCTAR. DECOR ET DECUS ECCLESIAR. DEVOTUS CHRISTO QUE TEMPLO SERVIT IN ISTO. FLORES VIRTUTIS CAPIET FRUCTUS Q. SALUTIS."

Other mosaics in Rome of this early style are in the apse of the Church of SS. Cosmas and Damian, built by Felix IV. (526–530) In the centre of the apse is a colossal figure of Christ; on the left St. Peter introduces St. Cosmas; on the right St. Paul introduces St. Damian; on the extreme left is St. Felix the founder, and on the right St. Theodore carrying his crown; the whole composition is enclosed between two palm trees. Beneath is a frieze with the usual subject of the central Lamb standing on the mount of Paradise with the sheep proceeding towards Him from the two holy cities. On the east wall of the nave above the arch of the apse is the Lamb enthroned, surrounded by the seven lamps, four angels, the eagle of St. John and the angel of St. Matthew.

In the later mosaics which still remain in the Roman churches we see a gradual transition in style. The mosaics above the arch at SS. Nereus and Achilleus (796) are remarkable as representing historical scenes instead of the usual Apocalyptic subjects. On the face of the Arch of the Tribune are the Transfiguration, and on either side the Annunciation and the Virgin with the infant Saviour. Those in the Church of St. Praxedes (820) are copied from those of SS. Cosmas and Damian, but in an inferior style of art. The last instance in the Roman series is that of the church originally called S. Maria Antiqua (858), in which the art is poor, and the execution rude, but it is interesting for the evidences of the introduction of a new idea and of ornamental treatment. The principal figure is the patron Saint, the Blessed Virgin Mary, now for the first time crowned, with the Holy Child on her lap, and the founder, Paschal I., kneeling at her feet; attended by saints, each under an arch of a continuous arcade, with tabernacle work spreading over the upper part of the design.

The ecclesiastical buildings of Ravenna still retain the mosaics with which they were originally decorated, and they are especially interesting as complete examples of the application of pictorial design and colour to the purpose of architectural ornamentation. These Ravenna mosaics are of different dates. The earliest are those which decorate the lower part of the orthodox baptistery (*c.* 430), and those which cover the whole interior of the Tomb of Galla Placidia (now known as the Church of SS. Nazaro and Celsus, *c.* 440). Like those which have been mentioned

Mosaic from the Tomb of Galla Placidia, Ravenna.

above, they are classical in style and feeling, and possess much merit, both in the elegant forms of the merely ornamental design and in the drawing of the human figure. The domes of this orthodox baptistery and also of the Arian baptistery (*c.* 553) are a century later in date, of the same school of classical art, but of inferior merit.

A third mode of treatment is seen in the mosaics of St. Vitalis and of St. Apollinare in Classe (*c.* 549).

To describe them without the aid of illustrations would be tedious to the reader. We are able to give a specimen of their beautiful effect in the accompanying illustration of the front of one of the upper galleries of St. Vitalis. The subjects from contemporary events in these Ravenna churches are very worthy of notice: for example, the important

Upper gallery, Church of St. Vitalis, Ravenna.

historical pictures in St. Vitalis of Justinian and his court, with the Bishop Maximinus (546-562) and his clergy, and the corresponding picture of Theodora and her attendant ladies. The walls of St. Apollinare in Classe are covered with whole rows of mosaic pictures, Christian symbols, portraits of archbishops, and scripture histories. The grand processions of male and female saints which decorate the wall-spaces over the nave windows of St. Apollinare Nuovo and lead up to the throned Saviour, attended by angels, in the apse, are also very noble examples of Christian art.

Of these frescoes at Ravenna, those in the buildings of Honorius and his sister were executed under the influence of Western Christianity; others, in the buildings of Theodoric, under the influence of Gothic Arianism; others, in the buildings of the reign of Justinian, under the influence of Eastern Christianity.

The Empress Theodora : St. Vitalis, Ravenna.

The decoration in all these buildings is fairly complete and perfect, so that they present a remarkable testimony to the prominent ideas of the Christianity of the period which they cover; it is very interesting to observe that the art teaching is perfectly scriptural and orthodox. Our Lord is the one Person presented to the adoration of the people; no special prominence is given to the Blessed Virgin; the saints are treated as historical persons; not a single doctrine or opinion contrary to those held at this day by instructed members of the Church of England finds expression.

There are some less important examples of mosaic of the early part of the fifth century in the churches of St. Lawrence and St. Ambrose at Milan, and (*c.* 543) at Parenzo in Istria.

St. Sophia at Constantinople still retains its original magnificent mosaic decoration, though in the interior it is covered with whitewash; during the temporary removal of this covering they were drawn by Von Salzenburg, and are published in his great work on the ancient Christian architecture of Constantinople. The mosaic in the exterior of the narthex, which represents the Emperor Constantine Pogonatus kneeling before our Lord throned, is of rather later date. The illumination of St. Dunstan kneeling at the feet of St. Gregory in a Saxon manuscript in the British Museum is clearly taken from this. Another grand example of the early part of the sixth century is the cupola of St. Sophia, Thessalonica. There are other mosaics at St. Catherine on Mount Sinai, Mount Athos, Daphne near Athens, and St. Luke in Livadia, and there is no reason to doubt that similar works were common in the churches of the East.

The church at Aix, built by Charles the Great, was decorated with mosaic. In the centre of the design of the apse is our Lord throned; seven small figures of the elders rise from their thrones and cast their crowns at His feet. The Church of St. Mark's, Venice, is a fine example of the revival of the art in the eleventh 'century. There are also in Rome examples of the revived art of the twelfth and thirteenth centuries.

The art has been again revived in our time by Salviati at Venice; the best examples which we possess at present are the spandrels of the dome of St. Paul's, London; small applications of mosaics to the decoration of reredoses and the like are not infrequent.

There are traces in scattered tesserae of the use of mosaics in the ornamentation of tombs in the catacombs. The only works which have survived are two. Marangoni mentions (Act, *s.v.*, p. 99) the tomb of an infant, named TRANQUILLINA, surrounded by a mosaic of white stones and coloured and gilded glass, upon which the epitaph is worked in the same materials. Marchi figures (v. tom. xlvii.) an arcosolium, in the crypt of SS. Protus and Hyacinth, decorated in this style with some of the usual subjects, Lazarus, Daniel, the paralytic, etc.

CHAPTER XVI.

IVORIES.

Consular Diptychs; Church Diptychs—Diptych of St. Gregory—Chair of St. Maximinus: of St. Peter—Book-covers—Pyxes and relic-boxes—Caskets and shrines—Doors.

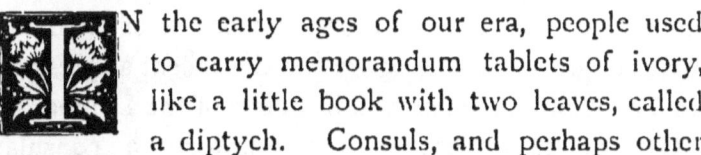N the early ages of our era, people used to carry memorandum tablets of ivory, like a little book with two leaves, called a diptych. Consuls, and perhaps other Roman magistrates, used to make presents of such tablets, on their election to office, and for new-year gifts, with their own effigies in official robes and insignia, sculptured on the exterior sides. The earliest existing example is that of Stilicon, attributed to A.D. 405. Many of these classical diptychs have been preserved through the accident of their having been used for the covers of the Gospels and other sacred books.

The early Church preserved lists of those whom it held in special honour—as saints, founders, bishops, benefactors, etc.—inscribed in similar diptychs, which were placed upon the altar at the time of the celebration of the Eucharist. The exteriors of these ecclesiastical memorandum-books were sculptured in relief, like those above mentioned, but with Christian subjects, such as representations of our Lord, of saints, and of scenes from the Old and New Testaments.

When the sarcophagi cease to afford us examples of the best art in sculpture, these ivory carvings happen to come in to continue the series. The subjects of them are the same as those on the sarcophagi, are composed in the same conventional way, and executed in the same style.

The woodcut represents the exterior faces of an interesting diptych at Monza, whose date and subject are matter of dispute. It is said to be one of the many pious objects which Gregory the Great sent as presents to Theodelinda, the orthodox queen of the Lombards; Martigny says that it was originally a consular diptych, and that Gregory had caused one of the effigies to be retouched in the face and hair, the robe, and the staff, so as to make it a representation of himself, and caused his name "SCS GREGR" to be inscribed over it; while the inscription of "REX DAVID" over the other effigy appropriated it to King David. Professor Westwood, however, says that, after careful examination of the ivories, with a view to this point, he comes to the conclusion that there has been no retouching of the original carving, and that the two names are certainly not palimpsest. He points out that this differs in design from all consular diptychs, and

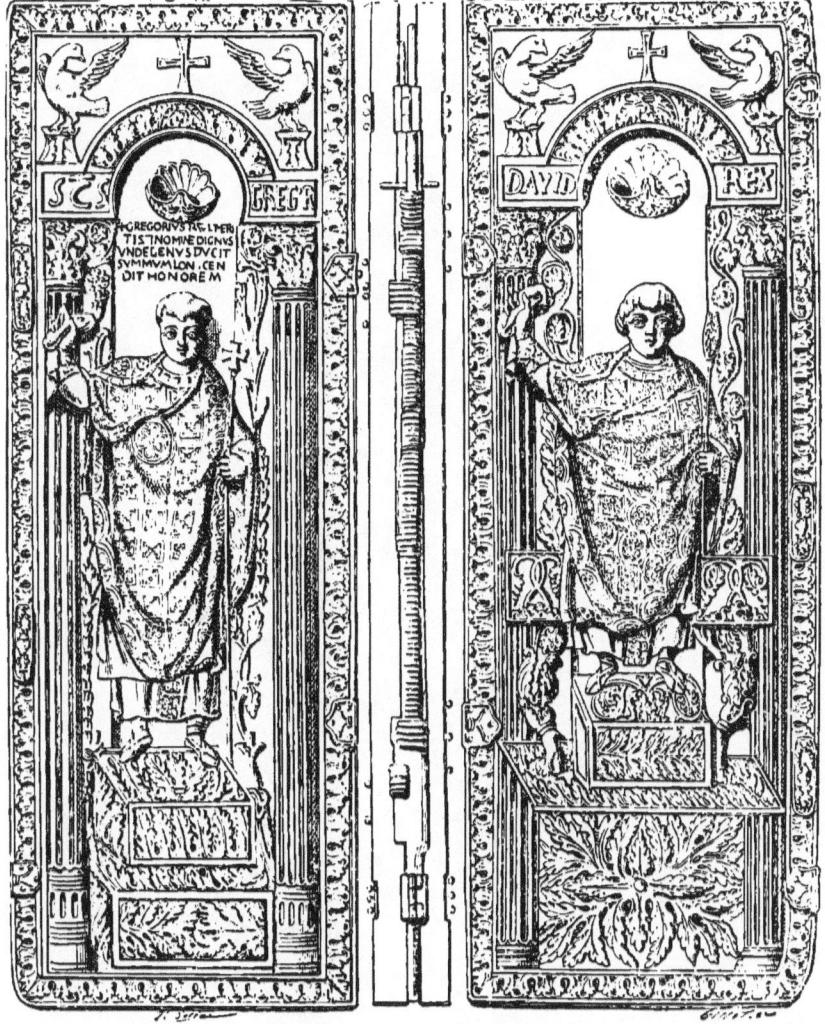

Ivory diptych at the Cathedral, Monza.

maintains that it is a genuine ecclesiastical work. The assigning of the title *sanctus* to Gregory would indicate that it is later than his lifetime, and therefore not one of his presents to Theodelinda. The ivory covers now contain a "gradual" of St. Gregory, written in gold and silver letters on vellum, and the subjects of the cover—David the psalmist, and Gregory the reformer of psalmody—suggest that the cover may have been expressly made for its present use.

The celebrated episcopal chair of Maximinus, preserved in the Cathedral of Ravenna, is decorated with a number of ivory plaques, representing subjects from the Old and New Testaments of the middle of the sixth century. The frieze of vine-scrolls with lions, deer, peacocks, etc., is full of freshness and spirit. It is the most magnificent work in ivory which has come down to us. The so-called Chair of St. Peter at Rome is ornamented with ivory carvings of the Labours of Hercules.

The woodcut on p. 300 represents a pax, probably of the eighth century, formed by a central plaque of ivory, sculptured with the Crucifixion, mounted in a frame of silver-gilt enriched with precious stones; it is preserved in the church of Cividale, in Friuli, and is probably the earliest remaining example of a pax.

A book-cover in the Cathedral of Milan, of the sixth century, is ornamented with scenes from the life of Christ, in which "the groups are finely arranged and in many respects savour of antique treatment."

The other examples of this early style of art (though their date is a little uncertain) catalogued by Professor Westwood are four plaques of red-stained ivory with scenes from the life of Christ, in the British Museum. Two sides of a book-cover in the Bibliothèque Nationale, Paris, with scenes from the life of Christ. Two tablets of the sixth

A pax of the eighth century, Cividale, Friuli.

or seventh century in the Kunst Kammer, Berlin, identical in design with the central portion of the last named, but more skilfully executed. Two leaves of a diptych in the collection of M. Carraud, with scenes from the life of St. Paul. Two leaves of a diptych of the sixth or seventh century in the collection of Mr. Bateman, with subjects from the life of Christ. The front of a book-cover in eight compartments, of the sixth or seventh century, in the Public Museum of Ravenna, with subjects from the life of Christ. The front of a book-cover in the Vatican Library, sixth to eighth century, one of the most important and admirable specimens of early Christian art: at the top, two angels support a circle containing a richly gemmed cross; in the centre, an admirable figure of a youthful Christ tramples on the lion and asp, under a round arch resting on fluted columns with Corinthian capitals; at the bottom is the Adoration of the Magi.

There are in the South Kensington Museum a considerable number of casts of round boxes of carved ivory, which are described in the catalogue as Pyxes. Some of them were perhaps used to contain the reserved Eucharistic bread; others were probably reliquaries—one when found contained a fragment of cloth such as was frequently treasured up as a relic from having wrapped, or at least touched, the body of a saint. One, of the fifth or sixth century, at the Vatican is carved with some of the miracles; another, of the sixth to the eighth century, in a private collection, with the healing of the demoniac; one, of the fourth or fifth century, in the Kunst Kammer, Berlin, has the sacrifice of Isaac, and Christ with Apostles. A very remarkable one is of the sixth to the ninth century, with a figure of St. Mennas, which probably contained a relic of that popular Alexandrian saint.

There is a very large collection of fac-simile casts of ancient ivories in the South Kensington Museum, including those above mentioned; and Professor Westwood's "Fictile Ivories," a *Catalogue raisonné* of the collection, gives photographs of some of the more remarkable examples.*

Ivory caskets and shrines are a numerous class of objects upon which the best art of their time has been bestowed, but few of them come within this early period to which we are restricted. The earliest and the most beautiful of these is the casket preserved in the Bibliotheca Quiriniana at Brescia, which is of the sixth or seventh century. The panels are sculptured with some of the usual subjects of the early classical school of Christian art—the Good Shepherd; Christ amid the Doctors; the woman washing Christ's feet with her hair; the raising of the daughter of Jairus; the raising of Lazarus, and the healing of the blind; Ananias and Sapphira.

Another casket in the British Museum, though below the limits of our period, is of so much interest that we shall be pardoned for introducing a notice of it here. It is made out of the bone of a whale, and has its sides and ends carved with historical and scriptural subjects. In front on the right-hand side is the Adoration of the Magi; the inscription over it is the word "MAGI." The inscription in front of the box relates, in Runic characters, the name of the Northumbrian hero who killed the whale and caused this casket to be made out of its bone in memory of the

* See also "Ivories, Ancient and Modern," W. Maskell.

exploit. It may be classed with the quaigh found at Long Wittenham * as interesting survivals of the classical school of Christian art in our own country.

Intimately related to these ivory panels, in choice of subjects and style of treatment, are the ornamental doors, of which the earliest examples are the doors of St. Sabina at Rome, of the sixth century. They are divided into panels which bear some of the usual cycle of Scripture subjects.† The famous bronze doors of the Baptistery at Florence, by Ghiberti (fifteenth century), are a revival of the ancient style.

* See p. 332.
† Garucci, "Storia della Arte Christiana," iv. 499.

CHAPTER XVII.

GILDED GLASS VESSELS.

Where found; mode of execution; subjects; inscriptions—Engraved glasses—Original use: memorial application.

AMONG the objects of early art is a series of glass vessels which seem to have come into use about the end of the third century, and to have ceased to be manufactured after about the end of the fourth. They have been found only at Rome and at Cologne; the larger number have been found in the Roman catacombs. About 340* have been published, and the British Museum is fortunate enough to possess a considerable number of them. Very few of them are perfect. They have been stuck into the wet plaster cementing the slabs or tiles with which the loculi were closed; and the greater part of them have been broken. Some appear to have been shallow bowls, others tazzi or salvers, the greater number drinking-cups of various shapes—some like

---

* Buonarotti's "Osscreazioni," etc., is the first adequate publication of these vessels. They are all figured in Garucci's "Storia della Arte Christiana."

egg-shells, one like a horn. Their great feature of interest is that the bottom of the vessel is ornamented with a circular medallion, which is a work of pictorial

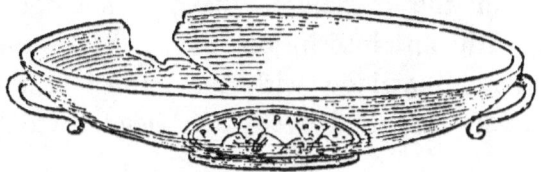

Gilded glass vessel, from the Roman catacombs. Side view.

art. It was executed in the following way: a round piece of glass of the size of the bottom of the bowl had a leaf of gold fixed upon it with some kind of

Gilded glass vessel, from the Roman catacombs. Full view.

cement; a pattern was traced upon the gold with a pointed instrument; the glass medallion was then fixed to the bottom of the vessel externally by the application of heat, so that the ornamentation was seen through the glass when in use. Silver leaf and colour were, very rarely, used instead of gold.

Some of the medallions have a subject in the centre, with an inscription over; the subject is frequently a marriage, with the names of the man and woman inscribed over their heads, which sug-

Gilded glass vessel: "Pompeiane, Teodora, vib(v)atis."

gests that the vessels were wedding presents; children sometimes accompany the adult figures. The figures of our Lord and of Apostles often occupy the centre, with their names inscribed over them; by far the most frequent are St. Peter and St. Paul in whole length, half length, or busts; another which very frequently occurs is St. Agnes; others which occur singly, or in pairs, or in threes, are Peter, Paul, Timothy, Simon, Luke, Judas; and saints, as Hippolytus, Laurence, Vincent, Callistus, Marcellinus, Ciprianus, Sixtus, Justus, Florus, Mary, Peregrina, Libernica, etc. Sometimes the central subject is from the Old or New Testament, and the most commonly found are those which we have seen were most frequently used in the paintings and sculptures: Adam and Eve, Noah, the sacrifice of Isaac, the stricken rock, Moses and the brazen serpent, the spies with the grapes of Eshcol, Daniel, Jonah. Our Lord appears as the Good Shepherd, between St. Peter and St. Paul, seated with lambs on each side, raising Lazarus, in the miracle of the loaves, and of the wine at Cana, and of the healing of the paralytic. It is notable that as the series of wall paintings includes three apocryphal subjects, that of Habakkuk bringing food to Daniel, and that of Susannah and the elders, and the ox and ass at the Nativity, so on these glass vessels there are Tobit and the fish,* and Daniel giving the balls of pitch to the dragon.†

Gilded glass vessel: "Angne."

A more elaborate design is exhibited in some

---

* Tobit vi. 3.   † Bel and the Dragon, 27.

examples, which reminds us of the painted ceilings of the catacomb chambers, where a central subject is surrounded by a number of others arranged outside, and sometimes radiating from it. Here is one

Gilded glass vessel. Bust surrounded by twelve figures.

of them, which, at first sight, looks like a bust of our Lord surrounded by full length figures of the twelve Apostles; but, on examination, the central bust might be that of a female, and there is nothing to indicate that the other figures are Apostles except their number. The name PETRVS, which catches the eye over the figure at the top of the design, turns out, on the reading of the whole inscription, to be that of the person to whom the vessel was to be presented. The inscription is of the usual convivial type, ELARE PIE ZESES PETRVS CVM TVIS OMNES ("Drink joyfully, long life, Peter, to you and all yours"). The groups of subjects from two examples have already been used in studying the symbolism of the art of the catacombs at pp. 231, 232. The design on another represents a heap of coins, among which are those of Caracalla and of one of the Faustinas.

Some of these vessels seem to be Jewish, from the subject of their designs, as the seven-branched candlestick, which is used in the Jewish catacombs, and the ark containing the rolls of the Law. Others have subjects from the old mythology, as Hercules, Achilles, and pagan deities. Others represent secular subjects, as hunting, chariots, a carpenter surrounded by scenes from his occupation.

The inscriptions are all of the same character, as, PIE, ZESES, πιε ζησῆς ("Drink, long life"); DIGNITAS AMICORVM PIE ZESES CVM TVIS OMNIBVS ("A token of friendship, drink, long life to you and yours").

There are a few examples of these bowls in which the ornamentation is executed by engraving upon the glass without any gold-foil.* One, in the shape of a truncated horn found at Cologne, and now in the British Museum, is incised with the subjects of Adam and Eve, and the stricken rock; another of similar shape, figured by Perret, is ornamented with a bird in a cage, and palms. One found at Podgoritza, in Dalmatia, has a series of Scripture subjects: in the centre the sacrifice of Isaac, and round it Adam and Eve, Lazarus, Moses-Peter striking the rock, Daniel, the Three Children, Susannah, Jonah. The subjects all have inscriptions.

* See Garucci, vi. 464.

The inscription to the stricken rock is, "Petrus virga perqod sit fontes ciperunt quorere," intended for "Petrus [? petram] virga percussit, fontes ceperunt currere," "Peter struck [or he struck the rock] with a rod, the fountain began to flow." (Note, *fontes* is the technical word for the baptismal font.) In the British Museum is also a plain glass beaker from the Roman catacombs.[1]

Various conjectures have been made as to the original use of these vessels, and the intention with which they were affixed to the graves.

As to their original use, the sacred subjects with which they are ornamented by no means imply that they were intended for sacred uses; such subjects were commonly used for the adornment of objects of ordinary domestic use, as lamps, buckles, dress, etc. On the other hand, the inscription πίε ζησῆς seems to be sufficient proof that they were intended for domestic use. The common formula seems to indicate a custom of drinking healths; the Teutonic "Drinc heil" of Geoffrey of Monmouth's story of Vortigern and Rowena is the exact equivalent of the πίε ζησῆς of these cups; while the fact that the formula is in Greek, even where Latin words are found with it, as *feliciter cum suis*, indicates that the custom came from the East.

As to the intention with which they were affixed to the graves, it has been suggested that they contained the blood of martyrs, that they were chalices, or had been used at the funeral feast. In favour of the theory that they contained the blood of martyrs, are the arguments that the faithful are known to have diligently caught the blood of the martyrs and to have preserved it as relics ; that a brown encrustation at the bottom of one or more of these vessels has been analyzed and pronounced to be blood ; that scratched in the damp plaster beside two of them are the inscriptions Sā Saturnū and Sang Sā. On the other hand, it is replied that the way in which the blood of the martyrs was preserved was by spreading cloths to catch it before the fatal blow was struck, as in the well-known case of Cyprian, or soaking cloths in it afterwards, which was the more usual way ; that the result of the analysis spoken of is not considered conclusive by those who have examined the subject ; and that the inscriptions mentioned are proved by the character of the letters and by the formula used to be forgeries of later date. It is especially a forcible argument that some of these vessels are accompanied by monograms which were not in use till after the last persecution was over, and some are actually dated, by the names of consuls, from A.D. 350 to 400. We hesitate to accept any more recondite explanation than that they were intended to identify the graves, just as we find coins and shells and such-like things impressed in the wet plaster of tombs, with the same intention. The great majority of the known examples have been published in Garucci's "Storia del Arte Christiana."

CHAPTER XVIII.

ILLUMINATED MANUSCRIPTS.

Earliest books, sacred and profane—Sacred MSS.—The Syrian Gospels of Rabula—Early MS. in England: the Genesis of the Cotton Library; the C. C. C. Cambridge and Bodleian Gospels—The Irish and Saxon MSS.

N treating of the art of painting as exhibited in written books, it is necessary to distinguish between merely ornamental forms of writing and pictures introduced into the text as illustrations.

The earliest books which remain to us depend upon the size and form of their letters for their beauty; in the sixth century, sometimes initial letters, or words, or lines are written in red pigment. In some early books the vellum leaves are stained of a purple colour, and the writing is in gold or silver; the intention seems to have been to do honour to the imperial or royal person for whom the book was written, rather than to the subject of the book.

The oldest manuscripts of the sacred Scriptures which have come down to us are the "Codex

Sinaiticus" and the "Codex Vaticanus," both of the fourth century, and the "Codex Alexandrinus," of the early part of the fifth century, which is in the British Museum; but none of these have either ornamental writing or illustrative pictures. Some very early secular books, enriched with pictures, have survived. A Virgil in the Vatican, with pictures, may be as early as Constantine the Great. A Roman calendar in the library at Vienna, with beautifully drawn figures of the months, has been thought to be as early as Constantine II., A.D. 338; but Professor Westwood's mature opinion is that it is a comparatively modern copy of a classical original. Probably the earliest sacred book with miniatures is a Greek manuscript of Genesis, written on purple vellum, with forty-eight pictures, in the same library, of the fourth or fifth century, engraved by D'Agincourt (IV., xix.), and still more satisfactorily by Garucci ("Storia della Arte Christiana," iii. 112–123). A history of Joshua, of the seventh century, is also a valuable monument on the history of the art (D'Agincourt, IV. 1. 23; Garucci, iii. 157–167).

One of the most remarkable and valuable of illustrated manuscripts is the Syrian manuscript of the Gospels preserved in the Laurentian Library at Florence. It was written in the year 586, by Rabula (as he himself records), a scribe in the Monastery of St. John, in Zyba, a city of Mesopotamia. The whole of these miniatures are given by Assemanni, in his Catalogue of the Laurentian Library, and still more accurately and beautifully by Garucci (vol.

iii. pp. 128-140). Many of the pictures, and the Eusebian canons, are placed under arches, which are sometimes of horseshoe form; the arches and columns which support them are ornamented with chevrons, lozenges, nebules, quatrefoils, zigzags, flowers, fruit, birds, etc., many of which strikingly resemble those found in the early Anglo-Saxon manuscripts, especially in the columns supporting the Eusebian canons in the purple Latin Gospels in the British Museum (Reg. I, E, 6). There is, however, none of the interlacing of the patterns so characteristic of the Irish and Anglo-Saxon manuscripts. Some of these arches, and their columns and capitals, are exactly like the Norman doorways which still remain in many of our churches; for example, that on Plate 128 of Garucci, beneath which stands a fine and dignified Virgin and Child. One feature of the work is the introduction, in the margins of the elaborate principal subjects, of very charming vignettes of the usual cycle of early Scripture pictures, treated with a certain originality, and sketched in with great firmness and skill, as the Annunciation, Baptism of Christ, massacre of the innocents, Nativity, healing of the woman, the paralytic, miracle of Cana, Jonah, entry into Jerusalem, Betrayal, Judas hanging from the top of a palm which bends with his weight (very clever and ghastly). The Crucifixion, Resurrection, Ascension, descent of the Holy Ghost, in a different style, occur on spare leaves at the end of the book. The woodcut represents the Ascension of our Lord, and if the date, A.D. 586, be correctly assigned to it, it is the earliest representation of the subject. The aureole round our Lord is supported beneath by the mystic living creature of Ezekiel (chap. i.) and St. John (Rev. iv.), and by two angels at the sides; two

The Ascension: from the Syrian Gospels, by Rabula, A.D. 586 (?).

other angels present crowns; the sun and moon are symbolized in the upper corners of the picture.

Beneath this scene in the clouds (not given in our woodcut) are the Apostles gazing upwards. In the middle is the Blessed Virgin Mary standing in the orante attitude, and on each side of her an angel delivering our Lord's message, "Ye men of Galilee," etc.

An account has recently been published by Dr. Josef Stryzgowski, of a manuscript of the Gospels at Etchmiadzin, which is bound in ivory plaques, and has miniatures at the beginning and end of the vol. The manuscript itself is dated A.D. 989, but the editor is of opinion that the ivory carvings and the miniatures are additions of Syrian origin, and probably of the sixth century.

The libraries of our own country possess some early manuscripts, which are valuable both as examples of caligraphy and of miniature painting. The Genesis of the Cotton Library,* in the British Museum, probably of the fourth century, is, or rather was, illustrated with pictures, for only fragments of it have survived the fire of 1731, which consumed so many treasures. There is also in the British Museum a fragment of a manuscript of the Gospels, written in large fine silver letters on purple-stained vellum (Titus, cxv.), which is, perhaps, the oldest manuscript of any portion of the New Testament now existing.

In the course of the "Life of St. Gregory the Great," written by John the Deacon, it is recorded that Gregory sent to Augustine, among other things, many books. In the "Annals of St. Augustine and Christ Church, Canterbury," compiled by a monk of St. Augustine, in the reign of Henry V., several books then in the library, and always regarded as having belonged to Augustine, are described. Two of these books are believed still to exist—one in the library of Corpus Christi College, Cambridge, the other in the Bodleian Library, Oxford. They contain Anglo-Saxon entries now a thousand years old, which connect them with the monastery of St. Augustine. The Cambridge manuscript is of the Gospels, written in fine Roman uncials, and probably of the fifth century. It has pictures of the Evangelists at the beginning of the several books, and has some small square pictures of scenes from the life of

* Engraved in the "Vetusta Monumenta," i. Plate LXVII.

Christ, brought together on separate pages and inserted; these bear traces of the conventional classical designs, but are treated rudely, and with a certain degree of freedom. They are the most ancient monuments of early Christian painting existing in this country. The Bodleian Manuscript is also of the Gospels. The text is ornamented with red letters in the first line of each Gospel and in some other places, but it has no pictures.

Another manuscript of the Gospels, which also belonged to the Monastery of St. Augustine, Canterbury, and is now in the British Museum (Royal I, E), may be of the seventh century; it is written on purple-stained vellum, with ornamental initials, etc., of the Anglo-Saxon school of art, and with pictures of the Evangelists of the Byzantine school.

The MS. Add. 11695 in the British Museum contains rude copies of paintings of much earlier date —horseshoe arches, and interlaced ribbands, which recall the Rabula Manuscript; a large cross with the $A\Omega$ suspended from its arms; at fol. 229 the Three Children in the Furnace in oranti attitude, with angels spreading out hands and wings over them.

The MS. Galba A XVIII. in the British Museum, of the eighth century, has an Ascension of the same type as that in the Rabula Manuscript.

From the sixth century the political troubles of the empire seem to have interrupted the work of the miniature-painter on the continent of Europe, until the revival of art by Greek artists in the time of Charles the Great. But in the seventh and eighth centuries the monasteries of Ireland, the Hebrides, and of Northumbria were producing books written in letters of a grand form, profusely ornamented with fanciful figures of birds, beasts, and lacertine creatures, and interlaced work, with borders and initial pages of ornament;* but the attempts at the drawing of the human figure in them are childish. In the Psalter of Athelstan we first see the revival of art in England, in miniatures which are clearly copied from ancient originals; the Ascension is so much like that in the Syrian manuscript of Rabula, as to raise the question how far our English art was indebted to Eastern sources.†

It is pleasant to be able to add that while the early English Church was indebted to more learned countries for books, in one instance at least a manuscript of the same Church is at this day one of the treasures of the Western Church. A huge and magnificent manuscript of the whole Bible, which Abbot Ceolfrid had written in A.D. 1716, either at Wearmouth or Jarrow, as a present to the Bishop of Rome, is accounted as one of the two manuscripts from which the text, as Jerome left it, may be best determined; it is known as the Codex Amiatinus, as having belonged to the convent of Monte Amiata; it is now in the Laurentian Library at Florence.

* For which see Westwood's "Palæographia Pictoria Sacra."
† The scribes of the East Syrian (Nestorian) Christians are to this day writing books in large bold minuscule characters, and ornamenting them with frontispieces of interlaced work, in the style of the Irish and Saxon manuscripts of the eighth century. It is a very curious survival of ancient art.

CHAPTER XIX.

GOLD AND SILVER VESSELS—HOLY OIL VESSELS— SACRED EMBROIDERY.

The altar and its canopy; altar vessels, etc.; censers; crosses; lamps —Holy oil vessels; their use; examples at Monza—Superstitions connected with: continued to the present day—Sacred embroidery: hangings in churches; clerical vestments.

IN the time of Constantine—and how much earlier we do not know—the altar in the more stately churches was overshadowed by a kind of canopy, which in Constantine's Church of the Holy Wisdom was a semi-dome, carried on four pillars with silver capitals. Two centuries later, when pictures and images were commonly used in churches, the presence of the Holy Ghost was represented by a silver dove hanging over the altar, and another over the font in the baptistery.

Even in primitive times the altar vessels, as chalices, patens, lamps, were of precious metals, and we cannot doubt that vessels of silver and gold would be wrought according to the use of their time. We have seen that in the upper room of Jerusalem it is probable that this was the case ; that it was so in later times we learn from several incidental notices. Tertullian,* in the latter part of the second century, speaks of the symbol of the Good Shepherd on the Eucharistic cup, from which we infer that the chalices and probably other sacred vessels were sometimes ornamented with the symbols and pictures which the piety of the time so freely lavished. Bishop Zephyrinus (A.D. 203) prescribed that the chalices should be of gold or silver. Urban I. (227) bestowed sacred vessels of gold and lamps of silver upon various churches. Part of the crime for which St. Laurence the Deacon suffered martyrdom under Valerian (c. A.D. 253) was that he refused to give up the golden vessels in which the sacred mysteries were celebrated, and the golden lamps used in the night assemblies, which were under his charge as deacon. In the Diocletian persecution, Mensurius, Bishop of Carthage, when (A.D. 303) ordered to Rome to be tried, left the gold and silver vessels of his church in the custody of the priests, and an inventory of them in the hands of a deaconess, with a charge that if he did not return she should give it to his successor. What this inventory contained may be inferred from another of the same period of the sacred vessels given up by Paul, Bishop of Cirta, to the persecutors ; it enumerated two gold cups, two silver cups, six silver water-pots, a silver *cumelium* (probably a flagon or bowl), seven silver lamps, etc. When emperors and kings became the "nursing fathers" of the Church, they lavished trea-

* Oxford translation, p. 111.

sure upon the fabrics and their furniture. To take the Basilica of St. Peter as an illustration. The doors were overlaid with silver plates, the pavement before the crypt was of silver. Besides the precious materials used in the construction of the *Confessio* for the relics of the Apostles, and the golden-plated vaulting of the apse, there was a cross of solid gold, an altar of silver gilt, adorned with four hundred precious stones, white, green, and blue; a golden paten with a cover of pure gold and a dove upon it (patenam auream cum turrem ex auro purissimo cum columbam), similarly adorned with jewels, together with five silver patens; three golden jewelled chalices and twenty silver ones; two golden and five silver *amæ*, apparently flagons for receiving oblations of wine from the faithful. Also a golden jewelled censer; four brazen candelabra, ornamented with silver medallions of Scripture subjects, and a golden corona—these stood before St. Paul's shrine; thirty-two silver *fara*, or pendants for light, in the nave and thirty in the aisle. The Lateran Basilica was still more splendidly furnished.

The furniture and vessels of Justinian's Church of Sta. Sophia were not less sumptuous. The altar was encrusted with gems set in gold; the baldachino over it had a cupola of gold and a cross of gold weighing 75 lbs., adorned with precious stones. The throne of the patriarch and the seats of the presbyters were of silver gilt. The pulpit had a dais of gold, with a cross of gold 100 lbs. weight, ornamented with carbuncles and pearls; the golden candelabra weighed

Y

6000 cwt., and the doors were of cedar, ivory, and amber. The sacred vessels of various kinds, which numbered 42,000, were of gold, and the chalices were ornamented with pearls and other gems. The catalogue reminds us of the list of the gold and silver vessels of Solomon's temple (1 Kings vi. and vii.).

The use of incense is mentioned in the Apostolic Constitutions not later than the early part of the fourth century, which implies censers of some kind. By the seventh century crosses of silver and gold, and adorned with gems, were placed upon the altar, and censers of precious metals were used in the service, since Chosroes gave such ornaments to the Church of Jerusalem (*c.* A.D. 616).

None of these works in the precious metals have come down to us. But we shall not err in taking for granted that they resembled, in their general forms, the secular cups and tazze and lamps whose forms we know from actual examples* or from pictorial representations.

Holy Oil Reliquaries.

Another interesting class of objects affording examples of early Christian art is that of the vessels to contain oil taken from the lamps which burned before the shrines of the martyrs. The custom belongs to that region of popular religious sentiment which so easily runs into superstition. Pilgrims to

* For example, those which have been found at Herculaneum and Pompeii.

the shrines used to carry these oils away as relics. At first, perhaps, they were not regarded as anything more than relics, but at an early period it began to be believed that the "holy oil" possessed miraculous properties, especially in the cure of disease. No doubt the foundation of this belief was the primitive practice of anointing the sick with oil, alluded to in Jas. v. 14. Septimus Severus was believed, in his early years, to have been cured of a sickness by a Christian who anointed him with oil. Ephrem the Syrian, who died *circa* 370, asserts that anointing with "oil wherewith the lights of the martyrs are kindled" would give spiritual healing;[*] so that the superstition dates back to the later years of the fourth century, and continued for many centuries afterwards. At all the famous shrines which were places of pilgrimage these holy oils were sold to the pilgrims. Probably a little of the oil from the lamp of the shrine was mingled with other oil. A bit of cotton wool was dipped into it, little flasks of glass, or metal, were made expressly to contain this relic; they were usually round and flat, about the size of a modern watch, with a short neck, and were usually ornamented with sacred symbols, or with the effigy of the saint, and had an inscription running round the edge or horizontally across.

In the latter half of the fifth century, among the pious articles which Gregory the Great sent as presents to Theodelinda, the orthodox queen of the Lombards, was a collection of these holy oils. Abbot

[*] Oxford Library of the Fathers, translation, p. 229, note.

John, by the bishop's direction, collected sixty-five from the principal Roman shrines; and the vessels which contained them, or some of them, still exist in the treasury of the Cathedral of Monza, together with a catalogue of them written on papyrus. Our woodcuts represent two of them. One has in the upper portion of the design a very curious shadowing forth of the Crucifixion. Instead of the cross of Calvary

Ampullæ, at Monza.

is a small jewelled cross with two persons kneeling at it; and instead of Christ hanging upon the cross is a head of Christ in glory. But the other usual accessories of the scene are there—the two thieves in the attitude of crucifixion, but with the crosses omitted; Mary and John; and the symbols of the sun and moon above. The lower subject is the sepulchre and the angel appearing to the Marys. The other has the Adoration of the Shepherds and of the Magi combined in one scene, with an inscription beneath, ΕΜΜΑΝΟΗΛ ΜΕΘ ΥΜΩΝ Ο ΘΣ ("Emmanuel, God with us"). Both have round the margin the inscription, ΕΛΕΟΝ ΖΥΛΟΥ ΖΩΗΣ ΤΩΝ ΑΓΙΩΝ ΧΡΙΣΤΟΥ ΤΟΠΩΝ ("Oil of the wood of life and of the holy places of Christ"). The flat sides form medallions which are ornamented with subjects of Scripture history, as the Annunciation, Salutation, Nativity, Adoration of the Magi, Baptism of Christ, Crucifixion, Ascension, the sepulchre with the Marys and angel, the cross, heads of the twelve Apostles, Christ and the Apostles. Similar vessels which contained oil from the shrine of St. Mennas, also exist. Such vessels were brought from all the great shrines, not only of Rome, but of Jerusalem, of Egypt, and probably of all the great saints of Christendom.*

Mr. J. Romilly Allen † points out that the treatment of the subjects on these vessels marks the transition between the art of the sarcophagi and that of the Saxon manuscripts and later works down to the

* Garucci ("Storia della Arte Christiana," vol. vi. Plate 443) figures several others of these vessels.

The author of "Mademoiselle Mori" says that it is still the custom in Italy to dip a bit of cotton wool into the oil of the small lamp burning at the altar of the Virgin, and to use it as a charm in cases of sickness. He adds that, in the Middle Ages, it was the custom, after the celebration of the saint's day at the Roman churches, for an acolyte to dip a piece of tow in the oil of the lamp which burned before the shrine, and to carry it to the pope, saying, "To-day the station took place in such a church, and the saint salutes you;" and that these locks of tow were carefully kept to form a pillow on which the pontiff's head might rest in the grave.

† "Early Christian Symbolism," p. 52.

twelfth century. The thought suggests itself that it might be the dissemination of these and such-like small portable objects, by the hands of traders and pilgrims, which helped to carry the conventional designs of ancient art over the length and breadth of Christendom, and afforded authorities to the native artists of every country.

A very similar custom was common in our own country in the Middle Ages. Pilgrims to St. Thomas of Canterbury, our Lady of Walsingham, and other great shrines, carried away holy water, in which the relics of the saint had been dipped, in small leaden ampullæ of the same general form as the earlier vessels, only that the ornaments upon the flat sides were pictures of the saint, or of his shrine, or initials of his name.*

SACRED EMBROIDERY.

From St. Jerome we learn that, in the fourth century, hangings embroidered with sacred subjects were beginning to be used in churches, and that the bishops did not all approve of it; for John, Bishop of Jerusalem, took down a hanging, "representing Christ or some saint," in a church of Palestine, giving it for a winding-sheet for the poor, and replaced it with one from Cyprus.†

In the fourth century Asterius, Bishop of Amasia,

---

* *Journal of the Archæological Association*, v. 124; *Archæological Journal*, vol. vii. p. 400; xv. 156; xvii. 68.

† Jerome, Ep., 51. This was perhaps the hanging which at certain times of the service screened the chancel from the rest of the church.

informs us that the rich people of his time had not only the walls of their houses decorated with pictures, but also their tunics and pallia; and the more pious of them, both men and women, chose scenes from the Gospels. "One sees there," he says, "Christ with His disciples, and each of His miracles as the history relates it; the marriage feast at Cana, and the water-pots; the feeding of the multitude, with the baskets of bread; the paralytic carrying his bed on his shoulders; the blind man cured with a little clay; the woman who touched the hem of the Saviour's garment; the sinner at the feet of Jesus; Lazarus recalled to life from his grave."* There is an interesting contemporary illustration of the custom in the mosaic portrait of the Empress Theodora, in St. Vitalis, Ravenna, in which the hem of her robe is adorned with the subject of the Adoration of the Magi.

During the first three centuries the dress of the clergy, both in ordinary life and in their ministrations, was that which has been already described at p. 9, viz. the long tunic and the pallium. In the fifth century new fashions of male costume seem to have come in, and gradually become general, which differed from the dignified simplicity of the old classical dress. The prestige of the ancient habit and its artistic merits caused it to be retained, as being more grave and dignified, by the officials of the empire and by the clergy. When civil dignitaries abandoned it, the clergy still used it in their

---

* "Homilia de Divite et Laz."

ministrations, and thus the tunic—under the name of the alb, because its colour was always white—and the pallium became distinctively clerical vestments. The new upper garment which superseded the pallium in general use was a circle of cloth, of larger or smaller diameter, with a slit in the middle through which the head was passed, and it fell in folds round the person. When this went out of fashion in civil use, it was retained by the clergy as the original of the chasuble, which has continued in use in the Western Church to the present day. The great dignitaries of the empire wore a richly embroidered pallium. And it was probably the presentation of such embroidered robes by emperors to the great dignitaries of the Church which led to the more common use, by bishops and priests, of such ornamented vestments. The figure of St. Cornelius, Bishop of Rome, represented at p. 157, is in the episcopal vestments of probably the sixth century. The figure of St. Gregory the Great, opposite p. 298, represents an embroidered vestment of about the same period.

CHAPTER XX.

RELIGIOUS SUBJECTS IN DOMESTIC USE.

Religion in daily life—Use of religious subjects in decorating houses; dress; water-vessels; wine-cups; buckles; hair-pins—Lamps.

IN order to understand the profuse use of Christian symbols at times and in places where our modern taste would regard them as incongruous, we must call to mind that, in the view of primitive Christianity, the Christian is a consecrated person, a member of the Body of Christ, and indwelt by the Holy Spirit; his life is a religion, and every act of it is done to the glory of God. As, according to the testimony of Tertullian, the primitive Christians, "in their coming in and going out, in putting on their shoes, at the bath, at the table, in lighting their candles, in lying down, in sitting down, marked their foreheads with the sign of the cross;" so in later times Christians saw no incongruity in sculpturing religious symbols over the doors of their houses, and painting Scripture histories on the walls of their rooms, embroidering them upon their garments, engraving them upon their seals, impressing them upon every article of personal and domestic use.

Among the miscellaneous objects of ancient Christian art which may be mentioned in this place, are secular vessels used for containing beverages.

The two woodcuts represent a leaden vessel found in the Regency of Tunis, the use of which is determined by the inscription, ΑΝΤΛΗΟΑΤΕ ΥΔΩΡ ΜΕΤ ΕΥΦΡΟCΥΝΕ ("Drink water with joy"). The figures cast upon it are a mixture of pagan and Christian subjects, and were perhaps chosen at random, out of the moulds which the maker had in stock, merely for ornament without any intention to convey a meaning. A mythological nymph mounted on a sea-horse, corresponds with the Christian symbol of the two birds drinking from a vase. The Good Shepherd is placed between a gladiator and a palm tree, an orante is between a palm tree and a mythological victory. The Christian symbol of the cross, on a mount from which flow the rivers of Paradise, with two stags drinking, is repeated; a vine pattern forms an ornamented frame.

Vessels, like small buckets of wooden staves mounted with metal, were intended apparently as receptacles for water or wine, or perhaps for ale or mead. One of these was found in a Merovingian grave at Miannay, near Abbeville, in France.

Later examples are one in the Duomo of Milan, and another in Mr. Attenborough's collection, one made for Otho II. (A.D. 973–978), and the other for Otho III. (born 980), of which there are casts in

Water-vessel from North Africa.

the South Kensington Museum. These also are ornamented with Scripture subjects.

A curious English illustration of the use of Scripture subjects in the ornamentation of objects of domestic use, was found in a Saxon grave at Long Wittenham, Berks; together with a spear, a bronze kettle, and an iron knife. It is a drinking-vessel, formed of staves and hoops, such as is not infrequently found in Saxon graves, and is still in use in Scotland, where it is called a quaigh.* The example in question had the following Christian subjects *repoussée* on the metal plates with which it was ornamented; the X P; and the A Ω within a circle; the Miracle at Cana; the Baptism of Christ, inscribed IΩANNHC; the Annunciation. The Greek form of the name of

Buckle of a belt. Daniel in the lions' den, and an orante.

the Baptist suggests the quarter from which came the designs of this vessel, if not the vessel itself.

Buckles for belts of bronze, in some cases plated with silver, have been found in the Jura, Switzerland,

* In the Mayer Collection at Liverpool, engraved in C. Roach Smith's Catalogue, and in the "Archæologia," xxxviii. 327.

and Savoy, which are probably not earlier than the sixth century, ornamented with Scripture subjects. Daniel in the lions' den seems to have been the most popular subject; figures in the attitude of prayer, and crosses, also occur.

Two objects found in England are worth mention here: in London a metal hairpin with a medallion at the top bearing a helmeted bust with a cross on its breast looking upwards towards a cross in the air; clearly an allusion to the vision of Constantine* (compare it with the gold coin described at p. 338); and a bone hair-pin at Colchester with a cross on the top.†

Lamps.

From the time of the Apostles downwards some of the most popular services of the Church were held in the evening, vigils lasted through the night, and the Eucharist was celebrated very early in the morning (Acts xx. 8). This involved the use of lamps; and these lights seem from the earliest times to have been regarded as having a symbolical meaning. Christ called Himself the Light of the world; St. Simeon called Him the Light to lighten the Gentiles; one of the names applied to baptism was *illuminatio;* again, oil was one of the symbols of the Holy Spirit. This will account for the lamps being reckoned among the sacred vessels of the churches, and for their being made of the precious metals.

* "Roman London," C. R. Smith, p. 128.
† "Historic Towns:" *Colchester,* p. 49.

At an early period, certainly within three centuries, the lamps were lighted before Vespers with certain appropriate prayers and psalms or hymns; and the ceremony gave to the Vesper service the name of Ἐπιλύχνιον, or in Latin *Lucernarium*.

Even in domestic use, when Christians lighted their lamps in the evening, Tertullian says they were accustomed to make the sign of the cross, and in later times they sang a hymn. The Greek hymn Φῶς ἱλαρόν ἁγίας δόξης ("Gladsome light of holy glory"), the thanksgiving at lamp-lighting, was old in St. Basil's day (A.D. 370).

We have seen that Christians ornamented all kinds of articles for mere domestic use with Christian symbols and subjects; the symbolical meaning which they attached to light, and the religious ceremonies connected with it, would lead them especially to the use of such symbols on their domestic lamps. Accordingly, in many countries are found in great numbers lamps of earthenware and metal ornamented in the style with which we are familiar. The ornamentation of the clay lamps was most commonly on the circular top, which formed a medallion, and consisted of figures of the Good Shepherd, a lamb, a bird, Jonah, the cross, the XP, etc. Metal lamps are sometimes made in the shape of a ship or a church, and the handle is often fashioned into a medallion ornamented with the same kind of figures as appear on those of clay.

Clay lamp, with XP ornament.

Earthen lamps have been found in our own country —at Newcastle, ornamented with the XP monogram; at London, with palm branches; and at Colchester, with the Good Shepherd and other early subjects.*

Garucci gives two plates of illustrations of metal lamps, and three plates of earthenware.†

* "Dictionary of Christian Antiquities:" *Lamp*.
† Vol. vi. Plates 469, 471, 473, 474, and 475.

CHAPTER XXI.

COINS, MEDALS, AND GEMS.

Coin of Severus with Noah's ark; of Trajan with XP; of Salonina with EN EIPHNH—Coins with Christian symbols: of Constantine, etc.—Medals: pectoral crosses—Gems: primitive use of them with Christian symbols—Clement of Alexandria—Examples in the British Museum, etc.

HE conversion of Constantine introduced the symbols of the Christian faith upon the coinage of the empire, at first in symbols sparingly introduced as mere accessories of the old-established types, then by allegories more plainly setting forth the faith, and at last by direct introduction of the effigies of sacred personages occupying the whole field of the coin.

There are, however, exceptional types of coins before the time of Constantine which are interesting enough to require notice.

Certain coins of Septimus Severus, which have the subject of Noah's ark on their reverse, must be noticed, if only to say that we do not claim a Christian origin for them. These were all coined at Apamea on the

Euphrates, and are connected with that city. The city was called (κιβωτός) Cibotos, and κιβωτός is the word used in the Septuagint and in the New Testament for the ark of Noah. Of the ancient legends

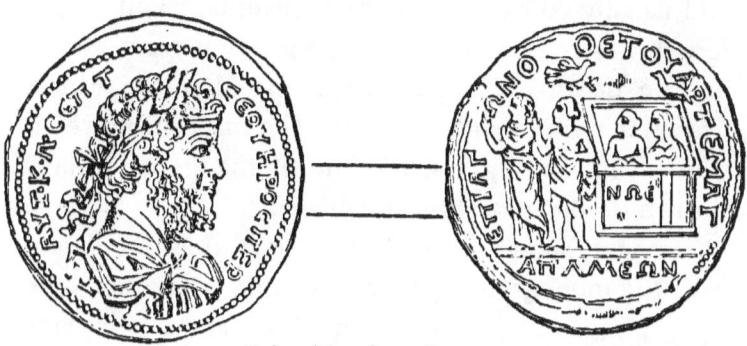

Coin of Septimus Severus.

of the Flood, one had taken root at Apamea, and thus the ark is adopted on the coin as a hieroglyph of the name of the city.*

A medallion of Trajan Decius (249–251) struck at Metonia in Lydia has on the reverse the inscription ΕΠ . ΑΥΡ . ΑΓΓΙΑΝΥΟ Β . Α ΧΡ . Α . ΤΟ . Β . ϹΤΕ- . Ι . ΑΝΗ . (ἐπί Αὐρηλίου ’Αφφιάνου δὶς ἄρχοντες ἀγωνοθέτι τὸ δεύτερον στεφανηφόρου). The engraver has contracted the PX in the word ἄρχοντες, so that it forms exactly the usual Christian monogram XP, and the monogram occupies a very conspicuous place at the top of the coin. It has been suggested that a Christian moneyer introduced this symbol of his faith upon the coin; and if so it would be valuable as one of the scanty evidences that the monogram was in use before Constantine.

* See p. 218.

We have already had occasion to mention the coins of Salonina, the empress of Gallienus, with the inscription, EN EIPHNH, "in peace," which is believed to be an exclusively Christian legend, and usually to have a funereal meaning; and therefore it has been assumed that the coins were struck on the death of the empress, and that she was a Christian; but some coins with the inscription which were struck during the lifetime of the empress, have thrown doubt upon this conclusion.*

The cut shows a coin of Constantine the Great with the monogram upon his helmet. Another coin of the same emperor shows on the reverse the Labarum between two soldiers. The monogram and the Labarum in various forms are the commonest of the Christian symbols of the coinage of this reign. A more important coin, both as a work of numismatic art and as a monument of Christian history, is an aureus presenting the emperor's head with eyes uplifted, and no legend round, executed in the very highest style of which the age was capable; its reverse always has reference in type and legend to triumph: as, GLORIA or VICTORIA CONSTANTINI AUG. The motive for this striking innovation in medallic portraiture is given by Eusebius.† "How great was the strength of the Divine faith which was the founda-

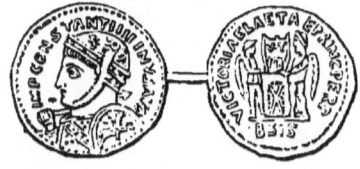

Coin of Constantine the Great.

---

* See "Dictionary of Christian Antiquities:" *Money.*
† "Vita Const.," iii. 15.

tion of his soul may be estimated from the consideration that he devised how his own portrait should be represented upon the gold coins in such a manner as to appear to be looking upwards, stretching himself aloft towards God, in the action of one praying. Now the pieces thus stamped are in circulation over the Roman world. Moreover, in the palace itself, at certain of the entrances, upon the pictures placed over the gateways, he had himself painted standing upright, looking towards heaven, and stretching forth his hands in the attitude of one in prayer."

There exists a scarce medal of CONSTANTINVS MAX AVG. Coronated bust to the right. Rev.: SPES PVBLICA, Labarum with three o o o on the banner and XP at the top of the spear, below is a serpent transfixed by the spiked end of the staff. The reader may remember that this enters into the subject of the great painting over the entrance of Constantine's palace at Constantinople, described in a former chapter.*

Lastly we may mention the medal struck in memory of Constantine's apotheosis. Down to his time the eagle bearing the emperor aloft is the established symbol of an apotheosis. In this medal a symbol clearly adapted from the horses of fire and chariot of fire of Elijah is adopted. For the emperor is seen standing in a chariot of four horses going at full speed, whilst the hand of God issues from the heavens, to which the emperor raises his eyes and hands. This interesting medal belongs to the mints of Alexandria, Antioch, and Carthage alone, but

* See p. 170.

must have been issued to a large extent, considering the numerous examples which remain to the present day.

Coins of the Emperor Constans have on the reverse a soldier holding the Labarum in his left and a little figure, perhaps a phœnix or a victory, in his

Coin of Constans.

right. The same reverse is found on coins of Constantius Magnentius and Constantius Gallus. A medal of Constantius II. shows that prince holding a standard emblazoned with the Christian monogram, the legend being "IN HOC SIGNO VCTOR ERIS," "Under this banner thou shalt be victorious;" probably the real words which Constantine saw in his dream, translated by Eusebius τούτῳ νίχα.

The monogram of the Saviour's name between the letters ΑΩ, with the legend SALVS AVGVSTI, is frequently the exclusive device of a medal's field under the two sons of Constantine.

During many reigns the usual reverse of the coins bearing the legend VICTORIA AUGUSTI was a figure of the emperor holding orb and Labarum and setting his foot upon the neck of a crouching barbarian. In the coins of Valentinian, Satan, in the form of a serpent with angel-head, is substituted for the barbarian. In the time of Majorian an angel is substituted for the figure of the emperor: this continued as the usual reverse of the solidi from 450 to 575, the workmanship becoming more and more rude and careless. The reverse of a coin of Flacilla, the wife

Coin of Justin I. (518 A.D.).

of Theodosius, has a winged figure—a victory—holding a shield marked with the monogram. In a coin of Placidia, the daughter of Theodosius holds a cross in the shape in which it first appears upon the sarcophagi.

Justinian II., on his recovery of the empire, placed a full-face bust of the Saviour on his solidi, holding

Coin of Licinia Eudoxia, wife of Valentinian III. (425-455 A.D.).

the Gospels in the left hand and giving benediction with the right. On the obverse is a full-length figure of the emperor grasping with one hand the cross planted on Calvary and holding in the other the mappa or rolled-up napkin with which the emperor gave the signal in the hippodrome, which was a badge of sovereignty. The coin is a great improvement upon those of the previous reigns. The Saviour's head is said to be a copy from the older statue over the palace gate, and that to have been copied from some antique statue. The portrait of Christ, with intervals of disuse, continued to appear on the coinage until the first capture of Constantinople. On the coins

Medallion of the eighth or ninth century.

of Basil the Macedonian appears a full-length figure of the Saviour seated on a throne. His son Leo the philosopher introduced a bust of the Blessed Virgin Mary, front face, with hands palm upwards, and not badly executed; over the head "MARIA" and on each side MR ΘY, mother of God. For many generations following this the Madonna seems to have been appropriated to the coinage of a female sovereign.

Some MEDALS exist, generally of bronze, of the third and later centuries, often pierced for suspension. On a large medal drawn by Buonarotti, but whose present whereabouts is not known, a Good Shepherd stands in the middle, bearing the sheep on his shoulders; the rest of the field is divided into four horizontal lines; on the first are Adam and Eve, and on either side Noah and Jonah under the gourd; on the second Daniel and the lions and the sacrifice of Isaac; on the third the healing of the paralytic and the smitten rock; on the fourth Jonah swallowed and disgorged. Other medals exist which bear some one of the usual cycle of early subjects, as the sacrifice of Isaac, Daniel, etc.

St. Paul and St. Peter (bronze).   Leaden medallion.

The remarkable bronze medal which presents the heads of St. Peter and St. Paul with unusual originality and great vigour is said to have been found in the Catacomb of Domitilla, and is considered by De Rossi to be of the third century.

The subject of the next example is the martyrdom of St. Laurence. It is remarkable as, perhaps, the earliest picture of a martyrdom; probably of early fifth century date. The figure in the attitude of prayer represents the soul of the dying martyr;

the hand stretched down from above is a symbol of God—it is prepared to give the martyr's crown. The legend upon it is "SUCCESSA VIVAS"—Successa being the name of the person for whom the medal was made.* Roller (Plate XLIV.) gives drawings of several medals, two of which represent the Adoration of the Magi, in which the Holy Child is distinguished by the nimbus, but not the Virgin Mother. They are not of earlier date than the fifth century.

At Carthage have been found moulds for casting little devotional medals and crosses; one of the medals has a XP in a circle, another a cross with AΩ suspended from the arms.†

GEMS.

In ancient times men used a seal where we use an autograph of our name, and in Eastern countries they do so to this day. This made it necessary for every man to possess a seal, which, for convenience of carriage and safety of custody, was often in the shape of a ring. Thus Clement of Alexandria discourages the wearing of rings as ornaments, but allows one signet ring as almost a necessity. "A man," he says, "should not wear the ring on the finger-joint, for this is effeminate,

---

* Smith's "Dictionary of Christian Antiquities." See "Early Christian Numismatics," by the Rev C. W. King; article *Numismatique*, in Martigny's "Dictionary;" *Money* in "Dictionary of Christian Antiquities;" figures of coins in Garucci, "Storia," etc., vi. 480, 381.

† "Revue de l'Art Chrétien," 1890, vol. i. liv. 2. For a bronze of Peter and Paul, and other very similar designs, see De Rossi's "Bulletino de Archæol. Christ.," fourth series, fifth year, Plate X., 1887.

but upon the little finger, as low down as possible; for the hand will thus be more free for action and the ring less likely to slip off, as being guarded by the larger joint. But let our signet devices be a dove, or

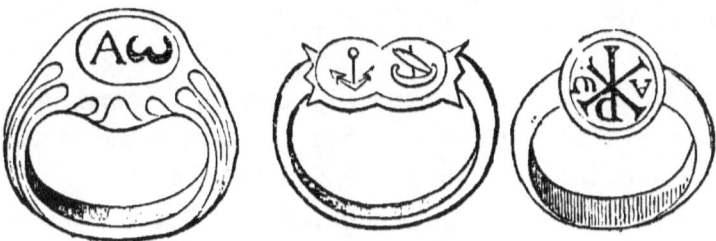

Early Christian rings.

a fish, or a ship coursing against the sky, or a musical lyre which Polycrates employed, or a ship's anchor which was the seal of Seleucus, or if it be a fisherman it will remind us of an Apostle, and of boys saved from water." A number of precious stones engraved with such devices, which probably were mounted in rings, have come down to us.* Several precious stones, probably of the third and later centuries, are engraved with the Good Shepherd; others with the fish, dove, anchor, etc.; one with an episcopal chair with ΙΧΥΘ (for ΙΧΘΥΣ) on the back, and a monogram, probably of the name of the owner of the seal, on each side of the chair; gems engraved with the sacred monogram are numerous. Mr. King specially mentions and gives engravings of the following :—

A fine large sapphire with monogram of Christ.

* Some are figured in the Rev. C. W. King's "Antique Gems and Rings," and others in the "Dictionary of Christian Antiquities."

A fine emerald, quarter inch square, set in a gold hexagonal ring with monogram.

Another in red jasper with legend ΙΗCΟΥC ΘΕΟΥ ΥΙΟC ΙΗΡΕ, "Jesus, Son of God, keep me." (All three are in the British Museum.)

The ship is frequent on gems of the Lower Empire; for cargo the ship generally carries a monogram XP; or cock with palm. A palm branch occurs on many signets with the name of the proprietor.

The Good Shepherd is engraved on a large carnelian from the north of India with I.X.Θ.Y.C. round the lamb, and on the reverse XPICTE CΩZE KAPΠIANON AEΠOTE (*sic*), "O Christ, save Carpianus for ever." The same figure of earlier and better work on a red jasper. A third in the British Museum represents the Shepherd in the middle of a landscape with dogs looking up to him, inscribed ECIΥKEΥ = "Kurie Jesu."

There are two intagli in the British Museum in green jasper, one with Christ's entry into Jerusalem, and the other with a Madonna and Child with angels ("Gnostic of the beginning of the third century"). In the same case two camei which cannot be later than St. Helena, one with John Baptist, the other with an Annunciation and the inscription OXAPETICMOC ΓABPIΗΛ, "The salutation, Gabriel."

A Gnostic gem, Good Shepherd with two sheep, and inscription IAH! (iv. Plate 9, Fig. 9). A martyrdom of a female with XP over her head (ix. Plate 8), and under ANFT ("Annum novum felicem tibi," a new year's present).

In the French collection of gems the following specimens which have been the signets of Persian (Nestorian) Christians are noticed by Chabouillet. No. 1330, the sacrifice of Isaac; 1333, the fish in the middle of the Christian monogram; 1331, Virgin and sacred Infant seated, with a Pehlevi legend; and lastly (without number) the bust of Christ in profile beardless, the fish below, and then the legend XPICTOY. Chabouillet considers all these earlier than the great persecution by Sapor II., A.D. 340.*

Innumerable other objects have been found in and near the loculi, chambers, and galleries of the catacombs, terra-cotta and bronze lamps, with monograms and symbols, vases of terra-cotta and other materials, unguent boxes, glass pastes, medals, rings, fibulæ, personal ornaments and utensils, ivory dolls, and playthings.

* King, "Antique Gems and Rings;" "Rings of the Early Christian Period," by C. D. E. Fortnam, copiously illustrated; *Arch. Journ*, xxvi. p. 139.

CHAPTER XXII.

INSCRIPTIONS.

History and character of inscriptions; prayers for the departed, and requests for their intercession; euphemisms; examples.

CHRISTIAN epitaphs of the first six centuries exist in large numbers in all Christian countries; they have been collected and annotated in many volumes, and form a special branch of archæological literature.* It will be enough for our present purpose to give a brief sketch of their general characteristics and some examples, and to note a few whose contents have a special bearing upon our subject.

* De Rossi has published two volumes, and has material for four or five others, of the Christian inscriptions of Rome earlier than the seventh century; the Abbé Guzzara has published those of Piedmont; Mommsen those of the kingdom of Naples; Le Blant those of Gaul; Waddington those of Central Syria; Renier those of Algeria. The early Christian inscriptions in Great Britain of the Roman period are in Haddan and Stubbs's "Councils and Ecclesiastical Documents," i. 39, 40; ii. p. xxii. and 51.

See the articles on the subject in Martigny's "Dictionary of Christian Antiquities," and in Smith's "Dictionary of Christian Antiquities." See also Dr. McCaul's "Christian Epitaphs," and "Britanno-Roman Inscriptions." Roller gives photographs of some hundred and fifty or two hundred of the more interesting inscribed stones as they are classified and arranged on the walls of the Vatican Museum.

During the first three centuries inscriptions are comparatively rare. As to their art, some are incised on the slab which closed a loculus, with all degrees of care, from the elegant caligraphy of the poetical epitaphs with which Pope Damasus distinguished the graves of his predecessors, down to very rude and illiterate scratchings; some are carefully carved upon the front of a rich sarcophagus. As to their contents, with few exceptions the earlier epitaphs are brief and simple, and without a date. Recent discoveries in the Cemetery of St. Agnes show that ninety-six out of a hundred of the earliest tombs are entirely without inscriptions, in contrast with the wordy elegies upon pagan sepulchres of the period. In the third century inscriptions became common, but are brief and undated. From the fourth century and onward they become more complex and ornate, and are carefully dated. Sometimes the day of the month of death is given, because that was the day on which the annual commemoration was to be held, but not the year; that was of little importance to those whose thoughts were of eternity. One characteristic which no doubt existed from the earliest times, but is only brought out by the language of the later inscriptions, is the existence of a strong feeling of family affection. In the open-air cemeteries epitaphs in verse abound; but formal eulogies and inscriptions are rare after the sixth century.

The briefest and commonest of the epitaphs is So-and-so EN IPHNH, or IN PACE. Brief as it is, it has two meanings; it is either an assertion that the departed rests in peace, or an aspiration or prayer that he may rest in peace, which latter meaning is brought out more clearly in some epitaphs, as " Dorme in pace," " Sleep in peace ; " " Semper vive in pace," " Live always in peace ; " " Vivas in pace," " Mayest thou live in peace." Many consist of an affectionate word of farewell on the part of the living to their departed relation : " Pax tecum," "Peace be with you ;" " Quiesce in pace," " Rest in peace ; " " Accepta sis in Christo," " Mayest thou be accepted in Christ ; " " Æterna tibi lux in xp," " May eternal light in Christ be with you ; " " Pax tecum permaneat," " May everlasting peace be with thee."

The principal symbols which appear on the inscriptions are the fish, dove, lamb or sheep, phœnix, cock, horse, stag, barrel, anchor, ship, lighthouse, cockle-shells, etc. Towards the end of the fourth century, or more surely at the beginning of the fifth, the cross begins to appear on the inscriptions at Rome.

Of requests for the departed to pray for the living, De Rossi says that among the inscriptions of the first three centuries the forms "Pete pro nobis," and " Pro parentibus," and "Pro conjuge," and " Pro filiis," and " Pro sorore," occur ; but Dr. McCaul adds that these are comparatively rare among the thousands, and that anything beyond these requests of the surviving relations to the departed to pray for the members of his family, is of extreme rarity. On the other hand, of requests to the living to pray for the departed, Dr. McCaul says that he only recollects, in the first six centuries, two of the addresses to the reader for his prayers which are so frequent in mediæval times.

The euphemistic phrases in which the heathen spoke of death, with a natural shrinking from the realization of its sadder features, are continued in Christian epitaphs with the strong faith which their religion gave them in the unbroken continuity of life and the certainty of a joyful resurrection. "RECESSIT DE SÆCULUM, DE SÆCULUM EXIVIT," "he departed this life;" "FUIT IN SÆCULUM," "he ceased to be of this life;" "VIXIT IN SÆCULUM," "he ceased to live in this life"—SÆCULUM being always used by Christianity of this present life; "REDDIT," or "REDDIDIT," viz. "DEBITUM VITÆ," "he restored his life to God who gave it;" "ABSOLUTUS DE CORPORE," "he was freed from the body." "DEPOSITUS" is the word for buried, which has the meaning of a treasure placed in safety.

Here are a few examples of epitaphs which have some special feature of interest.*

From Orleansville, in Algiers, Renier, n. 3701—

"HIC REQVIES
CITSANCTAE MEMO
RIAEPATERNOSTER
REPARATVS E. P. S. QVIFE
CIT IN SACERDOTIVM AN
NOS VIIII MEN-XI-ETPRE
CESSIT NOS INPACE
DIE VNDECIMV . KAL

* From Dr. J. McCaul's "Christian Epitaphs of the First Six Centuries." Toronto, 1869.

AVG PROVNC . CCCCXXX
ET SEXTA."

"Here rests our father of holy memory, Reparatus the bishop, who passed in his priesthood nine years eleven months, and went before us, in peace, on the eleventh day before the Calends of August, in the 436th year of the Province [*i.e.* July 22, A.D. 475]."

A lengthy inscription, recently found at Narbonne, recording the reparation of the church in A.D. 445, tells of another married bishop, "RUSTICUS EPISCOPUS EPISCOPI BONOSI FILIUS" (Le Blant, u.s. n. 489).

From the Cemetery of St. Agnes *—
"PRÆSBYTER HIC SITVS EST CELERINVS NOMINE
  DIC[tus]
CORPOREOS RVMPENS NEXVS QVI GAVDET IN
  ASTRIS
DEP VIIII KAL IVN FL SYAGRIO ET EVCERIO."

"Here has been laid a Presbyter called by the name of Celerinus, who, breaking the bonds of the body, rejoices in the stars [*i.e.* in heaven]. Buried on the ninth day before the Kalends of June, in the Consulship of Syagrius and Eucherius [*i.e.* May 24, A.D. 381]."

From the Cemetery of St. Paul, in the Ostian Way †—
"GAVDENTIVS. PRESB. SIBI.
  ET CONIVGI SVAE SEVERAE CASTAE HAC SANC
    [tissimae]
  FEMINAE QVAE VIXIT ANN. XLII. M. III. D.X.
  DEP III. NON. APRIL. TIMASIO ET PROMOTO."

* De Rossi, n. 303. † Ibid., n. 376.

"Gaudentius, a Presbyter, for himself and his wife Severa, a chaste and most holy woman, who lived forty-two years, three months, ten days. Buried on the fourth day before the Nones of April, in the Consulship of Timasius and Promotus [*i.e.* April 2, A.D. 389]."

To a deacon's wife and children:

"LEVITAE CONJUNX PETRONIA FORMA PUDORIS. IIIS MEA DEPONENS SEDIBUS OSSA LOCO.

PARCITE VOS LACRIMIS DULCES CUM CONIUGE NATAE . VIVENTEM QUE DEO CREDITE FLERE NEFAS.

DP IN PACE III NON OCTOB. FESTO VC CONSS

HIC REQUIESCIT IN PACE PAULA CLF. DULCIS BENIGNA GRATIOSA FILIASS

DP VII KAL SEPT .. .. .. T NANTO VC CONSS

HIC REQUIESCIT DULCISSIMUS PUER GORDIANUS FILIUS SS

DP ID SEPT . SYMMACHO VC CONSS

HIC REQUIESCIT ÆMILIANA SAC . VG . DPV . ID. DEC. PROBINO VC CONSS."

"I, Petronia, the wife of a deacon, the type of modesty, lay down my bones in this resting-place. Refrain from tears, my sweet daughters and husband, and believe that it is forbidden to weep for one who lives in God. Buried in peace on the third day before the Nones of October, in the Consulship of Festus, a most distinguished man [*i.e.* October 5, A.D. 472]. Here rests in peace Paula, a most distinguished woman, the sweet kind gracious daughter of the above mentioned; buried on the seventh day before the Kalends of September, in the Consulship of

Venantius, a most distinguished man [*i.e.* August 26, A.D. 484]. Here rests a very sweet boy, Gordianus, son of the above mentioned, buried on the Ides of September, in the Consulship of Symmachus, a most distinguished man [*i.e.* September 13, A.D. 485]. Here rests Æmiliana, a sacred virgin, buried on the 5th before the Ides of December, in the Consulship of Probinus, a most distinguished man [*i.e.* December 9, A.D. 489]."

"Levita" is used for "Diaconus," because the latter word is unsuitable for hexameters. De Rossi's comment upon it contains a most ingenious and conclusive argument that Gregory the Great was a descendant of the persons named in this epitaph.

In the basilica of St. Alexander, in the Nomentine Way, is an inscription to Appinnus, a subdeacon, who died in his thirty-fourth year, April 11, A.D. 448. The following is from the crypt of the Vatican*: —

" Locus Marcelli Subd. Reg. Sexte concessum sibi
    et pos
teris ejus a beatissimo Papa Joanne
que vixit ann plm lxviii dep p̄c basili v̄c ann xxii
    ind. xi. undecimu Kal. Januarias."

"The place of Marcellus, a subdeacon of the sixth Region, conceded to him and to his posterity by the most blessed Pope John, who lived sixty-eight years, more or less. Buried in the twenty-second year after the Consulship of Basilius, a most distinguished man, in the eleventh Indiction, on the eleventh day before the Kalends of Jan [*i.e.* December 22, A.D. 563]."

From St. Agnes (De Rossi, n. 1185) is an inscrip-

* De Rossi, 1096.

tion to Abundantius, an acolyte of the fourth Region, of the Title of Vestina, who died at the age of thirty. Opinions differ as to the date. De Rossi thinks it of the sixth or seventh century.

From Æclanum (Mommsen, " I. N.," 1293): an inscription to Cælius Johannes, an exorcist, buried December 6, A.D. 511.

From the Cemetery of Callistus and Pretextatus (De Rossi, n. 48): to Equitius Heracleus, a Reader of the second Region, who died in his twentieth year, Febuary 7, A.D. 338.

From the crypt of the Church of Æclanum (Mommsen, 1299): to Cælius Laurentius, Reader of the Holy Church of Æclani, who died about 48 years of age, May 9, A.D. 494.

From St. Paul (De Rossi, 1087): to Decius, custodian (*Cubicularius*) of the basilica, A.D. 534.

From the Church of the Holy Trinity, Ticinum (Muratori, 424, 426): Theodora, a Deaconess, aged 48, died July 22, A.D. 539.

From the Cemetery of Calistus (De Rossi, 497): Prætiosa, a virgin of only twelve years (ancilla Dei et XRI), died May 31, A.D. 401.

From St. Paul (De Rossi, 739): Gaudiosa, a most illustrious woman, a virgin (Clarissima fe nina, Ancilla Dei), who lived 40 years and 4 months, and was buried September 22, A.D. 447.

Roller gives inscriptions from the Roman catacombs to Dionysius, Presbyter and Physician; to Emmanius Opas, Lector of the Title of Fascicola, a friend of the poor, A.D. 377; to Prunus an Exorcist, to Secundius a Church Administrator, both probably of the fourth century; to Church Virgins (ancillæ dei); to Neophytes and Catechumens.

Inscription found in an arch of an ancient cemetery at Autun. Probable date latter part of fourth century :*

"Offspring of the heavenly Ichthus, see that a heart of holy reverence be thine, now that from Divine waters thou hast received, while yet living among mortals, a fount of life that is to immortality.

"Quicken thy soul, beloved one, with ever-flowing waters of heavenly wisdom, and receive the honey-sweet food of the Saviour of the Saints. Eat with a longing hunger, holding Ichthus in thine hands.

"To Ichthus... Come nigh unto me, my Lord [and] Saviour; [be Thou my Guide] I entreat thee, Thou Light of them for whom the hour of death is past.

"Aschandus, my Father, dear unto mine heart, and thou [sweet mother, and all] that are mine . . . remember Pectorius."

The inscriptions scratched by pilgrims upon the walls and stones in and about the objects of pilgrimage have been briefly noticed at p. 157.

In the fifth and following centuries it became the fashion to put inscriptions upon new churches and other buildings, recording the date of their foundation.

Many of the mosaics have inscriptions recording the name of the donor.

W. Marriott, " Vestimenta Sacra Antiqua."

CHAPTER XXIII.

SOME CONCLUSIONS.

IT may be useful to put together a summary of some of the conclusions which have been arrived at in the preceding chapters. The "Church of the Catacombs" is a beautiful myth. The assemblies for worship of the primitive Church were not held in caves and catacombs, except during the infrequent occurrence of general or local persecution, but in the upper rooms and halls of the houses of wealthy Christians.

Public churches were built probably as early as the first quarter of the third century, and were numerous throughout the empire by the end of the century.

The churches were built on the plan of the houses in which the congregations had been accustomed to assemble, with the modification of the apse suggested by the civil basilicas.

Of the Christian art of the primitive Church nothing has come down to us which can with any certainty be assigned to the *first century*, except a few insignificant inscriptions.

To the *end of the first and the second century* belong the early chambers of the cemeteries of Domitilla, Priscilla, Pretextatus, and Lucina, at Rome, before those family burial-places were opened to the use of the Church. We find in their wall-paintings the symbolical subjects of the vine, the fish, the dove, the anchor, the Good Shepherd, the baptism of Christ, Jonah, the stricken rock, Daniel in the lions' den, the agapæ, and the orantes, the resurrection of Lazarus, and a few others of the cycle of symbolic subjects; and De Rossi thinks the Virgin and Child with the man and star in the Cemetery of Priscilla, not later than A.D. 150. Others assign it to a much later date. The inscriptions are few, brief, and simple.

In the *third century* the preceding subjects develop, and others are added. The fish is often a dolphin, which is sometimes wreathed round the stock of the anchor; the ship of the Church appears. The water from the stricken rock forms a river, from which the fisherman draws out the mystic fish. In it Christ is baptized; it widens into a sea on which the ark floats, and which is the scene of the history of Jonah. We find new subjects in the wall-paintings: the sacrifice of Abraham, the miracles of Cana, of the paralytic, and others. Eucharistic symbols, as the tripod with loaves and fish, the fish with a basket of loaves and (?) a vessel of wine on its back, Orpheus, the peacock, and other symbols appear.

The inscriptions express aspirations on behalf of the departed: that they may be in peace, may be with the saints, may be refreshed, may enjoy bliss.

Friends offer for them to God the sacrifice of thanksgiving.

The peace of the Church at the beginning of the *fourth century* naturally leads to a great extension of Christian Art. The sculptured sarcophagi become very numerous, and are the most important existing monuments of the Christian Art of this and the following century. On these and other monuments we find all the old cycle of Christian subjects continued, with little or no change in their conventional treatment, with some new subjects, as our Lord before Pilate, and Pilate's declaration of His innocence; other Passion subjects begin to be introduced; the Nativity, with the legendary ox and ass, and the Adoration of the Magi, are more frequently found. The symbol of the cross is not at first openly put forward, but gradually the XP monogram takes the form of the cross, with the curl of the P attached to its upper limb; before the end of the century the cross is openly portrayed. The nimbus appears round the head of Christ before the end of the century.

A great development, due probably to the recent general persecution, has been given to the reverence paid to the departed. We find explicit prayers for the dead, and requests for their intercession: pray for such a one, be favourable to such a one, have such a one in remembrance in thy prayers. The inscriptions which Bishop Damasus caused to be placed over the tombs of his predecessors, in the Callistine Cemetery, mark the point at which prayers for the intercession of the saints came in.

Chapels begin to be made in the catacombs enclosing or adjoining the graves of saints and martyrs, and commemorative services are said there; a saint's tomb is sometimes used as the altar. Pilgrimages to the tombs of the martyrs become common; the pilgrims inscribe their names, invocations, and prayers upon the walls.

The ἰχθύς symbol gradually goes out of use, and the lamb becomes a popular symbol of Christ, of the Apostles, and of the Christian flock generally.

In the *fifth century* Christ is presented as the great Teacher of the Church, seated and delivering rolls (books) to the Apostles. Christ, standing or seated in the middle, with Apostles on each side of Him, is a very common subject; no special emblem distinguishes one Apostle from another. Sometimes two Apostles, no doubt St. Peter and St. Paul, are separated from the rest, and placed prominently on each side of our Lord, as the PRINCIPES APOSTOLORUM.*

* Bishop Leo I. (440-461) speaks of these two Apostles as those "whom the grace of Christ had raised to such a height among all the members of the Church, that they were as the two eyes of the body of which Christ is the Head, so that we ought not to think of them as differing in merit, since He made them equal by election, alike in labours, the same in their death" (Serm. lxxix.). St. Ambrose (374-397) says the primacy of Peter is in faith, not of order ("De Incarn.," c. 4); and, in another place, "neither was Paul inferior to Peter" ("De Spirit Sanct.," ii. 13). St. Augustine, speaking of St. Paul, says he is the head and prince of the Apostles (Migne's edition, iii. 2313). Pope Vitalian, in his letter to Otway of Northumbria (A.D. 665), exhorts him to "continue in all things delivered by the blessed Apostles Peter and Paul, whose doctrine daily enlightens the hearts of believers, even as the two heavenly lights, the sun and moon, clearly illumine all the earth." The heads of the two Apostles appear on the seal of the See from the earliest period; they were the joint founders and patron saints of the Roman Church.

Prominence begins to be given to St. Peter, but he is not yet represented with the keys. He is represented as Moses striking the rock, an allusion, perhaps, to his admission of Jews (at Pentecost) and Gentiles (Cornelius and his friends) to baptism. In the eighth century Art bears witness to the development of the papal idea in the mosaic* of the tribune of the greater triclinium, in the palace of the Lateran, where the principal subject is Christ with the Apostles, in which Peter is distinguished by the keys and a cross of two bars; in the spandrels, on each side of the principal subject, are, on the left, Christ giving the keys to Peter and the banner to Constantine; on the right, Peter giving the pall to Pope Leo and the banner to Charles the Great. Peter and Constantine have the circular nimbus, Leo and Charles the square nimbus. The representation of the cross becomes usual and replaces the XP monogram, but the crucifix does not yet appear. The use of pectoral crosses and medals with sacred subjects becomes usual.

The crucifix does not appear till the sixth century, and there is no attempt at realism. Christ stands in front of the cross, with arms extended horizontally, and is always clothed in a tunic. The miniature at p. 202 shows the sixth-century, and the ivory plaque at p. 300 shows the eighth-century modification of the subject.

The Byzantine epoch is the point from which a number of new ideas begin to appear in Christian Art.

* Bunsen's "Die Basiliken des Christ. Roms.," Plate XLIII.

The monuments of the Christian Art of the early centuries prove the non-catholicity of certain mediæval and modern doctrines and practices, and their silence with respect to others is a protest against them.

It is interesting to realize how different the external aspect of the civilized world had become during the latter part of the period which has been under consideration, from that which it wore in the earlier part of the period.

Then the great architectural ornaments of every city were the colonnaded façades of its temples; the subjects of art—statues, bas-reliefs, bronzes, paintings—were taken from the heathen mythology and the stories of the classic poets; every action of common life was attended by some superstitious custom; at every meal they poured out a libation to the gods; they beaded the thread of their discourse with frequent oaths: "by Jupiter," "by Hercules," and "by Bacchus."

Now the churches were the great public buildings of every city; the subjects of all art were taken from the Holy Scriptures; over the doorways in the streets were sculptured Christian symbols and sacred monograms; the public fountains in the squares were bronzes of the Good Shepherd and Daniel in the lions' den; the interiors, not only of the churches, but of the houses also, were covered with paintings of the cycle of symbolical and Scripture subjects with which we are familiar; the very dress and personal adornments of the people, and the utensils for common household use, were ornamented with Scripture subjects; the gestured sign of the cross hallowed every action; the whole external appearance of life was Christian; the common talk, the popular songs, were of religion.' Arius popularized his views in Alexandria by songs adapted to all classes, and Ambrose wrote popular hymns to fortify his Milanese against the proselytizing efforts of Justina. Jerome tells how, at Bethlehem, psalms and hymns were the ballads of the ploughman and the vine-dresser. In Chrysostom's time the favourite topic of the street and gossip of the market was the contemporary doctrinal controversy. It had become a Christian world; and not unfittingly, during the first half of the fifth century, the reigning empress, Pulcheria, was a Church virgin; in her palace the religious exercises and discipline of a monastery were maintained; and out of the midst of this seclusion the imperial nun ably and successfully administered the affairs of the East for nearly forty years.

Finally, there is nothing in the history of early Christian Art to discourage us—but rather the contrary—from frankly and fully using the Arts in the service of Religion. The æsthetic side of our nature, which recognizes the noblest aspect of things in the actual world and in ordinary life, and deals with human aspirations and ideals, is akin to the religious sentiment. Our English religion has long been cold and unlovely, to a degree which ought not to exist in a true representation of Christianity, not only by reason of some popular doctrines not really belonging to it, which shock the heart, but also owing to its repression of the imagination and taste. The Arts will receive a new impulse when Religion shall give them scope for works of the highest character for the adornment of its temples; and the Arts will repay Religion by teaching its lessons with a force with which mere words cannot teach, and by bringing out its poetry and beauty.

INDEX.

Ancyra, tombs of martyrs there, 149
Anicius Probus, sarcophagus of, A.D. 395, 271
Apostolic worship, 8; vestments, 9
Apse, modification of the tablinum, 33; western, 80
Architecture of early churches, 65, 66, 70, 76; Byzantine, 81-86
Art the handmaid of religion, 363
Atrium, description of, 18

Baptism, mode of administering, 90-92, 97, 98
Baptisteries, early, 93; design of, 94
Basilica in the house of Theophilus at Antioch, 15
Basilican church, description of, 40
Benedict Biscop, introduced Christian art into Northumbria, 167
Bethlehem, church at, 62
Buckles ornamented with sacred subjects, 332
Byzantine architecture, 81-86

Catacombs, a hiding-place from persecution, 141; violated by the Lombards, 127, 151

Catacombs at Rome, 107-123; Naples, 127, 128; Cyrene, 129; Alexandria, 129; description of their original state by Jerome, 125; by Prudentius, 125; disused for burial, 127; deserted, 127
Cemeteries, at Colchester, 103; family, 103; public, 119
Chair of St. Peter, 299; of Maximinus, 299
Chapels in the catacombs, 122, 151; in churches, 156
Chapter houses, 99
Christian art, definition of, 1; historical value of, 3
Churches, in houses, 11-23; public, first built, 29, 35; numerous before Constantine, 30, 31; plan of, 32; description of, at Tyre, 42
Church, the, represented as a woman, 245
Cœnaculum, 6
Coins with Christian emblems, 336-341
Confessio, 146
Constantine, arch of, 49; churches of, 53, 61-64
Constantinople, churches at, 63, 85

Conventional treatment of subjects, 179
Crucifixion, 199, 202
Crypts, reminiscences of the catacombs, 155; at Ripon and Hexham, 155; Canterbury, 155
Curtain between atrium and tablinum, 19
Cycle of scriptural subjects, 182, 214-233

Deceased persons, representations of, 235, etc.
Dome, introduced, 81-84; in Europe, 86
Drinking-vessels, 332

Emblems, 196; cross, 197; monogram XP, 201; A and Ω, 203
Emblems, personal, 249
England, early churches in, 87; paintings in, 167; sarcophagi in, 280, 281; illuminated manuscripts in, 316, 321; reliquaries in, 326; lamps in, 335

Funeral customs, classical, 102; Jewish, 104; Christian, 106
Funeral feast, 141, 143, 245, 246-248
Funeral rites, heathen, 141; Christian, 142

Gaul, churches of, at Lyons, 78; Tours, 79; Clermont, 79; Avignon, Alet, Poictiers, Roman Motier, 80; Arles, St. Gilles, Treves, 80
Gaul, sarcophagi of, 278, 280
Gems with Christian subjects, 344
Gilded glass vessels, 304; their original use, 310; secondary use, 311
Glass vessels, 309
Gold and silver vessels, 8, 320; of St. Peter's, 321; of Sta. Sophia, 321

Greek art, 2
Good Shepherd, 254-257
Graffiti, 156, 199
Groups of subjects, 227-233, 268-276, 307

Hippolytus, statue of, 258
House, the early Churches assembled in, 10-23; Christian symbols on exterior of, 74; description of Greek and Roman, 18

Illuminated manuscripts, 312
Incense, 321, 322
Inscriptions, 348, *et seq.*, 359
Invocations of the saints, 156, 157, 358
Irish examples of early school of sculpture, 282
Ivory carvings, 297

Jerusalem, churches at, 11, 63
Jesus Christ, representations of, 186
Junius Bassus, sarcophagus of, A.D. 359, 269

Lamps for sacred use, 322, 323, 333; for domestic use, 334
Lazarus, raising of, an illustration of early tombs, 152-155

Martyrs, honours paid to, 145, 146
Medals with Christian emblems and subjects, 342
Milan, Church of St. Ambrose, 69
Monumental stones, 137; at Prymnessos, 139; in England, 140
Mosaic, manufacture of, 284; designs of, 284

Oil from the lamps of the saints, 323
Oranti, 235-240

Painting, classical, 160, 265; Christian, 161; of different periods, 171; descriptions of, by ancient authors, 166, 183; in houses, 169, 329; Christian, early use of it, 165

Parenzo, church at, 77

Pax of ivory, 300

Persecutions, 25-29; Diocletian, 145

Pilgrimages to the catacombs, 125, 156, 323

Pillars, monumental, 132, 137

Pompeii, the street of the tombs, 132

Pyxes of ivory, 301

Rabula, Syriac manuscript of, 202, 313, 315

Ravenna, churches at, 76; sarcophagi at, 276, 278; mosaics at, 291

Relics removed from the catacombs, 151; placed in churches, 151, 155

Reliquaries of ivory, 301; of metal, 323

Rings with Christian subjects, 344

Roman art, 2

Rome, St. Peter's Church, 58; St. Paul's, 59; St. Agnes, 61; St. Clement, 67

Salone, sarcophagi at, 278

Sarcophagi, 259-281; pagan used for Christian burial, 279-281

Sarvistan, palace at, 81

Scribblings on walls and tombs, 156, 199

Scripture subjects on sarcophagi, 227

Sculpture, classical, 253; Christian, 261

Sepulchres, subterranean, at Rome, 104; Syrian, 136

Sextus, Bishop of Rome, martyred, 147

SS. John and Paul, house of, 150, 170; church of, 150

St. Alban, 152

St. Gregory the Great, his presents to Theodelinda, 298, 323; to Augustine, 316

St. Peter and Paul, patron saints of Rome, 360

St. Peter, statue of, 259

Symbolical subjects, 204; Good Shepherd, 204; lamb, 204; fish, 205; *Ichthus*, 205; fisherman, 206; ship, 206; anchor, 207; amphora, 207; vine, 207; olive, 208; palm, 208; birds, 209; sheep, 209; goats, 209; peacock, 209; Phœnix, 209; Orpheus, 210; ox and ass, 211; Mount of Paradise, 212; stag, 212; hand, 213; nimbus, 213; aureole, 214; from the Old and New Testaments, Daniel, 215; three children, 216; Jonah, 216; Lazarus, 217; Noah, 217; sacrifice of Isaac, 219; paralytic, 219; infirm woman, 220; blind man, 220; Red Sea, 221; Moses in various scenes, 221-224; Job, 224; Eve, 224; the Fall, 224; Abel and Cain, 225; Elijah, 225; baptism of our Lord, 225; triumphal entry, 225; arrest of Christ, 225

Symbolism, came from the East, 176; its growth, 178

Symbols of the Eucharist, 226

Syrian churches, 35-37, 70-73

Temples, classical, 55; converted into churches, 56, 57

Thessalonica, churches at, 75

Thorns, blocking church doors with, 150

Tombs, classical, at Rome, etc., 131; Jerusalem, 132; of St. Helena, 133; of Constantia, 133; at Hass, 134
Torcello, bishop's throne at, 69

Upper classes, converts of the, 12-15
Upper room, at Jerusalem, 6; Joppa, 12; Troas, 12; Rome, 16; of Mary at Jerusalem, service in it, 8; the Church of the Apostles, 10

Virgin Mary (supposed representations of), 239-244, 315

Water-vessels, 330

THE END.

PRINTED BY WILLIAM CLOWES AND SONS, LIMITED, LONDON AND BECCLES.

www.ingramcontent.com/pod-product-compliance
Lightning Source LLC
Chambersburg PA
CBHW032027220426
43664CB00006B/395